Thomas O'Loughlin

Liturgical Resources for Advent and Christmastide

YEARS A, B AND C

the columba press

First published in 2006 by
the columba press
55A Spruce Avenue, Stillorgan Industrial Park,
Blackrock, Co Dublin

Cover by Bill Bolger
Origination by The Columba Press
Printed in Ireland by ColourBooks Ltd, Dublin

ISBN 1 85607 554 0

Acknowledgement
I would like to acknowledge the feedback I have had from so many
people – priests in parishes, musicians, liturgists, scripture scholars,
and most importantly many who 'sit in the pews' – to the materials
printed here during the time that I was putting together this collection
of resources.

For Francisca Rumsey,
For inspiration and encouragement

Table of Contents

Preface

When, just over forty years ago, the Second Vatican Council began to carry out the most thorough reform of the liturgy of the Latin Church in its history with the object of restoring the liturgy to its pristine centrality in the life of the Body of Christ, few thought that this work would still be in progress now. Equally, few who embraced that work eagerly in the 1960s and 1970s realised just how much more demanding the celebration of this renewed liturgy would be for everyone involved. I recall standing some years ago as one of group of concelebrants in the sacristy of the Jesuit house in Milltown Park in Dublin waiting for a special celebration of the Eucharist to begin. Around us were fussing musicians getting their various instruments tuned and working out their parts relative to the organist. There were readers checking they had the right texts. There was to be a complex preparation of gifts and it too was being put in hand. There was to be a liturgical drama and that meant more people getting ready and moving hither and thither. And, of course there was the old problem of finding a smoker in the sacristy who would have matches to light a taper to light the charcoal for the thurible. I am sure anyone who has had any contact with liturgy knows the scene and could fill out more of the details. Just then, my eye and that of a colleague just happened to fall on a small notice, in Latin, now yellowed with age and pinned above the vesting bench: 'Priests are earnestly exhorted to celebrate Mass without raising their voices above a whisper. Remember, raising your voice will disturb every other priest saying Mass at the same time as you.' We both burst into laughter: the notice was still there, but it was from a foreign world. Gone were the days when celebrating the Eucharist was only a sacerdotal affair, and where few material concerns – a homily apart – had to be thought about in preparation for each celebration.

But if the restored liturgy makes far more demands in terms

of preparation and the stresses of presiding, there are still only twenty-four hours in a day and seven days in a week. It is in the light of this greater need for ideas and resources for the liturgy that I have produced this book. We humans tend to get good ideas in two principal ways. First, we see an idea somewhere, perhaps in a book, which strikes a cord with us and which we like; then we adopt the idea as our own, adapt it to our circumstances and then develop it within our own thought and work. Second, we hear or see something that appears so silly, daft, bizarre, or stupid that we reject it and as a consequence develop thoughts of our own by way of reaction. I would like readers of this book to find it helped them in the first way; but if it only generates thought in the second manner, then well and good. Either way, it will have served its purpose.

T. O'L
Lampeter
Epiphany 2006

The Themes of Advent's Sundays

Over the four Sundays of Advent the creators of the lectionary saw a definite evolution of themes, and it is these themes that form the overall texture of the season in the liturgy today. These themes were noted explicitly in the 1981 *General Introduction to the Lectionary*, n 93 (*Lectionary* vol 1, p xxxviii):

Each Sunday has a distinctive theme:

The Lord's coming at the end of time (First Sunday of Advent);

John the Baptist (Second and Third Sundays);

The events that prepared immediately for the Lord's birth (Fourth Sunday).

It is in accord with this scheme that the gospels for each day were chosen.

The Old Testament readings are prophesies about the Messiah and the Messianic age, especially from Isaiah.

So, unlike the pattern that links the first reading with the gospels on most Sundays during the rest of the year, there is no inherent connection between the first reading and the gospel reading.

The readings from an apostle serve as exhortations and proclamations, in keeping with the different themes of Advent.

Again unlike most of the year when the second readings are not linked to either the first reading or the gospel, during Advent there is some link between this reading and the gospel in so far as they can be seen to share a common theme.

Psalm Numbers

In the *Lectionary* and *Missal* the numbers given to the Psalms follow that given in the Latin *Ordo Lectionum* which, being in Latin, naturally follows the Vulgate numeration. The Vulgate numeration followed that of the Old Greek translation ('The Septuagint') as this was seen as 'the Psalter of the Church.' However, most modern books, apart from Catholic liturgical books, follow the numeration of the Hebrew text of the Psalter.

Since this book's primary referents are the books of the Catholic liturgy, the Septuagint number is given first and the Hebrew numeration is then given in (brackets). The same convention as is used in the English translation of the Liturgy of the Hours. See *Breviary*, vol 1, pp 640*-641* for further information.

For example: The Psalm that begins 'My heart is ready' is cited as Ps 107(108).

For convenience here is a concordance of the two numeration systems:

Septuagint	Hebrew
1 – 8	1 - 8
9	9 - 10
10 -112	11 - 113
113	114 - 115
114 - 115	116
116 - 145	117 - 146
146 - 147	147
148 - 150	148 - 150

Advent

'Advent has a twofold character: as a season to prepare for Christmas when Christ's first coming to us is remembered; as a season when that remembrance directs the mind and heart to await Christ's Second coming at the end of time. Advent is thus a period for devout and joyful expectation.'

General Norms for the Liturgical Year and Calendar, n 39

First Sunday of Advent (Year A)

Note

The liturgy communicates with us through all our senses for all of the creation is the handiwork of the Creator. However, when it comes to marking this new period in the year – this time of preparation of Christmas – there are few traditional symbols to mark it out and draw our attention to it. Most of those we have are borrowings from Lent – for as Advent emerged it became a kind of mini-Lent – such as violet vestments that are linked to penitence rather than preparation. However, while Lent begins with the wonderful symbol of ashes, there is no such equivalent for this day. This has led to a marvellous creativity in recent decades to find some rituals / objects / symbols that can mark this out as our period of specifically Christian preparation for the Christmas festival. Because there is no formal church-wide tradition, it is up to each community to be imaginative and find its own way of making this day, and these weeks, stand apart as special time. But it is also the case that most of this creativity is derived from catechetical sources and has the odour of the classroom about it: so that what we get is not a strong symbol with which we can relate, but a complex, sensible, *aide-mémoire* which cries out to be 'explained' – and that explanation is its meaning. What results is a set of codes – colours, dances, objects made in the classroom as 'symbols' – and then a set of decodings: usually a child reading a slip of paper which begins: 'we do this to re-mind ourselves that …' If this is what liturgy is about – re-minders of what we should be conscious of – then it is just an elaborate religion lesson and not an encounter with the sacred. Moreover, such so-called 'symbols' belong to the world of teaching, not the adult world of faith: symbols for adults do not need explanation and without any words can be embracing or dangerous: just observe the range of reactions to the secular symbol of flying a national flag.

So we need a symbolic opening for the season: it should be a genuine symbol belonging to liturgy rather than a visual aid supporting a lesson, and it should draw on the creativity of the community. However, if this seems too much then consider adopting a simple Advent wreath blessing as the introduction to this Sunday's Eucharistic assembly.

Introduction to the Celebration
If you do not use the Advent Wreath Blessing (see page 39), then:
Sisters and brothers, today is the first day of the season of Advent. In four weeks' time we will celebrate Christmas and the coming of the Son of God among us as our prophet, our priest, and our king. But to know who Jesus is, we must recall the faith of the people who looked out for him, we must look to the writings of the Old Testament to see what they say about the promise of God to visit his people – and during these coming weeks we will read much from the prophet Isaiah; we must recall those who prepared the way for his coming – and we will recall the work of John the Baptist; and we will reflect on how the Christ comes to birth in our world through our faith and discipleship – and we will remember Mary whose faith and acceptance of the invitation of God inaugurated the whole Christian era. Let us stop and in silence note that this moment is an important turning point in our year.

Rite of Penance
Lord Jesus, long ago you came among us as one of us
and proclaimed your gospel of peace, Lord have mercy.
Lord Jesus, you come among us today as we gather in your name and offer us your consolation, Christ have mercy.
Lord Jesus, you will come again as judge of the living and the dead according to your law of love, Lord have mercy.

Headings for Readings
First Reading
When the Lord comes he will inaugurate the reign of peace:
'nations ... shall beat their swords into ploughshares, and their
spears into pruning hooks; nation shall not lift up sword against
nation, neither shall they learn war any more.'

Second Reading
We are people of the day, we must act honourably for we walk
in the light of Christ, and must reflect that light.

Gospel
We Christians must stay awake: we do not know the moment
when we shall have to give an account of how we have lived our
lives as disciples.

Prayer of the Faithful
President
Friends, gathered here today we recall the first coming of the
Lord Jesus long ago, we remind ourselves that he will come
again, and we believe he is with us now in this assembly which
meets in his name. So in union with him let us pray to the Father.
Reader (s)
1. For all who embrace the name of Christ, that this will be a time
of a renewal of discipleship as we reflect that the Son of Man is
coming at an hour we do not expect. Lord hear us.
2. For all people of goodwill who over the coming weeks will see
Christian images and hear snippets of our story, that these religious pointers may help them discover a new spiritual depth in
their lives. Lord hear us.
3. For all who in the next month on hearing parts of our story
will be offended by it, or angered by it, that the Spirit will give
them a new tolerance and a new attitude of understanding. Lord
hear us.
4. For all who are ill, for all who are suffering, for all who are
persecuted for being followers of the Son of Man, that they may

experience the consolation of the nearness of the Christ. Lord hear us.

5. For all who will die this day, that the Son of Man will present them to their heavenly Father. Lord hear us.

President

Father, we are the people who long for the coming of your Son, hear our prayers and help us to be the presence of your Son in your creation, for we make these petitions through that same Christ, our Lord. Amen.

Eucharistic Prayer

Preface I of Advent (P1).

Invitation to the Our Father

In Advent we are recalling Jesus's first coming; we are looking forward to his final coming; meanwhile, with him we pray to the Father:

Sign of Peace

Isaiah prophesied that in the time of the Lord 'Nation shall not lift sword against nation, there will be no more training for war' – let us who celebrate here that the Lord has come, and reaffirm to each other that we will be peacemakers.

Invitation to Communion

Behold the One who has come, and who will come again, who today comes to us as our food and drink for our journey of discipleship, happy are we who share in this supper.

Communion Reflection

Read the first four paragraphs of the second reading (from the Catecheses of Cyril of Jerusalem) from today's Office of Readings (*Breviary*, vol 1, p 49 to the second line of p 50).

Conclusion

Solemn Blessing 1 for Advent (*Missal*, p 367).

COMMENTARY

First Reading: Is 2:1-5

One can think of the Book of Isaiah as the collection (i.e. the whole canonical book) of collections (i.e. [First] Isaiah – chs 1-39; Second-Isaiah – chs 40-55; and Third-Isaiah – chs 56-66) of collections of oracles and other materials. The opening line of today's reading is the introduction to one of these collections of oracles. The collection in question is 'Oracles concerning Judah and Jerusalem' and this collection embraces everything between 2:1 and 5:30. The remainder of the reading then stands as a nugget: the first oracle in this collection and it can be read as a single oracle to be interpreted as a message from the Lord through the prophet.

The oracle assumes a time of war when the nations do not know the Lord has his temple in Jerusalem and so attack his people. In contrast to this present state, the prophet looks forward to a future when the Lord is openly recognised as the universal king. In this 'new world order' the nations (Isaiah thinks of the world in terms of extended families each with a specific destiny within history) and their rulers do not come as conquerors to Jerusalem but as pilgrims. This is a reversal of history that takes place through the divine action, but the precondition is the abandonment of war by the nations.

This oracle has been read by Christians as looking forward to the time of the Christ who is universal king, brings peace, acts as the city on the hill that cannot be hidden, and whose message of salvation reaches out to nations (there are echoes of this oracle in Mt 5:14; Acts 2:17; Apoc 15:4; and Jn 4:22). But we should note that in Isaiah, this state of peace is placed in the indefinite future: it is not the promulgation of some earthly utopia, but a proclamation of the final victory of Yahweh and it is his gift presupposing covenant loyalty from his people. As such, the oracle can be read today as the promise of a world-to-come that God is preparing for his people beyond history; but that world sets the standard by which our actions in this world are to be judged.

The oracle supposes a tension: the reign of the Lord as the universal king is not some sort of perfection of this world 'when peace finally breaks out' – that would be to confuse the kingdom with an earthy utopia; but the coming kingdom does demand a way of living in the material world – to imagine that one could concentrate on heaven without working for peace on earth would be to separate God from his creation. The tension in Isaiah can be found again in the way we view Jesus as king (cf Jn 18:36), and in the way we set out the Christian hope alongside the Christian task.

Psalm 121(122)

This psalm picks up the theme of pilgrimage to Jerusalem. Within the liturgical imagination of Israel to arrive in the holy city, to enter the temple, is to arrive in the very presence of God. This coming into the holy presence of the temple can be understood by us by noting that it evokes the same ritual/liturgical response as that found in the post-Tridentine spirituality of a Visit to the Blessed Sacrament: here in the holy place, the Lord is present now, I am in his presence, here I can pray 'directly' to him. Read as part of the theme of this Sunday within Advent, it is the notion that we are the people on pilgrimage who are seeking the holy temple of the Lord, the heavenly Jerusalem as our final destination (see Gal 4:26): there we will encounter the Christ in his fullness.

Second Reading: Rom 13:11-14

This is the rhetorically rich conclusion to a section of the letter (12:1-13:14) dealing with the demands of upright Christian living. The key element in such a life is that the Father is worshipped in the Spirit. Now at the end of the section Paul wants to introduce a note of urgency: these are the end-times, action is required now rather than in some far-off time. This sense of the end-times is here a genuine attempt to draw out the eschatological nature of Christian existence rather than some simplistic notion that the end of the world was about to occur in a matter of a few years. For Paul, at this point in his development, the Christian destination is not to be confused with either an imminent Second Coming or some sort of perfection of the material world; the Christian must look forward to life in Christ with the Father; but the demands of that desire manifest themselves here and now. Hence the Christian must be putting on 'the armour (*ta hopla*) of light.' This is one of a set of images that Paul uses whose general sense is that the Christian must be Christ-like in 'fighting the good fight' of discipleship. However, in 1 Thess 5:8 Paul gives a neat explanation of what he means by 'the armour': faith, hope, charity. These are the ways that the Christian now must live for an upright, 'godly' life, and in that lifestyle s/he can be said 'to have put on Christ.'

In most contemporary western societies the notion of clothing denoting office or the assumption of responsibilities or lifestyles is now only a vague memory rather than a living metaphor – even those who still wear uniforms explain them in terms of utility for the job rather than as the insignia of office. In such a society the notion of 'putting on' or 'taking up the armour' is very distant; however, there is a contemporary image that conveys the notion: to set out on the work of discipleship we must be properly suited-up: that is, we have to have faith, hope and charity or else we will not survive in the hostile environment in which we find ourselves.

Gospel: Mt 24:37-44
The narrative time-setting of this passage is the first day of Holy Week, after the arrival in Jerusalem and before the anointing in Bethany. In all three synoptics there takes place at this point a series of statements about the end-times and this part of these gospels is referred to as 'the synoptic apocalypse'; in Matthew this takes the form of a long discourse (24:1-25:46) usually called the 'Eschatological Discourse'. The passage read today forms a unit in Matthew with the message: you must keep close watch for you don't know when the moment of the Son of Man will come. However, this is a matthaean construction because these

verses are found as two separate items in Lk: verse 37-41 in Lk 17; verses 42-44 in Lk 12.

The theme of watching and waiting for the coming of the Son of Man – read by Christians as the return of the Christ – is the central message of Advent, hence today's gospel passage can be seen as the perfect introduction to the whole season. However, it should be noted that it is taken into the liturgy without the apocalyptic baggage it has in Matthew. Here the watchfulness is seen to be part of the very condition of human existence and of Christian living – which is living in waiting and hope. However, the parousia of the Son of Man is imagined from the whole cloth of all we believe about the end-times with its images of completion, gathering in, restoration, healing, rest, and banquet. Here we take over Matthew's sense of urgency and need for care, but assume that it is linked to our whole picture of the Christ.

HOMILY NOTES

1. The time we are now entering is for most people 'the run up to Christmas'. It is that for us too, but it also has a far more serious side. To say that 'The Lord is coming' or to pray 'Come Lord Jesus' (*maranatha*) is part of the most basic Christian confession of faith: we are a people who are looking forward, who believe we are on a journey, a pilgrimage, towards a destination. This destination is an encounter with the Lord, and it is variously described as 'the Second Coming', the time of 'the return of the Son of Man', when he 'comes again to judge the living and the dead', of 'the Day of the Lord'. Indeed, we believe this journey toward the Day of the Lord is something that responds to a most basic instinct implanted within our humanity by the Creator: 'You [O God] have made us for yourself and our hearts are disquieted until they rest in You' (St Augustine, *Confessiones* 1,1,1). And, it is the Christian confession that we encounter God in his Christ. So part of our reflection in Advent is on the end-times and our encounter with the Lord when he comes again. So, in short, we are a people looking forward to the Day of the

Lord's Second Coming. And this is the time of year when our cycle of ritual puts these thoughts, as in today's gospel, before us.

2. To declare that we are waiting for when Christ 'will come again in glory to judge the living and the dead' (the creed), tells us nothing about the nature of the final judgment.

3. Since the first generation of Christians there has been a core belief that the time the people of Israel spent waiting for the coming of the promised Messiah is structurally similar to the time Christians spend waiting for the return of the Lord. Israel waiting for the first coming parallels the church waiting for the second coming. It is this logic of antetype and type that explains why we recall the waiting for the Christ in the first readings during Advent; while we then read about the Second Coming in the gospel readings in Advent. The common element between Israel and the church is that of waiting on the Christ to come; the difference is that Israel was waiting for the first coming, the church is waiting for the last coming. What Isaiah expected the Day of the Lord to be like is what we read in the first reading. 'He shall judge between the nations, and shall arbitrate for many peoples; they shall beat their swords into ploughshares, and their spears into pruning hooks; nation shall not lift up sword against nation, neither shall they learn war any more.'

4. If we want to know what the judgement will be like at the Second Coming, we look to the message of the Christ in his first coming. Many then thought that the Day of the Lord would be the 'great crunch' – a warrior messiah that would dole out vengeance and wrath. Instead the Lord came as the re-builder of Israel, the one who brought healing, who called disciples to love God and neighbour, and established reconciliation with the Father. This is the nature of the judgement we now wait for and proclaim. With truth we can call this, amidst the panics and fears that are always said to be on the horizon of the future, the good news. The Day of the Lord is not the 'great crunch', but the day of peace: 'He shall judge

between the nations, and shall arbitrate for many peoples;
they shall beat their swords into ploughshares, and their
spears into pruning hooks; nation shall not lift up sword
against nation, neither shall they learn war any more.'

First Sunday of Advent (Year B)

To mark the beginning of the new season, something like the blessing of the Advent Wreath, pp 39-42, is probably better than just a verbal introduction. However, if that is not an option then here are some notes.

Introduction to the Celebration

Today we begin Advent. This is the period when we prepare to celebrate the coming of the Christ among us two millennia ago, but we also believe that he is coming among us now and so we have to be prepared to receive him, and we know that he will come again at the End of time and we have to prepare the world for his coming. Everything we do as Christians is related to these three comings. We must now recall that it is because he first came in Palestine back then, that we are assembled here for the Eucharist today; gathered, here and now, we ask pardon of our sins that we might be prepared for his second coming in this Eucharist; and as a community let us pray that we will be ready to stand before him when he comes again in glory.

Rite of Penance

Lord Jesus, you came first in Bethlehem of Judea proclaiming the Father's love, Lord have mercy.

Lord Jesus, you come now into our gatherings with your for-giveness, Christ have mercy.

Lord Jesus, you will come again to judge the living and the dead, Lord have mercy.

Headings for Readings
First Reading

This reading announces the great theme of Advent: God our Father is sending the Redeemer into our midst. God made us, God cares for us, God looks upon us, God is with us.

Second Reading

Advent reminds us that we are a people who are waiting for the return of the Lord Jesus in glory; meanwhile, we must pray – as St Paul did for the church in Corinth – that we will not be without any of the gifts of the Holy Spirit.

Gospel

When will the Lord come to meet us? We do not know the day nor the hour. We are a people who are called to stay awake, to be alert to the demands of being followers of Jesus in every moment of our lives.

Prayer of the Faithful
President

On this first day of Advent we begin our annual recollection of the Lord's coming in human history, his coming in our lives as his disciples today, and his coming at the end of time. Knowing that he has come among us because we are gathered in his name, let us place our needs before the Father.

Reader(s)

1. For the whole church of God, that this time of recollection will renew us as followers of the Word made flesh. Lord hear us.

2. For all people of good will, that they may have wisdom and strength to do what is just and right. Lord hear us.

3. For ourselves in this church, that as we prepare for Christmas we may grow in wisdom and insight. Lord hear us.

4. For all who are in need, that the Lord might come to them with his comfort and healing. Lord hear us.

5. For all who have died, that they may rise with the Lord in his coming in glory. Lord hear us.

President

Father, hear our prayer to you at the beginning of this holy season and as once you heard the prayers of your people and sent them your Son, so now hear us and answer our needs through that same Christ, our Lord. Amen.

Eucharistic Prayer
Preface of Advent I (P1).

Invitation to the Our Father
Because Jesus came among us to give us a relationship to the
Father, we can now stand and pray:

Sign of Peace
Peace with God is our final destination. We must begin that journey by building peace with those around us. Let us offer each
other the peace of Christ.

Invitation to Communion
Behold the Lord who stands at the end of time beckoning us to
come to him, and who now calls us to share in this table.

Communion Reflection
The first Preface of Advent (*Missal*, p 404) is a splendid summary
of the faith of the church as it is celebrated in this season. Begin
reading it by changing the tense of the opening sentence: Father,
we now give you thanks through Jesus Christ our Lord. Then
read the next two sentences and conclude with Amen after 'will
come again in his glory'.

Conclusion
Solemn Blessing 1 for Advent (*Missal*, p 367).

COMMENTARY

First Reading: Is 63:16-17; 64:1. 3-8
This is an elegant selection of pieces out of a single section of the
work of Trito-Isaiah. The section in question (63:7-64:11) is a
confession of sin by Israel in the presence of God who is recalled
as a God of care and mercy. How do we know how loving and
caring God is? By looking at how he seeks out and offers new
life and love to the sinner.

This reading sets the tone of repentance in Advent: repentance is possible because God is so loving and repentance is desirable as it brings the Lord into our worlds and lives. There is a tendency in popular presentations of the scriptures to present a facile opposition between the 'Old Testament God of fear' and the 'New Testament God of love' – today's reading is a reminder of how silly such reductions are.

Second Reading: 1 Cor 1:3-9

This is Paul's opening to his letter that takes the form of a thanksgiving for the church in Corinth. Since it is a thanksgiving, that is, something which is equivalent to a blessing, he has to give the reason why he is blessing God, thanking God, for this church: the reason is that it is a community which has been brought into existence by a divine call and which, in accordance with that vocation, is waiting for the return of the Christ and has among its members all the gifts of the Spirit. Thus Paul's blessing functions as a reminder of the inner identity of what a church is: a community called in Christ, empowered by and using the gifts of the Spirit, waiting for the end, and living to the glory of God [the Father]. This ecclesial vision is Trinitarian – even if Paul would not have recognised such a language – in its elaboration of deep identity. Moreover, this vision of the church assumes that each community has an integrity given it by the Spirit in its actual structures. It is with regard to this latter aspect that the modern community is most at variance with Paul's understanding of an actual church. We can see this in that today there will be many communities who cannot gather for the Eucharist – fundamental to Corinthian identity – simply because no bishop has ordained someone to preside. This is unthinkable to Paul as the Spirit gives all the gifts needed within the church. Indeed, Paul would probably have seen the current situation in many communities as blasphemous because to assume that there is no one gifted by the Spirit to preside (and whom the rest of the church could authorise by the laying-on of hands) is tantamount to denying that the Spirit is working now in the churches.

If, by chance, this reading is being used at a 'Communion Service' which is 'replacing' the Eucharist due to the lack of someone with the licit use of valid Orders, it might be appropriate for the person with the canonical duty of the care of souls in that place to write something in the Newsletter, pointing out the absurd irony of reading this theology of the church (which assumes that the Spirit would gift someone so that he would be suitable to preside) and declaring it 'the word of the Lord', while at the same time assuming that there is no one suitable available so that that community could have the Eucharist (recalling that having the Eucharist on Sunday is also deemed to be the divine will).

Gospel: Mk 13:33-37

Mark introduced an apocalyptic section into his gospel (13:5-37) just before the account of the passion of Jesus; and this arrangement was later taken up by both Matthew and Luke. Since, therefore, this apocalyptic section is now found in all three synoptic gospels it has been given the name of the 'Synoptic Apocalypse' as if it were a distinct item found in all three; in fact, it is something found in Mark which is then adapted in various ways by the other two. However, the fact that it is found at all in Mark, and then struck a cord with both the others, shows that there was a strong apocalyptic element – not just a belief in an imminent parousia – among many people who joined the Jesus movement. Presumably, many who followed the religion of Israel with an apocalyptic mindset retained that vision of the universe when they became followers of Jesus. So following Jesus was retained together with an apocalyptic faith, and each was simply adapted and dovetailed to the other. This may seem strange to us for it seems that one of the distinctive features of Jesus's teaching – and which sets his teaching apart from that of John the Baptist – was the absence of apocalypticism. However, shaking off such beliefs is far harder than adopting new ones, and those who already viewed the world as just about to face the great crisis, disaster, and judgement simply continued to hold these while accepting Jesus as messiah and joining in the gatherings of his disciples. How deeply rooted these ideas were within their religious mindset can be seen from the fact that they transmitted that mindset to Christianity where it still thrives on the margins of most major churches and is central to many popular movements today.

What we have today is the concluding call, literally 'the watchword', of Mark's apocalypse. The section begins with a note on signs of the coming crisis, then a description of troubles, then the prediction of the breakdown of the sacred ('the desolating sacrilege'), then the prediction of the coming of the Son of Man as an end-times' figure, a reminder of the nearness of those times, and lastly, the bit we read, what must be the attitude of those who wish to survive: be alert! The overall message is that of any apocalyptic discourse: you should be nervous and on-edge and ready for action. It is interesting to note that while surveys now keep noting the death of formal Christian belief in western societies today, such apocalyptic versions of Christianity are actually increasing; and probably have not been as prevalent with Latin Catholicism at any time since the Black Death as they are today; witness such popular forms of piety as the so-called 'Divine Mercy' cult or the cult of 'the messages of Fatima'. Moreover, many politicians and much of the media thrive on a secular apocalypticism: there is some great disaster or ill-defined threat looming, and only urgent extreme action can 'save' the situation: hence their extreme actions are justified! It is important to note the prevalence of these attitudes in our world for there are many in the average gathering today who will find an immediate rapport with this snippet of gospel and find therein the justification for many of their most deeply held beliefs. Within the context of the liturgy, however, this section of text is expected to convey an entirely different message.

Within the liturgy the watching is for the coming of the Christ as that is celebrated within Advent: we are to be alert and sensitive to the coming of Christ now – in the liturgy, in the action of the People of God, within our society and culture, within our hearts, minds and imaginations. 'Watching' is thus a call to a new awareness, a new mind (literally *'metanoia'*), and a willingness to discover the Christ – who is the Logos who is present in the whole creation – in unexpected ways.

HOMILY NOTES

1. On this first Sunday of Advent the church's thoughts are concentrated not on the coming of the Lord in Palestine two millennia ago, nor upon the new liturgical year, but on the Second Coming at 'the end of time', the Last Days, the Parousia, the Eschaton, 'The End'. This is not a popular topic for preaching. Indeed when most preachers, excluding those from the fundamentalist fringes, are asked about the topic they say that it is one best left alone. However, while preachers are silent, that does not mean that this topic is not communicated in popular programmes, urban folklore, and ill-informed comment in the media. Most people think they are more than familiar with the Christian view of the end-times: it's the apocalyptic nightmare when God is going to come as fearful destroyer, give everyone their come-uppance, and it will be a combination of a horror film and a cataclysm. Such thoughts about 'The End' are seen to show that in the final analysis God is a mean brute exacting vengeance; and religion is just a scare story of a wicked father punishing misdeeds. This may seem a caricature, but it is widely held and one that many Christians are happy to adhere to as when there are calls for getting back to the real days of preaching when people were told what's what. Moreover, a glance at Christian religious TV from the USA will show you that there are more than enough communicators of the 'God as brute vengeance' message in the world today.

2. Given this fact of so much misinformation in the public imagination about The End, this opportunity to say something that is not sensationalist and does express the church's faith on the eschaton should not be passed over.

3. The place to begin is to acknowledge that there are two dis-

tinct views, schools of thought, about The End within the Christian tradition and that these views go back to the time of the earliest followers of Jesus. On the one hand there is the familiar view that God will come as avenging justice and repay the wicked with suffering: The End as the Great Crunch. A careful reading of the evidence in the gospels makes it almost certain that this was the vision of The End that was preached by John the Baptist: 'His winnowing fork is in his hand, and he will clear his threshing floor and will gather his wheat into the granary; but the chaff he will burn with unquenchable fire' (Mt 3:12). One of the matters where Jesus's teaching is very different from that of John the Baptist is on precisely this point: The End that Jesus announces as coming is one where suffering humanity is delivered through the Father's love. For Jesus, The End is the Great Banquet. He preached a future in terms of banquet, harvest, rest, and fullness. The stark choice between the message of Jesus and that of the prophet John is the choice between the Great Banquet and the Great Crunch. However, in so far as many of John's followers became followers of Jesus, they seem to have retained the Baptist's vision of the future; or they seem to have perceived Jesus's message as a refinement of John's, rather than its replacement.

4. Down the centuries these two visions of The End have exercised varying amounts of influence in preaching. Some parts of the church have read, indeed devoured, the Great Crunch approach which has its clearest expression in the Book of the Apocalypse. Other parts of the church have been so appalled by it – the Greek churches on the whole – that while they have kept it in the canon, they have refused to read it in the liturgy. Other parts of the church have preached the Great Crunch, but then used the Great Banquet language of Jesus as the key to imagery about the life of the world to come. Often the two have sat uncomfortably beside one another as if one was the 'real' message, while the other was 'the sugar-coated' variant. But we are called to make a clear choice between the message of John and that of Jesus.

5. The basic message of Jesus about the coming of the Lord is that of being brought into the Banquet of life: God is love, healer, restorer, mercy. If this is our faith, then this must form our vision of the Second Coming. Just as the First Coming was not the mighty warrior king that many hoped for, but love made flesh in Jesus Christ who reconciled the world to the Father, so the Second Coming is the mercy of God in Jesus Christ who reconciles us to the Father and bids us to takes our places in the Great Banquet. Hence our presence today at the Eucharist: this is the foretaste of that banquet. Christ's coming now in our gathering is the anticipation of his final coming.

6. To reflect on how we view the Second Coming is the challenge to purify our mind's images of the future, of the message of the Christ, and our image of God. It is to replace the image of the Great Crunch with the Great Banquet; to replace the image of vengeance with that of mercy; to replace the image of God is power with that of God is love.

7. For Christians, the future is good news!

First Sunday of Advent (Year C)

To mark the beginning of the new season, something like the blessing of the Advent Wreath, pp 39-42, is probably better than just a verbal introduction. However, if that is not an option then here are some notes.

Introduction to the Celebration

Today we begin Advent. This is the period when we prepare to celebrate the coming of the Christ among us two millennia ago, but we also believe that he is coming among us now and so we have to be prepared to receive him, and we know that he will come again at the end of time and we have to prepare the world for his coming. Everything we do as Christians is related to these three comings. So let us reflect on how it is because he first came that we are here at the Eucharist today; gathered now we ask pardon of our sins that we might be prepared for his second coming in this Eucharist; and as a community let us pray that we will be ready to stand before him when he comes again in glory.

Rite of Penance

O Son of David, you came announcing peace, Lord have mercy.
O Son of Man, you come now offering reconciliation, Christ have mercy.
O Son of God, you will come to share with us your glory, Lord have mercy.

Or use Option c. iii (*Missal*, p 392-3) which is appropriate.

Headings for Readings
First Reading

We recall that the Lord prepared the way for the coming of the Christ: he promised redemption to all who waited for the Son of David; now he promises redemption to us who wait for his coming in glory.

Second Reading

The Lord came once in Bethlehem to announce the good news; he will come again and gather together all his disciples: we who are called to be saints.

Gospel

The Son of Man will come again with great glory. Meanwhile we must be watchful and attentive disciples: careful builders of the Kingdom.

Prayer of the Faithful
President

Sisters and Brothers, as we begin this time of preparation for our joyful celebration of the coming of the Son of God as our brother, let us pray to the Father that we may become a people who express the shape of Christ in our world.

Reader(s)

1. That we may be found awake at the Lord's return, Lord hear us.

2. That we may have the confidence to stand before the Son of Man, Lord hear us.

3. That we may be the people of hope, Lord hear us.

4. That all who see the Christian people may see an expression of love, Lord hear us.

5. That all who are troubled may have the blessing of peace, Lord hear us.

6. That we may bring the Lord's love and comfort to all who suffer, Lord hear us.

7. That the dead be welcomed home by the Lord, Lord hear us.

President

Father, these weeks of preparation for Christmas remind us that you sent your Son among us, and that he will return. Meanwhile hear the requests your Son's people make to you through him, Christ our Lord. Amen.

Eucharistic Prayer
Preface I of Advent (P1).

Invitation to the Our Father
The Son of God invites us to pray to his Father and our Father,
and so we say:

Sign of Peace
Long ago people looked forward to the coming of the Prince of
Peace. Now we are called by him to be peacemakers. Let us
begin by expressing our desire to overcome divisions in our own
community by offering each other the sign of peace.

Invitation to Communion
He invited the shepherds and the wise men to Bethlehem,
He calls all to come to him at the end of time,
And now, here, he calls each of us to share his table.
Happy are we who hear this invitation.

Communion Reflection
Father,
We are waiting and watching for the return of Christ our Lord in
glory.
Long ago you anointed Jesus Christ with the oil of gladness as
our eternal priest and universal king.
As priest he offered his life on the altar of the cross and re-
deemed the human race by this one perfect sacrifice of praise.
As king he has dominion over all creation,
That he may present to you, his almighty Father,
An eternal and universal kingdom:
A kingdom of truth and life,
A kingdom of holiness and grace,
A kingdom of justice, love, and peace. Amen.

Conclusion
Solemn Blessing 1 for Advent (*Missal*, p 367).

COMMENTARY

First Reading: Jer 33:14-16

This is a prophecy about the future restoration of Judah and Jerusalem: God has not abandoned his covenant; the throne of David will be filled again. This loyalty to his covenant with Israel constitutes redemption; and when his promised one appears he will come bringing justice to the whole people. This theme of Christ as the virtuous branch from the tree of David was taken over by Christians from the earliest days (see the genealogy in Matthew) and stands behind the imagery of the Davidic family tree of Jesus.

Second Reading: 1 Thess 3:12-4:2

Thessalonica was an important city economically, politically, and culturally. While it had a sizable synagogue it would appear that the first Christians were mainly gentile converts, and they must have thought of themselves as just one more variant within the city's cosmopolitan religious landscape. However, this letter to them is one of the less well-known parts of the canon (by comparison, for instance, with Romans or the letters to the Corinthians) which is a pity as it is probably the earliest Christian text that we can date with anything approaching certainty. It would appear that it was written in AD 50 and it is Paul's first extant piece of writing. This in itself makes it a text of great interest.

However, it is also a letter that presents many problems: a quick reading of today's text would immediately suggest that this is the conclusion of a letter, a final exhortation, yet in fact this comes from mid-way through the text. This might be explained, as some maintain, by it being a collection of shorter letters preserved as a single text; or it could be that Paul wants to keep returning to the theme of exhortation. Whatever is the answer to that question, it is clear that Paul sees his task as encouraging his new converts to remain in hope and to look forward to the coming of the Lord with the saints. Thus this is an attempt to strengthen them to wait and to hope for the return of the Christ.

Gospel: Lk 21:25-28, 34-36
The apocalypse discourse of Luke's gospel (i.e. what we often think of as his version of the 'Synoptic Apocalypse') runs from 21:8 to 21:36. What we have here are two parts of that section, and from the point of view of the liturgical understanding of scripture what is omitted in today's reading is as important as what is included:
Verses 25-28
This is a unit concerning the parousia of the Son of Man
Omitted Verses 29-31
The parable of the Fig Tree – on how close in time is the parousia
Omitted Verses 32-33
On the timing of the parousia
Verses 34-36
Conclusion of the whole apocalyptic discourse.

The stress in the reading is on the final coming of the Lord in glory, while omitting any references that could be understood in apocalyptic terms, and which could give rise to millenarian questions. This careful avoidance of an apocalyptical framework in the reading indicates that such speculation should have no place in the homily or in the overall presentation of this Sunday's theme which is the Final Coming of the Christ.

HOMILY NOTES

1. On this first Sunday of Advent the church's thoughts are concentrated not on the coming of the Lord in Palestine two millennia ago, nor upon the new liturgical year, but on the Second Coming at 'the end of time'. What do we mean by this curious phrase: 'the end of time'?
2. Approaching this theme in a homily presents three difficulties. First, it can easily be heard as apocalypticism. That is, it seems to the hearers that there is a direct link between some breakdown in the world order now (either in the social order, the realm of justice, peace, or some vague threat from a monstrous other) and God's action of punishing or letting everyone get what they deserve. In this scenario, everything going

wrong is actually a bizarre proof that Christians are right and that the more disastrous things get the more it shows that God is in charge for he has already written the script. An example of this is the position of many American fundamentalists on the problems of climate change: no use doing anything about it, it is part of God's plan to punish the world for not being 'saved'. Such ideas are far from the perspective of most Catholics, but there has been an enormous growth in Catholic apocalypticism since the 1980s and many people in any average congregation will be disposed to hearing today's gospel, and any talk about the end times, in such millenarian terms. It is significant that the two sections of the discourse that are most explicitly part of the apocalyptic tradition are omitted today: clearly, apocalypticism has no place in Advent preaching.

3. Second, there is a danger that speaking about the end times is not about the consummation of the universe, but a finger-wagging exercise about the religious equivalent of what some cosmologists call the 'Great Crunch'. Whatever we say about the them end times must be clearly part of God's plan. Hence it is part of God's loving plan for the universe and so must be appreciably part of the good news. There has been a curious double think about this: God is love, but if you don't love, then God holds a stick! Such presentations are necessarily false: the coming to completion of the creation, the kingdom, is the completion of God's loving plan. It must be presented as analogous to the end of year party, not the end of term exams.

4. Third, there are few areas of our faith where we know less, where our language is more strained, and where our images are less precise. Ironically, the fact that there is so little we can say about the Consummation has actually left a gap which imagination has filled to overflowing, and not always with a profound outcome.

5. Here is a possible approach to the question. First, the 'End of the World' has two meanings. There is the very obvious one

of the cosmos coming to an end or the whole created order being radically transformed by God. The second meaning of the end of the world is the end of the world I as an individual inhabit: my world will come to an end at my death. In regard to the first meaning we have no information whatsoever within revelation as to when the universe will cease (this is a point worth making as there have been, and still are, many who engage in 'scriptural mathematics' using the Book of Daniel and the Apocalypse of John to find out how long more the world has got!). On the second meaning of the end of the world, my death, we are in a different situation: I may not know the day nor the hour (and am glad that I do not know this), but I am certain that I am going to die. Whatever happens in the future of my life, good things or bad things, I know that it will end. That end will be my end time, my eschaton.

6. Whichever meaning we use, there is a common feature: at The End we must not imagine a giant chasm, but the figure of the Logos who shares a human nature with all approaching him as their priest, prophet, and king. Christ as King stands at the end of time gathering all the fragments of each of our lives, and of the life of the whole cosmos, and refashioning that existence so that nothing is lost. He gathers and refashions our life so that as a new creation this existence, my life, can be presented to the Father.

7. The Good News is that the end is not a crunch, but the glorious figure of the Lord.

8. The end is the gathering of all the little pieces of our scattered and fragmented lives, all our joys, all our collaborations with the grace of God, all the goodness we have sought to create, the peace we have fostered, the reconciliation that we have sought, the acts of kindness and mercy, the attempts to witness to the truth in the face of falsehood or injustice. All these scattered actions are gathered into a new existence that the Christ can offer to the Father in the Spirit.

9. The word 'End' is a word with many sad connotations for us:

the end of a relationship, the end of a film or a moment of en-
joyment, the pain that is a common part of the ending of a
life. We look forward to the consummation, the completion
of the universe. Thus can we read in the gospel: 'then [we]
will see the Son of Man coming in a cloud with power and
great glory. Now when these things begin to take place, look
up and raise your heads, because your redemption is draw-
ing near' (Lk 21:27-8).

Blessing for an Advent Wreath

The Advent Wreath appeared in Lutheran Germany in the nine-teenth century as part of a renewed interest in celebrating the liturgical year. It soon spread within the German-speaking lands where it was a catechetical object in the church building and in the home. It was to be a specific symbolic object of 'what was really being celebrated' amidst the range of other prepar-ations and trimmings that were and are part of German Christmas festivities. It began to spread to other countries through catechetical materials borrowed from German and Dutch sources in the 1960s. It is now firmly established in most parishes as part of the Advent decorations and has a place in the catechetical programme for this time of year in most countries. However, there is little evidence that in English-speaking coun-tries that it has established itself as a domestic symbol. We should therefore note that its value as a symbol is more limited than some of the enthusiasm for its adoption would suggest. First, as yet it has little emotional currency for people in that it is not integrated within their family/household traditions. Put an-other way, if people were asked to think of things they associate with Advent, this wreath would come low down on the list. Second, it still is linked with the classroom: a little nice piece of craftwork/artwork/religion that belongs to the children of be-tween 8 and 10 years. This means that it can become so bur-dened with questions-and-answers about 'what does it mean?' that it cannot speak for itself. Third, because of its links with the classroom it can be seen as belonging to something that is 'done for the children'. A religious symbol must be able to speak to the whole community. Moreover, one of the secularising forces that undermines liturgy is the widespread notion that 'Christmas is really about children.' That reduces the celebration of our won-der before the incarnation to nostalgic retelling of fairytales. Hence any action that encourages the 'Christmas is the children's time' must be treated with suspicion in the liturgy. On the other hand, the wreath is a simple object, it uses candles as lights which is part of the basic vocabulary of our ritual; it can mark the passing of the time of preparation, and it can mark off this time as special: so until you conceive a better symbolic object, you should make use of this.

Form

The simplest form is that it is four thick candles in a wreath or bed of holly or other greenery. In some catechetical books – and in some of the 'off the peg' wreaths sold by church suppliers – it takes on more complex forms such as purple candles or three purple and a pink candle or a five candle arrangement that includes Christmas. Such added complexity miss the point: if you have to explain the pink candle then it turns it into a piece of code rather than a symbol; if you include Christmas you forget that it is to mark the movement of time up to Christmas: Christmas itself is something new, not the highpoint of Advent. And, as for coloured candles, they just make it harder to see the candles against the greenery. But it is important to use thick candles, as they have to be seen both lighted and unlighted (narrow candles are hard to see at any distance if they are unlighted). However, the whole arrangement must be large enough that it is visible to the whole community and be a public object in the liturgical space. Many of the wreaths used are based on those suitable in size for a classroom and are simply lost in a big building. Just look at the size of the Big Six candles of the former rite to see the size candles have to be if they are to make their presence felt in a building.

Location

The area near the eucharistic table, in what is in most church buildings is the former sanctuary, is where most wreaths are located. A moment's thought shows that this is not a good idea. Nothing should distract from the table around which we gather for the Eucharist – it is the centre of our worship and our building – anything placed near it piles on layers of complexity that can simply confuse. Moreover, the area around the table is already full of clutter: the ambo is often but a pace or two away, the chair likewise, sometimes a lectern, and a jumble of odd seats, stools, and kneelers – and this is not to mention a tabernacle. And, having everything near the president at the Eucharist can give the impression that the area around the table is a stage: you watch it to see what is happening up there. Yet liturgical space is something that envelops everyone at the Eucharist: the whole space is where we act our celebration. Probably the best place is near the door of the assembly. There can be a procession there to bless it, and it is seen close-up by everyone passing in and out over the four weeks of preparation.

Blessing
Here is a possible rite of blessing.
Form a procession with incense, cross, lights, and proceed to the wreath while one of the Advent hymns is sung; then begin the Eucharist at the wreath.

Dear Friends,
The time of Advent is once more upon us. In the coming days and weeks we will recall God's plan of salvation when he prepared his chosen people to receive his Son; we shall recall that we today are called to bring Christ to birth in our world and that we must renew our commitment during these weeks to being his disciples; we shall remind ourselves that he shall come again at the end of time, judging the living and the dead.

Let us pray.
Almighty God,
We pray you to bless + this Advent Wreath and make it holy.
Today we begin to recall how your Son's coming was proclaimed by all the prophets;
how the virgin mother bore him in her womb with love beyond all telling;

and how John the Baptist was his herald and made him known
when at last he came.
Grant that this time of preparation will increase our holiness and
give us new strength to follow in your Son's way.
We make this prayer through Christ our Lord. Amen.

Incense the wreath.

The Lord be with you.
And also with you.
The beginning of the holy Gospel according to John [1:1-14].
In the beginning was the Word, and the Word was with God,
and the Word was God. He was in the beginning with God; all
things were made through him, and without him was not anything made that was made. In him was life, and the life was the
light of men.
Pause while a new flame is struck and one of the candles lighted.
Then continue:
The light shines in the darkness, and the darkness has not overcome it. There was a man sent from God, whose name was John.
He came for testimony, to bear witness to the light, that all might
believe through him. He was not the light, but came to bear witness to the light. The true light that enlightens every man was
coming into the world. He was in the world, and the world was
made through him, yet the world knew him not. He came to his
own home, and his own people received him not. But to all who
received him, who believed in his name, he gave power to become children of God; who were born, not of blood nor of the
will of the flesh nor of the will of man, but of God. And the Word
became flesh and dwelt among us, full of grace and truth; we
have beheld his glory, glory as of the only Son from the Father.
This is the gospel of the Lord.

*The procession returns to area around the table, the celebrant going to
the chair to pray the opening prayer.*

Second Sunday of Advent (Year A)

Introduction to the Celebration

Christmas is coming! If you are not already busy preparing, then you will have at least heard many people telling you it is time you started getting ready. As the people of God we too need to start thinking about the welcoming of the Christ and the preparations that we are called upon to make as disciples. We must prepare the way for the Lord to enter our lives, to enter the lives of those around us, and to enter into our world with his word of peace and forgiveness.

Rite of Penance

Lord Jesus, your way was prepared by John the Baptist, Lord have mercy.

Lord Jesus, you are Son of God and Son of Mary, Christ have mercy.

Lord Jesus, your coming brought the kingdom of forgiveness and peace, Lord have mercy.

Headings for Readings
First Reading

Christ has come among us: he is the rallying point calling all nations to himself; he is coming with righteousness; he is coming in peace; he is coming offering us a whole new way to live with others; he offers a new way for humanity.

Second Reading

Christ's coming fulfilled the promises to Israel, but his coming was to all humanity so that all peoples might glorify God for his mercy.

44 LITURGICAL RESOURCES

Gospel

Today we recall the ministry of St John the Baptist. Jesus said about John: among those born of women no one has arisen greater than John the Baptist (Mt 11:11) for his mission was to prepare a people who would receive the Christ and announce him when he came. We see John as the culmination of the centuries of preparation and the work of the prophets, and now on the brink of the coming of the Christ he announces: 'repent, for the kingdom of heaven is near.'

Prayer of the Faithful
President

Friends, we are the people who are in the interval between the comings of Christ: we are preparing this month to recall his first coming; we are praying that we might be ready as a church for his coming in glory. Now in this interval time we walk by faith and call on our heavenly Father for our needs.
Reader(s)

1. For the whole church, that we will prepare the way of the Lord. Lord hear us.

2. For all people, that they may find the way of peace and goodwill, Lord hear us.

3. For this church gathered here, that we will witness to Christ's coming in our world. Lord hear us.

4. For all our needs: ... *insert some local needs and needs of the moment* ... That the Lord will hear his people's plea. Lord hear us.

5. For our departed brothers and sisters, that they may see the Lord's coming in glory. Lord hear us.
President

Father, recalling the advent of your Son and seeking to prepare his way now today, we make these prayers to you. Hear them and grant them for we ask them through Christ our Lord. Amen.

Eucharistic Prayer
Preface of Advent I (P1), (*Missal*, p 404.)

Invitation to the Our Father
As we wait in joyful hope for the coming of our Saviour, Jesus Christ, we pray:

Sign of Peace
St Paul tells us to 'Welcome one another, as Christ has welcomed you, for the glory of God': so, let us offer welcome and peace to each other.

Invitation to Communion
Behold him who has come among us and will come again in glory; in the meanwhile let us behold him in this supper to which he beckons us. Lord I am not worthy …

Communion Reflection
May the God of steadfastness and encouragement
grant us to live in such harmony with one another,
in accord with Christ Jesus,
that together we may with one voice
glorify the God and Father of our Lord Jesus Christ.
And, may we welcome one another,
as Christ has welcomed us,
for the glory of God.
Based on the second reading.

Conclusion
Solemn Blessing 1 for Advent (*Missal*, p 367).

COMMENTARY

We normally expect that there is some connection or common theme between the first reading and the gospel. However, today there is no such link. Within the lectionary's rationale, today and next Sunday focus on the preaching and work of John the Baptist (hence today's gospel), while the first reading is simply one that is in harmony with the main themes of the Advent season. So today, unless one takes a very generic Advent theme, one should not try to find 'common themes': we have, in effect, three distinct readings which severally are suitable to the time in one way or another.

First Reading: Is 11:1-10

This reading from proto-Isaiah, or at least the first nine verses of it, is an oracle belonging to the second group of oracles 'concerning Judah and Israel' (9:7-12:6). It presents an idyllic future king who has all the attributes of wisdom, is a manifestation in his work of 'the spirit of the Lord,' and whose images show up just what wicked and unworthy kings the people have now. Indeed, to get this perfect king it is not enough to have an improvement on the present situation or even to reform the existing monarchy. You have to go right back to before there was any king – to the time of Jesse the father of David – and start over from scratch. In Isaiah's eyes in this passage the whole monarchy, all the kingly structures, is corrupt and 'unfit for purpose': it is not simply a case that the institution has the divine favour and it's just now and then there is a bad incumbent; rather the whole tree is corrupt. Only by starting afresh can Israel get the blessings of righteous, holy, and priestly rule: the sort of image that sacral kings both in Egypt and Mesopotamia regularly presented as flowing from their priestly work of ordering the state and the cosmos. Such kings ruled with wisdom, they produced order, and they produced the fruitfulness of the land and people. How can his audience get this ideal sort of king? Well, the situation is so bad that they will have to start over and forget any notion of divine investment in the monarchy as such. The final verse is probably an addition to the original oracle acting as a summary of what has gone before and a link to the next oracle.

However, when this text is read by Christians it takes on a wholly different colour as one of the key prophetic texts speaking of a divinely appointed messianic figure who is the saviour of the people. Now the stump is the symbol of the royal 'genes' that produces the royal genealogy of Christ in Matthew's gospel, and this is a symbol of God's continuity in providential care throughout the history of salvation. The spirit of the Lord is the new gift of the Holy Spirit who here gives his seven-fold gifts to animate the new community. In the text as we read it (in either the NRSV, RSV, or JB) this Spirit can only be linked with six gifts (wisdom, insight, counsel, power, knowledge, and the fear of the Lord), however, the Holy Spirit is, on the basis of this text in the Septuagint, always linked with seven gifts within the tradition. This occurred by its rendering the Hebrew word for 'knowledge' by the phrase 'knowing and reverence.' It is this longer rendering that influenced the Latin (*spiritus sapientiae et intellectus … consilii et fortitudinis … scientiae et pietatis et … timoris Domini*), and so the list (wisdom, understanding, counsel, forti-tude, knowledge, piety, and fear of the Lord) that is used in the catechesis for Confirmation. When the new King appears, upon him rests the fullness of the Spirit and he imparts the Spirit's 'gifts' to his followers. This new age is the age of peace, harmony, and the reconciliation of the creation. This is now the perfect Christian future, and it presents one of the great Christian im-ages of the future and of the eschaton – so much at odds with the future preached by the gloom-mongers. The time of the Christ is the perfect time, the time of justice, and the time of perfect hap-piness. Within the Christian reading the final verse is the perfect ending of the oracle: the great ensign towards which all the nations are drawn and which finds its echo in Jn 12:32.

This text can really set the tone for Advent and our sense of joyful longing for the Christ: it is the image of the Kingdom at the moment of the fullness of the church as Christ's body.

Second Reading: Rom 15:4-9
The reader of the lectionary in English today might well wonder why this piece of Paul – it is not a well-rounded unit as can be seen in its opening phrase – was selected for Advent. The an-swer lies in the history of the lectionary's origins: this was the epistle for the Second Sunday of Advent in the Missal of 1570 and it was retained in the new lectionary as there was a desire to show some continuities where possible.

The reading in its Vulgate version points out a distinction between the time before the Christ and the time of the Christ that is
not nearly so obvious in English translations. Its key usage here
is that it states that the hopes of Israel which are written down in
the scriptures are fulfilled in Christ; the hope of the patriarchs is
fulfilled in Christ. For Paul, in what is his exhortation section of
the letter, then wants us to draw the conclusion that if hopes are
fulfilled in Christ, then the time has come when the gentiles (his
audience) can rejoice in the Christ. This implies that they behave
towards one another as Christ behaves towards them.

Within the context of Advent, this reading does show how
the theme of Christ as the fulfillment of the hopes of Israel and
the fulfillment of the promises made in the past – themes used
repeatedly in the Advent liturgy – have been themes within the
kerygma since the beginning.

Gospel: Mt 3:1-12
This gospel passage forms a unit within Matthew: it is his presentation of the preaching of John the Baptist in his role as har-
binger of the last times, i.e. the time of the Christ who is Jesus.
However, Matthew has retained much of the actual dynamic of
preaching that can be seen in the gospels as being that of John
the Baptist. John saw his role as preparing an elect people for the
final times that were just about upon them. This moment he understood in terms of a decisive judgement of the righteous and
the wicked with appropriate rewards. The moment of decision
had arrived: the good had to decide to become the new people
(who would survive the cataclysm) by repentance through the
new ritual of baptism. Anyone who had his/her sins thus forgiven would survive. For those who rejected this, or who did not
accept his preaching or message, i.e. the religious authorities
('many Pharisees and Sadducees') in 3:7, there was the end of
unquenchable fire. John also preached that there was an even
greater figure coming, the actual bringer of the last times, (vv 11-
12) whom he assumed would carry out the act of judgement and
do the separating. This leads to questioning by John about Jesus

in Mt 11 – could Jesus be the one who is to come – and, indeed, to Matthew presenting Jesus in terms of such a separation of 'sheep and goats' in Mt 25:31-46 but then making the judgement part of the eschatological times when 'the Son of Man comes in glory with his angels'. Thus, over the course of his gospel, Matthew maintains the message and role given by the Baptist to himself, but transforms it so that it integrates with the preaching of Jesus and the faith of the church in him as the anointed one and the one who comes at the end of time.

HOMILY NOTES

1. Do you know this text:
   > Christmas is coming,
   >
   > The goose is getting fat,
   >
   > Please put a penny in the old man's hat.

   A few simple comments on this little rhyme can provide a checklist for people to remind themselves of what we celebrate during Advent.

2. Christmas is coming.

   This is a time when preparation is everywhere in the air: preparations for holidays, for all the festivities, buying presents, sending cards, arranging food, everyone is 'getting ready'. Everyone is looking forward to the period around 25 December. 'Looking forward' and 'getting ready' are basic Christian activities: we are looking forward to the coming of the kingdom, we are looking to the return of the Christ in glory. We are looking forward to the life of the world to come. We are always getting ready to be better disciples, to be witnesses, to be the eyes and hands and feet of Jesus.

   What we are looking forward to right now and working so busily to prepare for is 'Christ Mass': the Christian feast. The feast that proclaims that the Son of God has come among us, walked with us, talked with us, suffered with us, and offered us adoption as daughters and sons of God. He is coming among us now, and will come again to judge the living and the dead.

3. The goose is getting fat.

   If God has sent his Son among us, then this is a cause for joy. We as Christians can be truly party animals for we are celebrating the depths of the Father's love. It is right that we should have the great party that the thought of a fat goose brings to mind. We are a loved and redeemed people: we have more to celebrate than we can even imagine.

4. Please put a penny in the old man's hat.

   But if we rejoice that the Father loves us and has sent his Son among us, then it also make demands on us. Being disciples means we have to be doers. We cannot be indifferent to sufferings and needs of others. God loves us, we must love others; God has forgiven us, we must forgive others; God provides for us in our need, we must provide for others. We cannot party with honest hearts until we have sought to relieve suffering. The image of the old man with his hat on the ground in front of him begging reminds us of all the work we must do to bring about the kingdom.

5. We Christians rejoice as we wait for the Lord when he comes again in glory to say:

   'Come, you that are blessed by my Father, inherit the kingdom prepared for you from the foundation of the world; for I was hungry and you gave me food, I was thirsty and you gave me something to drink, I was a stranger and you welcomed me, I was naked and you gave me clothing, I was sick and you took care of me, I was in prison and you visited me. Truly I tell you, just as you did it to one of the least of these who are members of my family, you did it to me.' (cf Mt 25:34-40).

Second Sunday of Advent (Year B)

Introduction to the Celebration

Today we move along our Advent journey towards our celebration of the Son of God entering our world, our humanity, and our community. On this Advent journey, our memory this Sunday concentrates on the figure of St John the Baptist: he went before the Lord and prepared his way and made his path straight. He is our model as witnesses to Jesus the Christ: we have to create a path for Jesus to enter our world and we have to remove the obstacles we place, both as a community and as individuals, to his being recognised in our world today.

Rite of Penance

Lord Jesus, come and console your people, Lord have mercy.
Lord Jesus, deliver your people from slavery, Christ have mercy.
Lord Jesus, forgive your people their sins, Lord have mercy.

Headings for Readings
First Reading

God's people are those who seek to prepare in the wilderness a path for our God.

Second Reading

We are the people who are waiting for the coming of the Day of the Lord and the way we live our lives must reflect this.

Gospel

John the Baptist was the one who went out into the wilderness to prepare a people for the coming of the Lord.

Prayer of the Faithful
President

Dear friends, today as we recall the ministry of John the Baptist
we must pray that the Father will give us the wisdom, strength
and courage to prepare the way for the Christ today in the rough
places of our lives, in the places desolate of faith, and amid the
darkness of our world.

Reader(s)

1. As we wait for the Lord's coming, that we may become a community of love and forgiveness. Lord in your mercy, hear our
prayer.

2. As we wait for the Lord's coming, that we may become a community promoting peace in the world. Lord in your mercy, hear
our prayer.

3. As we wait for the Lord's coming, that we may become a community seeking justice for the poor. Lord in your mercy, hear
our prayer.

4. As we wait for the Lord's coming, that we may become a community seeking freedom for the oppressed. Lord in your mercy,
hear our prayer.

5. As we wait for the Lord's coming, that we may become a community which protects the environment. Lord in your mercy,
hear our prayer.

6. As we wait for the Lord's coming, that we may become a community which cares for the sick. Lord in your mercy, hear our
prayer.

President

Father, we seek your face through our following of Jesus in
whom you are revealed; grant that this period of preparation for
the feast of Christmas will be a time of return and renewal for all
Christians and especially for the church that is gathered here, for
we pray to you through Christ, your Son our Lord. Amen.

Eucharistic Prayer
Preface I of Advent (P1); if Eucharistic Prayer III is used then the name of John the Baptist can be inserted after 'the apostles, the martyrs …'.

Invitation to the Our Father
Waiting for the Christ to come again, let us say the prayer of God's new people:

Sign of Peace
We are called to become the new people who have been baptised into Christ, let us show our love for each other in this community.

Invitation to Communion
John announced his coming and declared him to be the Lamb of God who takes away the sin of the world; now we gather at his table; happy are we to be his new people.

Communion Reflection
Lord, you came long ago in Bethlehem,
Lord, you shared your table with all who would learn to love,
Lord, you called on us to remember you by sharing at table.

Lord, you came among us here today.
Lord, you have given us each a part of your body and life,
Lord, you have given each of us a share in your cup.

Lord, you will come again to judge the living and the dead,
Lord, grant us a place at table at the heavenly banquet,
Lord, give us a share in your life with the Father.

Conclusion
Solemn Blessing 1 for Advent (*Missal*, p 367).

COMMENTARY

First Reading: Is 40:1-5, 9-11

This passage describes the hope of Israel that after the exile they
will find a wilderness turned into that joy of a society living in
close contact with food-production: a pasture. The perfect time
will be when a land familiar with warfare will encounter the
God of peace, and human death will encounter divine life. The
use of this reading today provides a context in which to hear
today's gospel.

Second Reading: 2 Pet 3:8-14

The vision of the end in this passage is that which has given rise
to the phrase much used in older blessings 'and the judgement
of the world by fire'. The Day of the Lord is the judgement day
for people and the day the material universe will end by being
burnt up. The writer wanted to affirm the Christian belief in the
coming judgement, while not making it an immediate prospect,
yet at the same time not allowing for complacency. This was
achieved by a complex cosmology based on the fire that existed
in the heavens slowly destroying the cooling water so that the
universe was moving inexorably towards its finality. However,
one could not make calculations based on this as time is itself
relative to the divine will (a day can be a thousand years and *vice
versa*). While this is one of the more unusual cosmologies from
the early Christian period, by the time of Basil (late fourth century)
it was becoming mainstream and through Ambrose and
Augustine became the standard Latin cosmology until the late-
twelfth century.

    This reading serves to highlight the eschatological character
of Advent: the coming of the Lord long ago is recalled while we
wait for the coming 'to judge the living and the dead.'

Gospel: Mk 1:1-8

This is the beginning of Mark and so you should introduce the
text with the formula: 'The beginning of the holy gospel according to Mark.' Mark sees the story of Jesus the Christ as beginning

with the ministry of John of the Baptist and in order to describe his work as the preparation for the work of the Christ he quotes Is 40 to locate John and Jesus within the whole history of salvation.

In order to have a prophecy about 'the messenger preparing the way' (1:2: 'Behold, I send my messenger before thy face, who shall prepare thy way') he combines two other scriptural quotations (Ex 23:20 and Mal 3:1) and gives these words also to Isaiah.

Today's first reading and gospel is a perfect couplet: Mark made sense of the events in terms of Is 40, and then quoted it as the anticipation of his gospel. Both texts taken together capture the message of Advent: we are looking forward to the salvation of the Christ, and we do so within the context of those who have in earlier times looked forward to a time of deliverance and lived within a time in which preparing the way was the task of the followers of God.

HOMILY NOTES

1. When we read Mark's presentation of the ministry of John the Baptist we are confronted with his role as the one who preached 'a baptism of repentance for the forgiveness of sins'. The immediate thought may be to take this as a cue for preaching the need for the Sacrament of Reconciliation or the need for individual confession. This has been a very common reading of the Baptist's cry and has the effect of making Advent and Lent seem very similar in many places. However, this approach fails to do justice to the kerygma and obscures our understanding of the nature of the preparation Mark understood John to have carried out; and that preparation is a central part of the work of the gospel for Mark. So avoid in the homily any linking of this text with individual sacramental reconciliation or using it as a cue to draw attention to a Reconciliation Service that is scheduled for Advent.

2. The key element in John the Baptist's preaching was the preparation of a new people, a distinct community, the Israel of the last times of the Day of the Lord's [judgement]. This

was not an individualist cleaning out of sins, each putting his or her house in order; but encouraging people to join a new society that would be able to withstand the coming judgement because of the purity of its observance of how the People of God should behave and live as a group. The event that marked one as a member of this new People, new group, was to be baptised by John. His baptism marked the border between being a member of the old community now destined for punishment because of its unfaithfulness to the Law (i.e. sin) and the new community that observed the Law with purity such that it could survive the Day of Lord. The important point to remember is that salvation is corporate, the forgiveness is corporate and the new way of living is corporate. We should think of John's baptism as being more like the day novices enter a monastery, thus beginning a new community life, rather than in terms of individual 'confession'. Or more metaphorically, it is all rowing in a lifeboat together rather than having individual lifebelts.

3. Jesus takes over from John the message of the new community of the Last Times, the New Israel with its twelve new foundation members: the Twelve. But unlike John, this new Israel is not the group that can survive the wrathful judgement, but the new People who can keep the Law in spirit and truth and who can rejoice because the Father loves them.

4. By contrast with the picture of the new People that is defined by Jesus's baptism, i.e. our baptism, John's community is but a forerunner, a foretaste, a dry run.

5. To welcome Jesus we must become the new community, the new People of God, the new Israel, the holy royal, priestly people of our baptism. This is the call of today's gospel. But this means a whole new vision of what it is to be a Christian, and abandoning any notion that Christianity is a religion system for individuals or a salvation system for individuals.

6. So what actions is the community taking this year to help it realise its calling to be the new community that is 'in Christ'?

• Has it any plans for a more perfect liturgical gathering?

In many places people still sit at the Eucharist using the individualist model of 'getting Mass': can people actually gather
around the table so that it is clear that they are not just getting
something but are at the Lord's banquet?

- Has it any plans to have a programme of prayer which unites
  it in spirit when it is dispersed?
  The early Christians offered united prayer by all praying at
  the same times each day and fasting on fixed days. More recently Christians were united by the Angelus at fixed times.
  Can the community's members agree to say the Our Father at
  a fixed time each day so that they are uniting in prayer even
  if not physically in the same place?
- Has the community any plan to grow in knowledge and
  awareness?
  Is there any plan to have a group that will study who we are
  as Christians or study how best to celebrate Christmas? Are
  there any ways of witnessing to the Christ and his message in
  the world in which we live?
- Has the community any plans to re-dedicate itself as a
  People, the new people, the people who are welcoming the
  Son of God into their midst? And, how would it do this?
  This act of rededication of the community could be an
  Advent reconciliation service, but if so then it has to have the
  community dimension foremost rather than the individual
  confession-absolution agenda.
- Has the community plans to act collectively to ease suffering,
  poverty, and injustice in our world?
  There is need to 'get organised' so that as a community we
  are making a difference and we are acting in a new way as a
  new people. You cannot be the New People if the group is
  still behaving in its way of life in the old way of injustice and
  exploitation. This new way of acting is essential if we are to
  be the people of the Christ, but it is not a substitute for renewing the liturgy, having a plan of prayer, and having an
  awareness of the need to fast as a community.

- How will the community express its joyfulness and thankfulness for what it is?
  Will there be other opportunities to show that being a people is not just a collection of individuals, but being part of a society, a living entity? What activities can we engage in that will act as a glue between us and help us overcome the fragmentation that is such a part of modern western post-industrial living?

7. Advent poses us hard questions. Questions much harder to answer and do something about than those linked with the individualist notion of God-and-me that is inherent in 'going to confession'. 'Preparing a people' is far harder task for the president of a community than many hours sitting in the confessional!

Second Sunday of Advent (Year C)

Introduction to the Celebration

Why do we gather here each Sunday to celebrate the sacred meal of the Lord? Because as we say later: when we eat this bread and drink this cup we proclaim the Lord's death until he comes. Now in Advent we recall the past when Jesus first gathered disciples, but we also remember the future when he will come again in glory. Then we will be delivered from all that binds us, but before then we must take John the Baptist as our model: 'we must prepare a way for the Lord' within the world we live in.

Rite of Penance

Lord Jesus, your coming was prepared by John the Baptist, Lord have mercy.

Lord Jesus, you came among us with forgiveness, Christ have mercy.

Lord Jesus, you will come again with salvation for your people, Lord have mercy.

Headings for Readings

First Reading

In this reading, Jerusalem stands for the whole people of God who await deliverance from sadness and oppression: at the Lord's coming they will become the royal people and become the messengers of the good news of the Holy One.

Second Reading

St Paul reminds the church in Philippi that while they wait for the Day of the Lord to come, they must set about the tasks in hand: they must deepen their knowledge, they must increase their awareness of what being a Christian in the world means, and they must spread the good news.

Gospel

Luke is anxious to remind us that the message of salvation is not in some far away alternative world: it entered our real world of suffering at a definite moment in history. Christianity is alternative in that its gospel calls us to live in this world in an alternative way.

Prayer of the Faithful

Use the Sample Formula for Advent given on pp 996-7 of the Missal. Choose one of the options given for each of the four intercessions marked A, B, C, D.

Eucharistic Prayer

Preface of Advent I (P1); Eucharistic Prayer III contains the notion of the universal gathering as part of the work of the Christ (in the form of the perfect sacrifice of praise offered from east to west) that is also found in today's first reading.

Invitation to the Our Father

Awaiting the final coming of the Lord, let us pray for the coming of the kingdom:

Sign of Peace

To welcome the Lord into our lives is to be willing to bring him into the world in which we live, and the first step in bringing the Lord to the world is to establish the reign of peace.

Invitation to Communion

This is the Lamb of God who has come into the world and whose final coming we await in hope. Meanwhile, happy are we who share in his supper.

Communion Reflection

This is the time of Christmas parties: we somehow know that it is important to gather together and celebrate.

These gatherings tell us about who we identify with, our memories, our hopes.

Christ chose this gathering, his holy meal, as our way of getting together.

Week in, week out, it tells us who we are, recalls our memories, expresses our fears, needs, and hopes.

We gather and share his food and drink, we become his body and have his blood giving us all life.

This gathering to celebrate transforms us, we become one with the Christ whose coming we are celebrating.

The cup of blessing we have just shared is a participation in the blood of Christ.

The loaf we have just broken is a participation in the body of Christ.

Because there is one loaf, we who are many are one body, for we all partake of the one loaf.

Our Christmas parties come and go, our meeting here with the Lord of Christmas prepares us for the banquet of heaven.

Conclusion
Solemn Blessing 1 for Advent (*Missal*, p 367).

COMMENTARY

First Reading: Baruch 5:1-9
Baruch is one of those books that Catholics and Orthodox accept as part of the scriptures – for the simple reason that it was part of the Septuagint which was 'The Scriptures' of the first Christians – but which others do not accept as part of 'The Bible.' However, even among the churches that do accept Baruch, it is a text that rarely appears in the liturgy. It presents itself as being written in the immediate aftermath of the destruction of Jerusalem in 587, but in fact is a collection of bits and pieces which may vary in date from 300 BC to 70 AD. These pieces seem to have been written with the Jewish diaspora in mind and to offer them the promise of speedy assistance from God couched in terms of a restoration of the land, the city, and the temple. The reading

today is the latter half of one of these pieces: the prophet addressing Jerusalem and announcing the coming time of joy and deliverance (4:30-5:9). When the great day of deliverance comes it will be a gathering of the scattered people from east and west and then the offering of the prefect praise. This is a theme that is found in many other late texts (e.g. Malachi) and we know that it was a central feature of the thanksgiving that early Christians offered the Father for the work of Jesus: he was the promised regathering of scattered Israel (we see this in the Eucharistic Prayer of the Didache, which in turn inspired our Eucharistic Prayer III).

Its link to today's gospel is complex: both this reading and the gospel make use of Is 40:3-5 – the filling in of the valleys to make the ground level, and then this reading is presented in the liturgy so that it can be seen as anticipating the gospel. The historical reality is even more valuable: it shows how the biblical interpretation that is found among the early Christians is in perfect continuity with the Jewish communities out of which they sprang – for it was those very communities that produced Baruch, and Malachi, and many other so-called 'inter-testamental writings' which became the immediate backdrop to the early churches.

Second Reading: Phil 1:3-6, 8-11

The key to this reading's place in the Advent lectionary is to be found in its references to 'the coming day of Jesus Christ'. By this phrase, used in verses 6 and 10, Paul was looking to the eschaton when all the desires of his churches would be fulfilled; we too are looking to that day (Advent as the time when we look forward to the Final Coming), but also to its ritual anticipation in our celebration of the Christmas festival. Then the agenda of the Christians looking forward, and celebrating Christmas, becomes clear: there must be a growing love between the members of the church, a willingness to deepen knowledge and perception about what it is to be a Christian, and a desire reach perfect goodness. The community that achieves this in Christ is then offering praise and glory to the Father.

Gospel: Lk 3:1-6

The majesty of the opening of this passage – the most elaborate chronograph found in any early Christian document – alerts us to the fact that Luke sees this passage as marking a major division in his whole narrative: the story of the infancy and youth of Jesus is over, the great work of proclamation is about to begin. This is the parallel passage within his telling of the story of Jesus to the opening lines of Mk; and from Mk he takes over Isaiah 40:3 and then adds another two verses from the same prophet so that at the end of today's reading we have Is 40:3-5 (neither of the other synoptic writers have such a long quotation from Isaiah).

Luke's aim is to make one point with the greatest force: at a precise moment in history something happened, but that event was not random but part of the long-revealed divine plan. The outsider might think of Jesus's coming as just the appearance of one more person on the religious scene, but that event was prepared by the work of John the Baptist, and that work of John was itself foretold in the ancient scriptures. Jesus is to be seen as the fulfillment of the history of revelation. This is a theme found throughout first-century Christian writing, but no writer is as insistent as Luke in repeating the theme: if you want to understand Jesus, you must know how he fulfills God's plans long-revealed to Israel. For Luke, only history explains Jesus; and indeed, in turn, only through Jesus does that history make sense. We see Luke's approach to the first part of this in the way that he writes sermons in Acts which he then puts into the mouths of the apostles; and to the second in the Emmaus 'lecture over supper' when all the scriptures (i.e. the accounts of the history of Israel) are explained by Jesus in terms of himself.

However, why the elaborate chronograph (from which, incidentally, all our AD dating is ultimately derived)? At first sight the reason is obvious: he has to locate the moment of the Christ whose history he is going to narrate so that all events prior to it are clearly so labeled. However, it is possible that Luke wishes to make a more elaborate theological point: the coming of Jesus is the entry of God into the particularity of human existence, and this particular individual, while sharing the limitations of every other human being (we only come into existence in one place at one moment in one situation in one culture – and have all the limitations that historical natures impose on us), is also of relevance on a much larger scale. So it is the appearance of another preacher from Galilee, but it affects the Temple (Annas and Caiaphas) which is the focus of the whole scattered people of Israel; it affects the whole of the Land given to their Fathers (hence Pilate, Herod, Philip, Lysanias who represent each of the regions that made up the historical 'Holy Land'), and all humanity (the *oikoumene*/empire represented by Tiberius). Luke seems to be implying that while Jesus was a discreet individual at a precise point in time, he was also the person to whom all history relates.

HOMILY NOTES

1. We can view repentance in two ways. Looking backwards it can be a question of making up for what has been done in the past. Looking forwards it can be getting the matter sorted out and making sure that, as far as possible, the problem does not come back. As with all such 'two ways of looking at something', people will then say that this is just a matter of whether you are an optimist or a pessimist, or whether you think that the bottle is half-full or half-empty. But the issue of repentance is more complicated that just manifestations of two ways of looking at life. We can see this by asking which view is embodied in most institutions in the societies to which we belong? We want criminals to go to prison: it is a time to 'pay back' for the past. We want criminals 'to get what they deserve' on account of their deeds in the past. We want compensation for the past, we want reparation for the past, and we very often want vengeance. Penitence – as the word is used in such words as penitentiary or penal – is linked to a belief that if someone has done something wrong, then later they must suffer for that crime, and somehow that

later suffering 'makes up for the past'. How it could make up for the past is another question: we seem to certainly want 'people to pay'. This notion that penitence is linked to the past, that it is someone 'getting his/her just deserts', is found in every society. Indeed, paying up for the past with suffering is often seen as the essence of justice. The people who come out of a court when a criminal who has hurt them has been sentenced to a long sentence often say 'we have finally got justice!'

2. This is certainly the human perspective, but is it something that we as Christians who believe in a God of love can accept as just a 'fact of life'? Certainly, many Christians in the past, and indeed today, imagine God as the great score-settler: if people don't pay in this life, then 'divine justice' will get them in the end. Hell, then, is imagined as God's final reckoner. Indeed, many contemporary Christians are schizophrenic about hell: they find it repulsive to believe in hell for themselves, but are quite happy that it should be there so that God can finally grind out his justice – on others. But is this view, however common, an adequate expression of what Christians hold as their story of God's dealing with humanity?

3. The prophets – we have the examples of Isaiah and John the Baptist in today's readings -- were in no doubt that people sinned and that the people of God had fallen into sin. Yet, when they call the people 'to repent' they start looking forward not backwards. To repent is to start anew, to make sure that the former ways disappear, that a new way of living appears. The repentance is the act of preparing the way for the Lord to come along. Repentance is change so that in the future all can see the salvation of God.

4. Christians have never been in doubt that humanity had fallen into sin and needed a redeemer. But to say it needed a redeemer is to look forward. God's justice was not the destruction of the sinful people, but to send his Son. When Jesus came he was not here to punish for the past, but to be the redeemer who would open up the future after sin and its ef-

fects. Jesus called us to a new way of living, he did not come 'to call to account' for the past.

5. When the church has preached penitence, it is as a medicine to train the person in a new way of living. We come as sick people to the source of healing (St Thomas). 'God the Father of mercies, through the death and resurrection of his Son has reconciled the world to himself and sent the Holy Spirit among us for the forgiveness of sins' (Formula of Absolution). God is love, not vengeance – but this is a very hard notion for us to grasp and to believe. The problem is as old as Ezekiel: 'Have I any pleasure in the death of the wicked, says the Lord God, and not rather that he should turn from his way and live?' (18:23); 'For I have no pleasure in the death of any one, says the Lord God; so turn, and live' (18:32); 'Say to them, As I live, says the Lord God, I have no pleasure in the death of the wicked, but that the wicked turn from his way and live; turn back, turn back from your evil ways; for why will you die, O house of Israel?' (33:11). And we, two millennia after seeing how God deals with his people – he sent them the Christ whose coming we are preparing to celebrate – seem to have as much difficulty in looking forward and seeing repentance as starting afresh with God's love.

6. But believing that God gives a new future to those who turn to a new way of thinking, living, acting, loving is just part of the task. We are called not merely to follow the Christ who brought the Father's love in his coming among us. We are called to become like him in our lives. As there is no place for vengeance, and no place for getting a 'pay back' for the past in God dealing with us; then there must be a similar desire to let people start over again among us. This is what we pray: 'forgive us our trespasses as we forgive those who trespass against us.'

7. Christmas recalls God's great new start with humanity: Jesus the New Adam. We hear that proclaimed today in the call to repent and to prepare the way. But if we want Jesus to come within our own lives today as he once came in Bethlehem,

then we must be prepared to turn from notions of vengeance and become people of forgiveness who look forward. Looking forward is far more difficult than looking backwards – we should honestly admit that as a fact about the human condition, most of us both as individuals and as groups are better at raking over old hurts than at looking for new ways to co-operate with one another. Yet it is only when we adopt this habit of looking forward that we can truly become Christ-like. We see Jesus's way of looking forward in what he said to the woman they wanted to stone as payment for her past: 'Go your way, and from now on do not sin again' (Jn 8:11). The task was to set out into the future: 'Go'; and start a new way of living: 'do not sin again'.

8. We are looking forward to Christmas: the Christ we seek to welcome calls us to look forward in the way we live – this is repentance and preparing the way; and he calls us to look forward to his own coming in glory.

December 6: Feast of St Nicholas

Note

This is not a significant day in the English-speaking world, but in many countries it is a kind of foretaste of Christmas when St Nicholas comes, dressed as the bishop he was, to visit the children. St Nicholas then goes through the good and bad deeds of the past year, and then extracts a promise of improvement. Finally, as an encouragement he presents each child with a small gift while asking audibly what the child hopes for as a gift at Christmas. There are umpteen variants on this tradition; but it is this tradition that was deliberately mutated by commercial interests in the mid-twentieth century to produce 'Santa Claus'. The name change went from Nicholas (Latin form) to Nikolaus (German form) to Klaus (familiar German form) to Claus or Clause (American form during Second World War when German name-forms would have been commercially counterproductive). It is now reported that he has married for in this age of equality between the sexes there is now a 'Mrs Clause'. This image now is a central part of the commercialism of this festival, and is so secularised that when 'religious winter festival images' are suppressed in the public domain, Santa gets away with it: his pointed red hood with a bobble is sufficiently unmitre-like as not to raise the suspicions of those who believe religion should be a wholly private affair.

While Christians have to openly embrace the natural calendar that produced mid-winter festivals not only in the religion of ancient Rome but those of the other European peoples (and which it then suited us to express as the feast of Christ's birth), equally we have to reclaim as part of our contribution to the larger culture those aspects of the feast that arose within Christianity. This, therefore, it the feast of the real 'Santa Claus' – and to know the background to 'Santa' is to know about Bishop Nicholas of Myra.

What do we know about the man? Virtually nothing except that he was a bishop of Myra, probably in the early fourth century. Later accounts say he was imprisoned in the Great Persecution of Diocletion (303) and/or took part in the Council of Nicaea (325). The first detail could be true, the second is unlikely: both are just 'suitable' things for a bishop from Lycia to be doing in the early fourth century if that was when he lived. He first enters the realm of definite records when – his cult already flourishing – Justinian build a basilica in Myra in his honour in the early sixth century. Gradually his fame spread to both east and west. In the east he became patron of Greece and Russia, in the west we know his cult was popular in the mid-ninth century and he became patron of Lorrain. The growth of his fame can be followed in the umpteen churches all over Europe dedicated to him. In 1087 his relics were stolen from Myra and brought to Bari in Italy, where they still are; hence he is sometimes called St Nicholas of Bari.

So why did he become popular? The earliest evidence we have for the stories behind Santa Claus date from the eleventh century. Then he is credited with providing three gold coins to provide dowries for three poor girls (these become the three balls of the pawnbroker's shop-sign; and St Nicholas is patron of pawnbrokers); or that he rescued three officers who were wrongly imprisoned; or that he saved three children from death. It is a combination of these stories, combined with the idea of children preparing for Christmas, that lie behind the St Nicholas traditions in many countries in mainland Europe, and so behind the contemporary Santa story.

We have here a classic example of how a legend has sparked off new forms of celebration and new concerns within the Christian community. In a way, Santa Claus is just the latest secular twist in the evolution of the legend: he is now the secular patron of Christmas. However, it would be both out of touch with our larger culture and a failure to point out how the Christian calendar still has echoes in a 'shopping festival' not to draw special attention to St Nicholas of Myra, of Bari, and of 'Santaland.'

Introduction to the Celebration
Today we celebrate one of the most well known saints in the whole year, St Nicholas of Myra, better known as Santa Claus. All around us we see his image, with his big bulging sack of gifts. But this sack of presents all too easily becomes a message of greed centred on getting more and more for myself. We are here because of the Father's great gift to us: his Son's coming – the great gift that we are all busily getting ready to celebrate. But St Nicholas's feast reminds us of the words of the Lord Jesus, how he said: 'It is more blessed to give than to receive.' So to welcome the Christ-child we must be people who give to the poor and needy, who use our talents for the common good, who brings the gifts of peace and joy into the world.

Rite of Penance
Option c. ii (*Missal*, p 392) is appropriate.

Headings for Readings
The Advent readings for the day.

Prayer of the Faithful
President
On this day in Advent we celebrate the feast of St Nicholas famed in our history for his care for the poor, and famed now as 'Santa Claus' and a part of Christmas for children; let us now pray.
Reader(s)
1. For all who are poor and all who are exploited in their poverty, that the Lord will move hearts to help them and to act with justice towards them. Lord hear us.
2. For all who are busy preparing for the feast of Christmas, that this will be a time of happiness and rest. Lord hear us.
3. For all children who are looking forward to Christmas, that they will enjoy a special happy time, and also enjoy the wonder of the coming of the Christ as a child. Lord hear us.

4. For all whom you have called to the ministry of bishop, especially N. our bishop, that St Nicholas's care for the poor will inspire them. Lord hear us.

5. For everyone engaging in the coming celebrations, that pointers of faith, such as the varied references to St Nicholas, might call attention to the world as God's handiwork. Lord hear us.

President

Father, on this day we rejoice because of St Nicholas whose image is used far and wide at this time; grant us that faith that when we see the image of St Nicholas we will recall that his joy and merit were in being a disciple of Christ and a servant of his church. We make this prayer through Christ our Lord. Amen.

Eucharistic Prayer

Preface of Pastors (P67), (*Missal*, p 470); and Eucharistic Prayer III which allows the saint's name to be included.

Invitation to the Our Father

Today we recall St Nicholas who helped people in their everyday needs. Let us now ask the Father to help us in our needs and give us our daily bread:

Sign of Peace

The image of St Nicholas in shop windows tells us that Christmas is coming, the time of the Prince of Peace, so let us exchange peace with one another.

Communion Reflection

St Nicholas is revered as the great bringer of gifts;
let us thank the Lord for all his gifts to us.
St Nicholas is revered for the wise use of his riches;
let us beg the Lord for wisdom to use our riches well.
St Nicholas is revered for bringing joy to children;
let us ask the Lord to care for all children.
St Nicholas is revered for his care for the poor;
let us promise the Lord that we will care for the needy.

St Nicholas is revered for his care for prisoners;
let us pray to the Lord for all who are in prison.
St Nicholas is revered as a bishop
who ministered at this holy table;
let us rejoice in the Lord who has now shared his table with us.

December 8: The Solemnity of the Immaculate Conception

Introduction to the Celebration

In a just a few more days Christmas will be upon us, and we as God's People will be celebrating the coming of God the Son into our world to make us children of the Father. During this time of Advent we are recalling how God prepared a people to receive the Christ, and today we recall how his love prepared Mary to be the mother of the Christ. God loves each of us and takes an interest in us from the first moment of our being – so today we are having a festival to celebrate the first moment of the existence of the woman to whom we Christians owe so much.

Rite of Penance

Option c. iii (*Missal*, p 392-3) is appropriate.

Opening Prayer

The alternative form dwells less on the formal language used within the theological debates on the Immaculate Conception.

Headings for Readings

Note: Today the first reading is the classic text predicting the New Eve on the basis of the divine judgement given to the first Eve in Paradise. This was often referred to until the 1960s as the *'protoevangelium'* (this is a technical term applied to a snippet of Genesis; it is not to be confused with the early Christian narrative text called the *Protoevangelium of James*): that in the very moment of the commission of the first sin in which human nature was corrupted, there was the promise of the uncorrupted seed, Mary who would crush the serpent's head (a detail that can be seen on many statues of Mary). However, the text raises all the problems of the stories from the first chapters of Genesis and raises far more curious questions (was there really an Eve? Why do we read these myths? Isn't all that Old Testament stuff bunkum? Did Mary's heel really get bruised?) than it provides light for faith. So it might be wiser to avoid introductions today as the way to draw least attention to the first reading.

Prayer of the Faithful
Note: There is a confusing tendency in some places to insert a prayer addressed to Mary into the Prayer of the Faithful; this is wholly inappropriate as this is the prayer of the church addressed to the Father.
President
Friends, today we celebrate a great feast of Mary. Her willingness to accept her call to become the Mother of God gives her a unique place in the history of salvation for it is her giving birth to our Saviour that we are preparing to celebrate in just over a fortnight's time. So now as her children gathered by her Son, let us pray to the Father.
Reader(s)
1. That we will grow in wonder of the Word made flesh in Jesus, born of the virgin Mary, Lord hear us.
2. That we will grow in our appreciation of the care given us by Mary and the saints, Lord hear us.
3. That we will grow in faith that God loves each of us and cares for each member of the human family, Lord hear us.
4. That we will grow in discipleship following the example of Mary, Lord hear us.
5. That we will grow in our unity as Christians and behold in Mary our common mother, Lord hear us.
6. That we will grow in our love for all humanity and, like Mary, bring Jesus to birth in our world, Lord hear us.
President
Father, on this day when we celebrate Mary in whom we see in a most wondrous way the new creation brought by your Son, hear our prayers and grant that we may live the life of the new creation in Jesus Christ, our Lord. Amen.

Eucharistic Prayer
Preface of the Immaculate Conception.

Invitation to the Our Father
We are the New Creation, reborn in God's love, forgiven our trespasses, taught how to pray by the Christ. So let us pray:

Sign of Peace
Christ the Prince of Peace was born of Mary. On this festival let us celebrate that peace which is a hallmark of the new creation.

Invitation to Communion
Behold the Prince of Peace, who takes away the sins of the world, happy are we who gathered here to share in his supper.

Communion Reflection
There is a Prayer to the Virgin Mary in the *Missal*, p 1023, which is suitable for today.
If there is time for a more extended reflection: then a slow recitation of the whole Ephesian hymn – the version in the *Breviary* is more eloquent – would fit the day perfectly.

Conclusion
Solemn Blessing 15 for the Blessed Virgin Mary (*Missal*, p 374).

COMMENTARY

First Reading: Gen 3:9-15, 20
This text's origins and its place within the larger Genesis narrative have been at the centre of a century and a half of scholarship. However, all of that is irrelevant to the text's meaning within today's liturgy which derives from the role that the stories of Gen 2-4 were read by early Christian writers – most famously Paul in the Letter to the Romans – as the story of a fall from a sinless human existence, and thus providing a rationale for why the Christ had to come as a saviour. As those texts continued to be used in the church, they became the primary texts

upon which the theology of Original Sin was based, and in turn
they developed a marian emphasis as Mary came to be seen as
instrumental in countering Original Sin.

The key 'marian text' within this reading is Gen 3:15, but this
is far less marian as it is read today in most lectionaries than it
was to Catholic theologians of even a generation ago. Now we
read in the Jerusalem Bible version 'I will make you enemies of
each other; you and the woman, your offspring and her offspring. It will crush your head and you will crush its heel.'
While in the RSV (and almost identically in the NRSV) it reads: 'I
will put enmity between you and the woman, and between your
seed and her seed; he shall bruise your head, and you shall
bruise his heel.' But the Vulgate reads: *inimicitias ponam inter te
et mulierem et semen tuum et semen illius ipsa* ['she'] *conteret caput
tuum et tu insidiaberis calcaneo eius* ['her' to agree with ipsa].' So
for generations preachers asked who was this woman, and
agreed that the only woman it could be was Mary: therefore,
they exclaimed, in the very first days of human history there
was a reference to a specific woman who was to come, a prophesy that was fulfilled in Mary. Today this interpretation is most
often heard only in the hymns, for example the line: 'When creation was begun, God had chosen you to be mother of his
blessed Son.' The manner in which Gen 3:15 was used, and
which inspired its choice for today's feast is best explored by
looking up the use of Gen 3:15 in pre-Vatican II manuals of mari-
ology or soteriology.

The reading today closes with verse 20 where the woman is
given a name by Adam, and then that name is interpreted in the
story that it means 'mother of all the living'. This is the conclusion to the reading as that verse was seen as the basis for the Eve-
Mary parallel, 'the first Eve' who brought human life to her offspring but also sin, 'the last Eve' who brought eternal life to her
children and the deliverance from sin. The first mother was a
sinner, the latter mother was sinless. This interpretation of Gen
3:20 is, of course, widely found in traditional piety. In the *Salve
Regina* the 'poor banished children of Eve' look to Mary as the

new source of 'our life, our sweetness and our hope'. However, it can only be used in preaching where one can assume that the congregation is already familiar with the hermeneutic that sees all Old Testament texts as directly related to the events of the New Covenant – but while that is a hermeneutic found in the Lectionary – it is also one that is very far from most contemporary preaching, and when used often stirs up for the hearers the notion that the whole of revelation is some elaborately coded game.

Second Reading: Eph 1:3-6, 11-12
This is an early Christian hymn – probably the earliest piece of specifically Christian liturgy that was committed to writing – preserved in the text of Ephesians. It is a celebration of the cosmic care of God for his creation, which is equally his care of each individual. This is the song of the assembly of the Christians celebrating the providence of God that is also salvation in Jesus the Christ. Since today we are celebrating that salvific providence in the life of Mary this makes it an ideal reading for this feast. However, one wonders what has been gained by excising the four verses from the hymn that locate salvation in Christ: everything we say about Mary must also be referred to its relationship to the life and work of her Son.

Gospel: Lk 1:26-38
This is the great text of Mary's willing co-operation within the divine plan. From the perspective of the immaculate conception the key verses are 28 which in Latin reads: *Aue, gratia plena* (hail, full of grace), and 30: *inuenisti enim gratiam apud Deum* (for you have found grace [already is implied] with God). These verses have been seen as implicit confirmation that there was no stain of Original Sin in Mary, and the presence of sanctifying grace, at the time of the annunciation. However, from whatever perspective we approach Mary – or the mystery of the incarnation – this passage is foundational. The Word enters his creation within the manner of the creation and with the wondrous co-operation of a

creature for whom God has proclaimed his interest and respect. Mary is no mere instrument of the divine power, nor is she coerced in her vocation: rather she is the perfect case of a joyful and loving response to a loving God.

HOMILY NOTES

1. While it is a coincidence that this feast always falls in Advent – today's celebration is calculated on the older feast held on 8 September – there is a long tradition of seeing this as Advent's marian feast (see Paul VI's *Marialis cultus*).

2. In Advent we are reflecting on God moving in history: he prepared a people as we are reading each day in the prophets. He sent John the Baptist to prepare the way before him. He called Mary to be the mother of Jesus. This part of our faith is not something that is easy for us to accept for we have become suspicious of stating that God's hand is in events after the most destructive century in human history. However, part of our good news is that in the face of that destruction there is a caring God: a God who cares, who listens, who brings new life, and who offers us the life of heaven. The alternative to this good news is that we are but barges on the torrents of history. We may feel mighty forces are tossing us about, but we are also attentive to the sign of hope that such forces are not the final word.

3. Believing in a caring and loving God we seek out the signs of his care in our lives. We have to try to become attentive to what place each of us has in his desire to renew the creation, to stem the effects of human destructiveness, and to challenge the forces of evil.

4. The most shining example of someone being called to have a specific role in bringing about the coming of the kingdom (for which we constantly pray), to make the Anointed One present in our world (for which we ask strength at every Eucharist) and to take a part to stem the torrents of destruction (something for which each of us has committed him or herself in baptism) is Mary. We are celebrating that during

the whole of her existence God was interested in her as an individual: let us pray that each of us may have the faith to know that the Father is just as interested in each of us.

5. The Ephesian hymn sums up this whole notion of God's living providential care. That hymn can be said today to be the hymn of Mary. It was also the hymn of many of the earliest churches: can we make it our hymn?

APPENDIX: THE HISTORY AND THEOLOGY OF THIS FEAST

Origins of this Feast

At some time in the early middle ages a series of feasts began to appear celebrating various moments in the life of the Blessed Virgin Mary. This seems wholly fanciful to us, but we must bear in mind that there was a general lack of hesitation, indeed acceptance, of a range of traditions about the life of Mary (such as stories about the Marian events witnessed in texts such as the *Protoevangelium of James*) which now only survive in fragments in popular belief. One of the central events in these traditions was the account of Mary's birth to the barren parents Joachim and Anne. The actual day that was held to be that of her birth varied from region to region, as did the date of her death / falling asleep / assumption. Gradually, 15 August emerged as the most widely favoured date for her death (the day of death is normally the feast day of a saint) and 8 September as her birthday (apart from Jesus, the western church only celebrates the nativities, as well as the deaths, of Mary and John the Baptist). However, just as 25 March was then celebrated as the conception of Jesus followed nine months later by his birth, so the logic of celebrations dictated that if 'we know' the birthday – and 'we must know it for we have been celebrating it for generations!' – then we can easily know yet another feast of Mary that we can celebrate: her conception nine months before her birthday. And, moreover, there were traditions about Mary's wondrous conception to barren parents. Hence this feast falls on this day. When St Bernard said 'Of Mary, there is never enough!' he was not merely stating his own interest in writing about Mary, but expressing a more general attitude: if we could find another Marian feast to celebrate, then let us find it and celebrate it!

However, at the time this feast is first evidenced in surviving calendars (eighth century), what was being celebrated was simply the day of Mary's conception because that was itself a significant moment to recall in the life of the all-holy Mother of God; it was not yet a feast because that conception was 'immaculate' (i.e. conceived free of the infection of Adam's sin) for such ideas had not even been imagined. Today we celebrate it because that conception was, in the belief of the western Catholic Church, unique; but the feast began simply as one more joyful anniversary relating to the life of Mary. Here lies the major difference between the origins of the feast and what we are now celebrating: yet, it is the actual celebration of the day of conception, not its specific 'theological' quality, that, first of all, marks the long-standing tradition of the church (as Prosper of Aquitaine remarked: *lex orandi legem credendi statuat*), and, secondly, it was the interest in this annual major feast that prompted the theological speculation that eventually resulted in the notion that Mary's conception must have been unique and hence the whole doctrine of the Immaculate Conception that reached its peak in the formal definition by Blessed Pius IX in 1854. Of course, there is a specious apologetic that unless they knew there was 'something' special then the feast would not have been celebrated and then, eventually, after sufficient 'development' it was realised that this 'something' was the 'immaculate conception'. This sort of reasoning – and it can still be found in polemical textbooks – makes a nonsense of the actual notion of the 'mind of the church' it seeks to defend for that 'mind' is thereby given 'mindlessness' as its chief characteristic (since there is no abuse that could not be developed out of an 'inchoate something'); and secondly, it fails to take account of modern historical scholarship which has been at the forefront of the liturgical renewal of recent decades and that can trace the development of interest in the immaculateness of Mary's conception as a way of justifying the already existing feast.

Problems of Comprehension

Today's feast presents us with problems of comprehension at several levels. First, there are the problems associated with our perceptions of what we know about the life of Mary. For most preachers today detailed accounts about the life of Mary, and life within the 'Holy Family' (i.e. Jesus, Mary, and Joseph), belong to the 'fringes' of Catholic belief and practice. I have never seen a seminary course that, for example, studied the 'revelations' of Mary of Agreda or Maria Valtorta for information on the historical Jesus or his historical background. Yet, much of what those books contain can be traced backwards through hagiographical accounts – now excised from the Liturgy of the Hours – to the texts we label with the health-warning: 'early Christian apocrypha.' But it is worth noting that these 'fringe' notions are vibrant at the popular level where much formal theology never reaches: one only has to note the prominence such books have in many religious bookshops. When I asked in an academic theology bookshop, just to see the reaction of the shop assistant, if they stocked these I was surprised at this reaction. 'If you want to buy either author I can fetch them from the stock room. We do not keep them on the shelves because clergy, when browsing, object. But for the people who come in here off the street it is these books that are wanted and they don't browse, but simply ask here [at the counter] and we get them.' 'And,' I asked, 'do they sell well?' 'Well, I don't think I will ever see them being remaindered!' However, like it or not, if we continue to celebrate this feast we must see it as part of the 'larger' life of Mary that was part of the inheritance of all Christians until the Reformation and, until a few generations ago, part of the standard imagery of Catholics. Today we look only to the gospels for our information on Mary, but the longer memory tells of her parents Joachim and Anne, their wonder at conceiving their child, then how they 'presented her' in the Temple in Jerusalem [a ritual otherwise unknown in Second Temple Judaism], and many other events afterwards. We cringe at all this as 'apocryphal' lore, but the memory is still there in the

Roman liturgy (the feast of Saints Joachim and Anne on 26 July; the feast of the Presentation of the BVM on 21 November) and in Catholic folk-practice: chapels to St Anne where there is still a tradition of *superadultae* going to pray for a suitable husband. Within such a rich memory about the life of Mary as that older tradition, when one already has spoken of the time when St Anne conceived, then it makes perfect sense to celebrate it! Our history and our memory and our liturgical praxis are not neat; but it is better, I believe, to face up to this messiness than trying to sweep it into obscurity hopeful that 'from now on' everyone will accept a cleaned-up and logical version.

Second, the theological worldview that produced the theology of the Immaculate Conception is now one that causes unease among most theologians and many Catholics. This theology, its perception of the mode of transmission of Original Sin, its inherent view of sexual activity, its implicit view of what constitutes holiness, and the celebration of this feast are intimately intertwined. Once the feast was established and annually celebrated with ever greater solemnity / fervour / exuberance, speculation about what the feast entailed took on a life of its own within formal theology. Could one actually celebrate a moment of conception since that was glorifying an instant of carnal passion in which was transmitted the stain and effects of the Fall? It was not open to these theologians to ask 'should one so celebrate' as the actual celebration was a datum; it came with the most significant of ritual sanctions: a place in the calendar. One can imagine this as the clash of a dour Augustinian theology of Original Sin of the academic clerical few, with the simpler joy of the many wanting as many Marian fiestas as possible upon which to celebrate, relax and make merry on a happy anniversary. However, using a lawyerly approach to the discovery of truth more suited to maths than theology, it was easy to observe that both festival and theology were part of the tradition (hence neither could be wrong for that would imply that the tradition could err) yet were contradictory (so one must be false). The conundrum was solved by saying that Mary must have been free from the stain of

Original Sin in the moment of her conception: thereby one could still preserve the doctrine of Original Sin in its common western form, yet celebrate the feast. Subsequently, the questions emerged of how to explain how and why Mary should be so preserved. That debate which lasted from the thirteenth century until 1854 (at least officially that was when debate ended) produced the preaching that then became the focus of interest in this feast. It was no longer a celebration of a moment in Mary's history, but a celebration of what made her uniquely distinct among those born by sexual generation (the reason for the technical formula 'born by sexual generation' became necessary as to say 'born of humans' or 'woman' would also include Jesus). It is this uniqueness of Mary and her ontological status *vis-à-vis* every other human that has been the focus of most preaching on this feast and in its popular celebrations, for instance, the Virgin's title in Lourdes. In brief, the doctrine is that while Christians are only freed from the stain of Original Sin by baptism which is seen to 'flow from the cross'; Mary was freed by a unique and unrepeatable act of divine grace at the very instant of her coming into existence. 'Mary is different' is what the feast cries out, yet much recent Marian preaching (in the light of the final chapter of *Lumen gentium*) has emphasised Mary's commonality with other Christians. Then there is the question of what Mary was preserved from: Original Sin as that which is transmitted in the action of sexual generation in a line of physical descent reaching back to Adam. This is the biological view of Original Sin that is only found in the Latin church in the aftermath of St Augustine, and which is widely challenged today as a way of explaining the human condition's need of the Christ as a saviour. However, as the doctrine of the Immaculate Conception was defined it depended upon a particular way of viewing both the mystery of Original Sin and a specific way of explaining the transmission of Original Sin from 'our first parents' to each member of the human race, Mary alone excepted, through sexual generation. This manner of explaining Original Sin has fallen into abeyance since the 1950s. Today that approach, quite apart from its implications for reading the Genesis story of Adam and Eve as a matter of biological history, raises so many issues relating (1) to the notion of the inherent disorder in all human sexuality – which only becomes acceptable through the 'goods' of marriage, and (2) the inherently holier state of virginity / celibacy, that it is probably best left in the file marked: 'Doctrines: Past Sell-by Date.' This is not to deny such doctrines, but merely to state, as with all attempts to relate the mystery of the divine in human words, it operates within the world of human understandings of the time. And as our world of understandings changes, so must the way that we work out the implications of faith in the coming of the Son as the individual Jesus whose mother was Mary. Doctrines do not evolve like a mathematical game, nor through a web of syllogisms where one relates one 'fact' labelled 'true' to another 'fact' also labelled 'true' in the manner of a theological Sherlock Holmes (this was the great desire – and fundamental weakness – of post-Tridentine scholasticism), but by a series of glimpses. Each is a new imaginative picture that relates the mystery of the Christ to the world in which we live. However, the language of today's liturgy, the Preface for example, does evoke that older world; and it leaves many confused and lacking in comprehension. Again, the reality of our believing and doctrine is messier than a systematic primer ever reveals.

Third, this feast has curious ecumenical implications that are worthy considering at a time when many Christians seek to share calendars and festivals. When one asks eastern theologians if they accept this feast – and they are usually more comfortable with the details of the life of Mary found in the *Protoevangelium of James* than westerners – they usually give a polite answer such as 'If we accepted a Latin notion of Original Sin, then we would have to accept this feast; but [and here is the rub] we could not accept that notion of Original Sin.' Among non-Catholic westerners there is the problem of the apocryphal origins of the feast as such; and it is worth noting that such traditions still cause allergic reactions that are far more virulent than among Catholics. Then there is the whole problem of the theology of Immaculate Conception: this seems a wholly gratuitous notion arising out of excessive Marian piety supported by fanciful theological gymnastics. Celebrations that emphasise what divide are hardly in keeping with the prayer of Jesus in Jn 17:11 and 22.

Fourth, it is worth checking out the following with your congregation. Can they distinguish the following: (1) the virginal conception; (2) the Immaculate Conception; (3) the virgin birth; (4) the continual virginity [i.e. Mary as *aeiparthenos*]; and (5) between 'the blessed virgin Mary' (see the Nicene Creed) and 'blessed Mary ever virgin' (see the Confiteor of the Rite of 1970). When one has to engage in preaching with making the language of our theology transparent because it appears to be a confusing argot, it hardly helps set a festive tone for the celebration.

Evolving a new theology for the Feast
The feast needs to be re-imagined and given a new theological focus. Mention of such an idea as finding a new theology tends to generate suspicions that there is about to occur some dangerous rupture with the tradition. However, it is the celebration of the feast that is at the core of the tradition, and the doctrine of Immaculate Conception was an earlier generation's attempt to justify its celebration – a justification that was successful at enormous cost! A new theology for this feast can hardly be more divisive than the last one, and may be grounded on a more adequate basis than the propositional notion of truth that drove the last theological development. The actual form of the 1854 definition also allows some scope for re-interpretation for those for whom apparent logical consistency between one theological paradigm and another is a central plank of Catholic theology. The doctrine as defined in 1854 stressed that Mary was freed from the 'stain' (*labia*) of Original Sin (some theological extremists averred that she was also freed from the effects of Original Sin, namely: a darkening of the understanding, a weakening of the will, and an inclination to evil). Thus, as defined, the doc-

trine, in effect, means that Mary's immaculate conception put her in the same position as all other Christians are after baptism: new creations and members of the new creation which is the church. What is unique is the mode of her being created after the New Adam.

This allows us to say that this is the feast of Mary as the archetype of the whole new People of God and as the model for every Christian as they begin their pilgrimage of life and faith. Mary is thus to be celebrated as the holiest among us, the first member of the Body of Christ, the one who reached the perfection of the pilgrimage of discipleship. Meanwhile, we avoid the 'how did it happen' questions as generating more heat than light.

So why celebrate this aspect of Mary on the feast of her conception? Because we have believed since the early centuries that God has a specific interest in each of us and calls each of us personally to discipleship from the first instant of our existence. We Christians do not worship some impersonal supreme being, but a loving God who is interested in us as beings given life in the Word. To celebrate one Christian life, that of Mary, from its beginning, this feast, to its end, 15 August, is a witness to that belief. Let us celebrate the loving interest of God, his providence, and his plan to bring his Word to birth within his creation in Jesus – a providence that involved Mary from the outset of her being.

Carol Services

A carol service can be an opportunity to let people reflect on parts of the Christian tradition that are least appreciated today, or it can be a liturgical traffic jam: everyone wants to move but each in a different direction. There are two pit-falls to be negotiated: first, that it becomes a carol concert; and second, that it becomes a school event. If it is simply a concert – an opportunity for the choir or choirs to show off their stuff – then it is not really liturgy and an act of recollection of the mystery of the coming of the Christ. If it is just elaborate carols, Christmas motets, and a couple of popular pieces 'for everyone to join in', with a blessing tagged on, then it is most unlikely that it has created a space for prayer and reflection by the community. Yet, this is the most common form of carol service: the choir director creates a 'liturgy' determined by the musical abilities and tastes of the specialist singers. There may be a place for this, but it should not be confused with liturgically preparing for Christmas. The other pit-fall is that it is an assembly that is prepared by the school for the school and the only others directly involved are the parents participating as an admiring audience. This is an important part of the school's preparation for Christmas, but it will not involve the whole community as a liturgy in which they as adults can take part. When it is organised around the school the primary intention is to celebrate and communicate the memory of Christmas; when it is celebrated as an liturgy of the whole community this service can be a celebration of the Old Covenant as leading to the coming of the Christ. Carol services in the form of 'Nine Lessons and Carols' were an invention of the early twentieth century, but in that form they give liturgical expression to a Christological theme as ancient as Mt 1:1-18: the history of Israel becomes fully comprehensible with the birth of Jesus. If the carols are located within this frame of the 'book of the generations' of Jesus the Christ (cf Mt 1:1), then it can be a true liturgical event.

In an age when 'Christmas' is a time when many people scatter to every corner of the globe, the carol service also serves another purpose. A generation ago the idea of being 'at home for Christmas' seemed as 'natural' as apples falling from trees in autumn; today, Christmas is the mid-winter break when some of the most regular participants in the Eucharist throughout the year may be in the tropics or on the ski slopes: the carol service is often the last chance for the regular worshipping community to be together and specifically celebrate the Advent/Christmas season. In effect, the carol service becomes the community's actual Christmas celebration, because it is only part of the regular community that is there for Christmas Day along with visitors whose demeanour shows that they do not regularly join this community around the Eucharistic table.

Because this event is not an 'official' liturgy, it is one that can adopt many forms without difficulty, becoming a vehicle for expressing the particular gifts and creativity of the community. For example, in communities where there is a permanent deacon, this is one of the Christmas events over which he can preside.

One other aspect of this liturgy should not be forgotten. Many people who find the Eucharist threatening or off-putting, can find this acceptable because it is a 'cultural' part of Christmas. Such visitors can become fully part of this assembly in a way they might never feel comfortable or participant at the Eucharist, and if the liturgy has a narrative structure they hear the story of Christmas in a convenient form. Moreover, because the Eucharist can often be the marker of divisions among Christians, indeed can often deepen a lack of sympathy with Catholic Christians among those who feel excluded by Catholic regulations on inter-communion, such liturgies as this can have an ecumenical value: here is one of those few liturgies that all can share fully.

A Theology for a Carol Liturgy

'But when the time had fully come, God sent forth his Son, born of woman, born under the law, to redeem those who were under the law, so that we might receive adoption as sons. And because you are sons, God has sent the Spirit of his Son into our hearts, crying, "Abba! Father!"' (Gal 45: 4-6). This line from Paul captures a way of looking at the mystery of the Christ with which we are only vaguely familiar: the Christ came at the end of a long providential preparation that reached back into the earliest history of humanity. This is the theme of the genealogies in Mt and Lk, and the theology behind the line in the creed: 'God ... the Holy Spirit ... who has spoken through the prophets.' Our belief is that the Christ brings us to a perfect relationship with the Father and that that coming has been prepared by the Spirit. In a myriad of ways the world was silently prepared by the Spirit so as to be ready to welcome the Lord when at last he came. Likewise, it is our faith that the Spirit is silently preparing minds and hearts today to welcome the Christ who is the fullness of all human desires for the good. The Christ is not presented in this theology as standing as the alternative to our human existence, but rather the perfect expression of all that is honourable, just, pure, lovely, gracious, excellent, and worthy of praise (cf Phil 4:8). In him all desires for the good and the holy are fulfilled; we see our God made visible and are caught up in the love of the God we cannot see.

Finding Carols

Every hymnbook has a selection of carols, but this is often quite limited as the aim of most hymnbooks is to supply that slightly distinct item: the Advent or Christmas hymn. One of the best collections of carols available is *The New Oxford Book of Carols*, edited by Hugh Keyte and Andrew Parrott (Oxford 1992, paperback 1998).

Selecting Readings

There is no end to the various ways that readings can be selected for this: your favourites, the liturgy group's favourites, any of the sequences of readings that can be found in the lectionary. And, of course, there are well-tried formulae like that, widely used by Anglicans, which is based on a selection made for King's College, Cambridge. It has a lot to recommend it. Here is the selection: (1) Gen 3:8-15; (2) Gen 22:15-18; (3) Is 9:2-7; (4) Is 11:1-9; or Micah 5:2-5; (5) Lk 1:26-35 and 38; or Is 60:1-6 and 19; (6) Mt 1:18-23; or Lk 2:1-7; (7) Lk 2:8-16; (8) Mt 2:1-11; (9) Jn 1:1-14. This selection could be called 'the history of salvation' approach to Christology with a very definite classic theological dynamic, beginning with the promise made in the moment of judgement after the sin of Adam and Eve – what Catholic theologians referred to as the *protoevangelium* – and ending with the Joannine prologue. It has two less obvious dynamics as well: to use all the core bits of the narrative that an audience (e.g. on the radio) who might have only a sketchy knowledge of the Christian narrative could associate with; and secondly, to make sure that their narrative seemed consistent: there is a quiet harmonisation of Mt and Lk so that 'curiosity' questions are not raised.

Whatever readings are chosen there are three factors to bear in mind. First, once you have made a selection, then you have committed yourself to a particular theology of the Christ-event in exactly the same way that Mt and Lk have different theologies of the event due to the way that they use particular quotations and themes from the Old Testament. Every selection carries an inherent theology. Hence you have to think of the overall picture you are creating rather than just picking 'all our favourite bits'. When I have done this with liturgy groups – helping them to pick the nine readings – it has either been a learning experience *par excellence* on how the church relates to its memory or has shown that the group had not the slightest clue as to why we read 'all that stuff'! So selecting the readings can be a valuable part of Advent preparation. A useful trick is to start with the final reading and then select the others in so far as they help to bring a deeper understanding to it. Second, one has to arrive at

the Christmas narrative as laid out in the gospels, and this en-
tails some use of the familiar Bethlehem scenes. Not to have
such pieces read would not accord with the tone of the season.
This implies that no matter what large christological picture one
might want to present, it will never be clear-cut or neat: this is
just as well as the mystery of the Christ is always greater than
the frameworks in which we try to present it. Third, stick with
the canonical scriptures. Someone will always suggest some
'meaningful' reading that could be included – but this questing
after 'relevance' is to be resisted for four reasons. (1) This is the
time in the church's year where we especially reflect on the Old
Testament: there is such a wealth of material there for reflection,
that there can hardly be said to be a shortage of suitable passages. (2) The whole Advent liturgy is heavily dependent on the
Old Testament for its lectionary and re-use of that lectionary
here adds to a more general appreciation of the whole season.
(3) In a carol service there is already a heavy emotional and nostalgic input in the carols. Part of the purpose of reading from a
canon is to avoid a concentration on 'what is meaningful to me':
a use of what is less 'attractive' but appropriate can extend the
imagination of the faithful and challenge them in a way that 'the
meaningful' rarely achieves. (4) Lastly, and most important of
all, it was in reflecting on 'the scriptures' (which we now call the
'Old Testament') that the Christian community from the very
beginning made sense of the mystery of the Christ-event as we
can witness in the use made of quotations from the prophets in
the infancy narratives in Mt and Lk. We, each Advent, are engaged in this very process: we seek to make sense of what we
know of Jesus through the reflection on the Old Testament. Only
when we reflect on the appropriate passages of the Old
Testament can we make sense of what is written in the earliest
Christian accounts (what we refer to as the New Testament) and
thus reflect on the great Prophet, the Anointed One of the Lord.

   No matter what choice of readings is put forth, someone will
object that their favourite is omitted (usually a reading with
verses also found in Handel's *Messiah*): such protestors can be

invited to be part of the liturgy group for next year. Lastly, this is a very wordy service, but is it also one that can have a very celebratory tone due to holly and lanterns and jolly carols: it is not an event that needs a homiletic or catechetical input 'explaining' the readings or suggesting why they were chosen to fit a theme. The readings are best left to be their own communication. Likewise, complex histories of the carols or singing instructions by the conductor are out of place as they fragment the flow of the liturgy and smack of the master-class. All such instructions can be put on a service sheet. Exegetical 'explanations' can just add words without extra enlightenment and cloud a very simple sense of celebration with the deadly spectre of the classroom. If you want to do catechesis on this, then do it in a proper class environment (perhaps making such a group the group that prepare the carol service), not here. It is also best to avoid this as a 'good advertising moment' for even the best causes such as announcing when the penitential service is going to take place or the times of Christmas Masses: such info can be appended to the service sheet. Information of that sort makes this seem less than a simple celebration of Advent/Christmas joy and more like a sprat to catch a salmon: 'to get people to hear that they should be going to church more often'. People may need to hear this message, but in a media-savvy environment, to suggest it at this service is counter-productive. If people are to be enticed back to celebrating with the community, then this is more likely to be achieved by making them feel welcomed, not being under pressure, and somehow more aware of the mystery that draws humanity to itself.

A POSSIBLE CAROL SERVICE

1. *Opening carol while choristers, the nine readers, and ministers enter the church.*
A good idea is to have acolytes with candles to flank the lectern during the readings. Equally it is a good idea to bring the lectionary in the procession. The appropriate vestment for all such solemn but non-Eucharistic liturgies is the cope – preferably a violet cope to indicate that we are in Advent.

2. *Introduction*
My friends,
We are assembled to bear witness to our faith that when the time had fully come, the Father sent forth his Son, born of the woman Mary, born under the law, to redeem those who were under the law, so that we might receive adoption as sons and daughters. In our readings and carols we are going to celebrate this story of the coming of Jesus as the Christ.
Let us pray
Father, with joy we recall the ages when you prepared a people to receive the Anointed One; we recall your promises in the prophets, in the work of John the Baptist, and in your calling of the virgin Mary to become the mother of your Son. Grant that we will be like the shepherds and behold the infant Jesus with holy wonder, and like the wise men and offer our gifts to him and worship him. We make this prayer through our Lord Jesus Christ, your Son, who lives and reigns with you and the Holy Spirit, one God, forever and ever.

The book is placed on the lectern; and if a thurifer has led the procession, then the book can now be incensed.

3. *First Reading*
A reading from the prophet Isaiah. (Is 9:2-7)
The people who walked in darkness have seen a great light; those who lived in a land of deep darkness – on them light has shined. You have multiplied the nation, you have increased its

joy; they rejoice before you as with joy at the harvest, as people exult when dividing plunder. For the yoke of their burden, and the bar across their shoulders, the rod of their oppressor, you have broken as on the day of Midian. For all the boots of the tramping warriors and all the garments rolled in blood shall be burned as fuel for the fire. For a child has been born for us, a son given to us; authority rests upon his shoulders; and he is named Wonderful Counsellor, Mighty God, Everlasting Father, Prince of Peace. His authority shall grow continually, and there shall be endless peace for the throne of David and his kingdom. He will establish and uphold it with justice and with righteousness from this time onward and forevermore.

This is the word of the Lord.

4. First Carol

Carols fall somewhere between hymns and popular songs: this is their strength as bearers of the tradition. So it is important that as many popular carols as possible are sung so as to involve, primarily, the community rather than the choir. This means that out of the eleven carols that are sung in this liturgy, at least five should be for the entire congregation to sing. We sometimes look down on carols as just 'Christmas trimmings' but many are real theological gems. For example, just read 'Ding dong merrily on high' and note how its theology of liturgy is virtually the same as the Letter to the Hebrews except that it comes in an easy to digest Christmas wrapping.

5. Second Reading

A reading from the prophet Micah. (Mic 5:2-5)

But you, O Bethlehem of Ephrathah, who are one of the little clans of Judah, from you shall come forth for me one who is to rule in Israel, whose origin is from of old, from ancient days. Therefore he shall give them up until the time when she who is in labour has brought forth; then the rest of his kindred shall return to the people of Israel. And he shall stand and feed his flock in the strength of the Lord, in the majesty of the name of the

Lord his God. And they shall live secure, for now he shall be great to the ends of the earth; and he shall be the one of peace. This is the word of the Lord.

6. Second Carol

7. Third Reading
A reading from the prophet Isaiah. (Is 60:1-6)
Arise, shine; for your light has come, and the glory of the Lord has risen upon you. For darkness shall cover the earth, and thick darkness the peoples; but the Lord will arise upon you, and his glory will appear over you. Nations shall come to your light, and kings to the brightness of your dawn. Lift up your eyes and look around; they all gather together, they come to you; your sons shall come from far away, and your daughters shall be carried on their nurses' arms. Then you shall see and be radiant; your heart shall thrill and rejoice, because the abundance of the sea shall be brought to you, the wealth of the nations shall come to you. A multitude of camels shall cover you, the young camels of Midian and Ephah; all those from Sheba shall come. They shall bring gold and frankincense, and shall proclaim the praise of the Lord.
This is the word of the Lord.

8. Third Carol

9. Fourth Reading
A reading from the prophet Jeremiah. (Jer 30:18-22)
Thus says the Lord: I am going to restore the fortunes of the tents of Jacob, and have compassion on his dwellings; the city shall be rebuilt upon its mound, and the citadel set on its rightful site. Out of them shall come thanksgiving, and the sound of merrymakers. I will make them many, and they shall not be few; I will make them honoured, and they shall not be disdained. Their children shall be as of old, their congregation shall be established before me; and I will punish all who oppress them.

Their prince shall be one of their own, their ruler shall come
from their midst; I will bring him near, and he shall approach
me, for who would otherwise dare to approach me? says the
Lord. And you shall be my people, and I will be your God.
This is the word of the Lord.

10. Fourth Carol

11. Fifth Reading
A reading from the prophet Zechariah. (Zech 8:1, 3-8, 12-17, 20-23)
The word of the Lord of hosts came to me, saying: Thus says the
Lord: I will return to Zion, and will dwell in the midst of
Jerusalem; Jerusalem shall be called the faithful city, and the
mountain of the Lord of hosts shall be called the holy mountain.
Thus says the Lord of hosts: Old men and old women shall again
sit in the streets of Jerusalem, each with staff in hand because of
their great age. And the streets of the city shall be full of boys
and girls playing in its streets. Thus says the Lord of hosts: Even
though it seems impossible to the remnant of this people in these
days, should it also seem impossible to me, says the Lord of
hosts? Thus says the Lord of hosts: I will save my people from
the east country and from the west country; and I will bring
them to live in Jerusalem. They shall be my people and I will be
their God, in faithfulness and in righteousness. For there shall be
a sowing of peace; the vine shall yield its fruit, the ground shall
give its produce, and the skies shall give their dew; and I will
cause the remnant of this people to possess all these things. Just
as you have been a cursing among the nations, O house of Judah
and house of Israel, so I will save you and you shall be a blessing. Do not be afraid, but let your hands be strong. For thus says
the Lord of hosts: Just as I purposed to bring disaster upon you,
when your ancestors provoked me to wrath, and I did not relent,
says the Lord of hosts, so again I have purposed in these days to
do good to Jerusalem and to the house of Judah; do not be afraid.
These are the things that you shall do: Speak the truth to one another, render in your gates judgements that are true and make

for peace, do not devise evil in your hearts against one another, and love no false oath; for all these are things that I hate, says the Lord. Thus says the Lord of hosts: Peoples shall yet come, the inhabitants of many cities; the inhabitants of one city shall go to another, saying, 'Come, let us go to entreat the favour of the Lord, and to seek the Lord of hosts; I myself am going.' Many peoples and strong nations shall come to seek the Lord of hosts in Jerusalem, and to entreat the favour of the Lord. Thus says the Lord of hosts: In those days ten men from nations of every language shall take hold of a Jew, grasping his garment and saying, 'Let us go with you, for we have heard that God is with you.' This is the word of the Lord.

12. Fifth Carol

13. Sixth Reading
A Reading from the Book of Psalms. (Ps 72:1-19)

Give the king your justice, O God, and your righteousness to a king's son.

May he judge your people with righteousness, and your poor with justice.

May the mountains yield prosperity for the people, and the hills, in righteousness.

May he defend the cause of the poor of the people, give deliverance to the needy, and crush the oppressor.

May he live while the sun endures, and as long as the moon, throughout all generations.

May he be like rain that falls on the mown grass, like showers that water the earth.

In his days may righteousness flourish and peace abound, until the moon is no more.

May he have dominion from sea to sea, and from the River to the ends of the earth.

May his foes bow down before him, and his enemies lick the dust.

May the kings of Tarshish and of the isles render him tribute, may the kings of Sheba and Seba bring gifts.

May all kings fall down before him, all nations give him service. For he delivers the needy when they call, the poor and those who have no helper.

He has pity on the weak and the needy, and saves the lives of the needy.

From oppression and violence he redeems their life; and precious is their blood in his sight.

Long may he live! May gold of Sheba be given to him. May prayer be made for him continually, and blessings invoked for him all day long.

May there be abundance of grain in the land; may it wave on the tops of the mountains; may its fruit be like Lebanon; and may people blossom in the cities like the grass of the field.

May his name endure forever, his fame continue as long as the sun. May all nations be blessed in him; may they pronounce him happy.

Blessed be the Lord, the God of Israel, who alone does wondrous things.

Blessed be his glorious name forever; may his glory fill the whole earth. Amen and Amen.

This is the word of the Lord.

14. Sixth Carol

15. Seventh Reading
It is best to treat these gospel readings ritually in the same way as the others rather than as 'the gospel' at Mass. So no incense or having people stand. The aim is to reflect on a whole sequence of readings rather than see just one as the most important. Moreover, since this is legally a para-liturgy, the reading of gospel passages here does not presuppose deacons' orders: this allows a wider sweep of the community to take part. The president (be he a deacon or a priest) can sit back and preside until the last prayer.

A reading from the holy gospel according to Luke. (Lk 1:67-79)
Then [John the Baptist's] father Zechariah was filled with the
Holy Spirit and spoke this prophecy:
'Blessed be the Lord God of Israel, for he has looked favourably
on his people and redeemed them.

He has raised up a mighty saviour for us in the house of his servant David, as he spoke through the mouth of his holy prophets
from of old, that we would be saved from our enemies and from
the hand of all who hate us.

Thus he has shown the mercy promised to our ancestors, and
has remembered his holy covenant, the oath that he swore to our
ancestor Abraham, to grant us that we, being rescued from the
hands of our enemies, might serve him without fear, in holiness
and righteousness before him all our days.

And you, child, will be called the prophet of the Most High; for
you will go before the Lord to prepare his ways, to give knowledge of salvation to his people by the forgiveness of their sins.

By the tender mercy of our God, the dawn from on high will
break upon us, to give light to those who sit in darkness and in
the shadow of death, to guide our feet into the way of peace.'
This is the word of the Lord.

16. Seventh Carol

17. Eighth Reading
A reading from the holy gospel according to Luke. (Lk 2:1-20)
In those days a decree went out from Emperor Augustus that all
the world should be registered. This was the first registration
and was taken while Quirinius was governor of Syria. All went
to their own towns to be registered. Joseph also went from the
town of Nazareth in Galilee to Judea, to the city of David called
Bethlehem, because he was descended from the house and family
of David. He went to be registered with Mary, to whom he was
engaged and who was expecting a child. While they were there,
the time came for her to deliver her child. And she gave birth to
her firstborn son and wrapped him in bands of cloth, and laid

him in a manger, because there was no place for them in the inn. In that region there were shepherds living in the fields, keeping watch over their flock by night. Then an angel of the Lord stood before them, and the glory of the Lord shone around them, and they were terrified. But the angel said to them, 'Do not be afraid; for see – I am bringing you good news of great joy for all the people: to you is born this day in the city of David a Saviour, who is the Messiah, the Lord. This will be a sign for you: you will find a child wrapped in bands of cloth and lying in a manger.' And suddenly there was with the angel a multitude of the heavenly host, praising God and saying, 'Glory to God in the highest heaven, and on earth peace among those whom he favours!' When the angels had left them and gone into heaven, the shepherds said to one another, 'Let us go now to Bethlehem and see this thing that has taken place, which the Lord has made known to us.' So they went with haste and found Mary and Joseph, and the child lying in the manger. When they saw this, they made known what had been told them about this child; and all who heard it were amazed at what the shepherds told them. But Mary treasured all these words and pondered them in her heart. The shepherds returned, glorifying and praising God for all they had heard and seen, as it had been told them.
This is the word of the Lord.

18. Eighth Carol

19. Ninth Reading
A reading from the holy gospel according to Matthew. (Mt 2:1-11)
In the time of King Herod, after Jesus was born in Bethlehem of Judea, wise men from the East came to Jerusalem, asking, 'Where is the child who has been born king of the Jews? For we observed his star at its rising, and have come to pay him homage.' When King Herod heard this, he was frightened, and all Jerusalem with him; and calling together all the chief priests and scribes of the people, he inquired of them where the Messiah was to be born. They told him, 'In Bethlehem of Judea;

for so it has been written by the prophet: "And you, Bethlehem, in the land of Judah, are by no means least among the rulers of Judah; for from you shall come a ruler who is to shepherd my people Israel".' Then Herod secretly called for the wise men and learned from them the exact time when the star had appeared. Then he sent them to Bethlehem, saying, 'Go and search diligently for the child; and when you have found him, bring me word so that I may also go and pay him homage.' When they had heard the king, they set out; and there, ahead of them, went the star that they had seen at its rising, until it stopped over the place where the child was. When they saw that the star had stopped, they were overwhelmed with joy. On entering the house, they saw the child with Mary his mother; and they knelt down and paid him homage. Then, opening their treasure chests, they offered him gifts of gold, frankincense, and myrrh. This is the word of the Lord.

20. Ninth Carol

21. Prayer:
My sisters and brothers, when the time had fully come, the Father sent forth his Son, born of the woman Mary, born under the law, to redeem those who were under the law, so that we might receive adoption as sons and daughters. And because we are daughters and sons, God has sent the Spirit of his Son into our hearts, crying, 'Abba! Father!', so now let us pray: Our Father ...

Let us pray
Father, we have been reflecting on the wondrous mystery by which you prepared the world and a people to welcome your only Son, our Saviour Jesus the Christ. Look upon us and grant that we may be your people today and bring your Son to birth in the world in which we live. We make this prayer through Christ our Lord. Amen.

Solemn Blessing:
Solemn Blessing 2 for Christmas (*Missal*, p 368).

22. Recessional Carol as choristers and ministers leave

23. Conclusion: Mince Pies and Mulled Wine

This might seem like an optional extra, but reflect for moment. If
we are celebrating liturgically as a community the Lord's coming, then we must be able to celebrate simply as a community
that the Lord's coming has made us this community. After all, it
is the gathering to eat and drink together, and so participate in
the Christ, that is our basic ritual: the Eucharist. But if a community rarely simply celebrates its happy news, its happy time,
then it will be much harder for that community to feel itself as a
community *en fête* when it comes to liturgical celebrations. Until
recent times the celebrations of the village community for
Christmas were the platform upon which the more obviously
liturgical celebrations were built. Today, a Christian community
rarely meets except for the liturgy and then the liturgy's celebrations are often in mid-air: people are expected to be intimate
spiritually and refer to each other as friends and brothers/sis-
ters, but they might not even have chatted to anyone in that
community over a cup of tea. If the Eucharist is to be the 'centre
and summit' of a church's life, then there has to be a hinterland
around that centre and summit. So if the food of the Eucharist is
to be appreciated as the food for the community, that community
has to come together to eat and drink in other ways apart from
the Eucharist. This is one such occasion when drinks and nibbles
together is not something for the pious few or something forced:
at almost every event around this time there is some equivalent
use of mince pies and mulled wine, so it seems wholly appropriate, if this is a community celebrating Christmas, to offer such
fare. It is a fact of our human nature that sharing food and drink
– even if it is just mince pies and mulled wine – forms us into
communities, and you do not have to be an anthropologist to

think of umpteen examples; it is thus a case of grace building on nature that the Christ chose to bring us into his presence as his body in the context of a meal. This little Christmas 'meal' of mince pies and mulled wine is part of preparing ourselves to be a community of one mind and heart thus being able to welcome him in our Christmas eucharistic gatherings.

Lastly, do not charge for the pies and wine or even make this a way of getting some money for charity: this is the community's celebration, so let us celebrate. Would you like to be invited round to someone's house for 'Christmas Drinks' and then be charged for them? The same rationale applies here. After all, one of the signs of the times of the Lord is the invitation to 'everyone who thirsts, come to the waters; and you that have no money, come, buy and eat! Come, buy wine and milk without money and without price' (Is 55:1).

Third Sunday of Advent (Year A)

Note

This Sunday is still sometimes referred to as 'Gaudete Sunday' (the title derives from the opening words of the entrance antiphon) and was seen (by analogy with the Fourth Sunday of Lent) as a deliberate lightening of the penitential tone of Advent expressed in special rose-coloured vestments. However, it is doubtful if making a point about any of this at the liturgy is of anything but antiquarian interest. First, it is difficult enough to explain the themes that run right through Advent – and this Sunday is no exception: Christ is near; therefore we rejoice and become newly aware of this presence. Second, the paralleling of Advent with Lent tends to draw attention away from what is specific to Advent. Third, now that the liturgy is in the vernacular, there is less emphasis on such matters as details of vestments and the entrance antiphon is not a significant choral piece. It is doubtful if the average congregation are that aware that the assembly's president is wearing a specially coloured chasuble only taken out a couple of times a year!

Introduction to the Celebration

In these weeks before Christmas our reflection and prayer as a community focus on the various ways that the Lord is near to us: he is the One who is continually coming into our world with his good news of liberation and joy; we are the people who welcome him and become his hands, and mouth, and feet. So we can now reflect on the joyfulness that is ours because we are in Christ's presences – he is near to us; but we must regret the times when our actions have been far from him.

Rite of Penance

For the times when we have not proclaimed the good news to the poor, Lord have mercy.

For the times when we have not brought comfort and help to those in need, Christ have mercy.

For the times when we have not helped the blind to see, the lame to walk, and the deaf to hear, Lord have mercy.

Headings for Readings
First Reading
The time of the Lord's coming is a time when the whole creation is renewed: the wasteland will rejoice and bloom; it is a time of justice and salvation: he is coming to save you; it is a time of healing: the blind see, the deaf hear; the Lord's coming, our feast of Christmas, is a time of joy: sorrow and lament are ended.

Second Reading
To be a Christian is to be a person of patient hope: the Lord has come, but the Lord is still to come. We must wait and not lose heart.

Gospel
This gospel picks up, through the answers sent to John the Baptist's questions, the various points in today's first reading: Jesus is the One promised to Israel: his coming inaugurated the reign of God's kingdom.

Prayer of the Faithful
Use the Sample Formula for Advent given on pp 996-7 of the *Missal*. Choose one of the options given for each of the four intercessions marked A, B, C, D.

Eucharistic Prayer
Unless today is 17 December – and this happens whenever Christmas Day will fall on a Monday – when Preface of Advent II is used; today uses Preface of Advent I. By now most celebrants are more than familiar with this preface – just one preface for more than a fortnight is exceptional in the 1970 *Missal* – however, most of the assembly will not have that sense of familiarity

– and it is a most succinct statement of what we celebrate in
Advent.

Invitation to the Our Father
Jesus proclaimed the good news of the Father's love, and taught
us to pray:

Sign of Peace
The coming of the Christ inaugurated the reign of God: that
reign demands that we establish reconciliation and peace in all
our relationships.

Invitation to Communion
Behold the One who came first in Palestine, who will come again
in glory, and today comes among us his people as our food and
drink; happy are we who share this banquet.

Communion Reflection
Lord, grant that we may be patient, until your coming.
Lord, grant us the wisdom to be like the farmer who waits for
the precious fruit of the earth, being patient over it until it re-
ceives the early and the late rain.
Lord, grant that we may not lose heart.
Lord, grant us the wisdom to know that your coming is at hand.
Lord, grant us to know your closeness now in our sharing of
your loaf and cup with one another.
Lord, grant us the strength to avoid grumbling and complaining
against one another, so that we may not be judged; for behold,
you are the Judge who is standing at the doors.
Lord, grant that we may take as an example of suffering and
patience the prophets who spoke in the name of the Lord.
Adapted from the Second Reading.

Conclusion
Solemn Blessing 1 for Advent (*Missal*, p 367).

Bear in mind that this is often the last Sunday on which the 'normal' community is present. People have not gone away yet for Christmas holidays, visitors (either Christians in the locality who rarely participate in the Eucharist; or from elsewhere) have not arrived; it is therefore useful to acknowledge this and wish everyone present that as a community, even if dispersed, all should have a happy Christmas.

COMMENTARY

First Reading: Is 35:1-6 and 10
This is an image of the new creation that will result when Israel returns to the way of the Lord and to loyalty to the covenant. We read this in Advent messianically in that the new world comes about through the coming of the Lord's anointed; we do this because this is the way it is used in today's gospel: 'Then the eyes of the blind shall be opened, and the ears of the deaf unstopped; then shall the lame man leap like a hart, and the tongue of the dumb sing for joy' (35:5-6). It is this statement which was read as a prophecy that was thus presented as fulfilled in Jesus in Mt 11.

It is because of the use of the text of Isaiah in Mt 11 that we are reading this piece of Isaiah today; and since the key verses are 5-6, the literary unit in Isaiah (1-10) has been cropped midway through verse 6 with the latter half of verse 10 used as a finale.

Second Reading: Jas 5:7-10
The key to the role of this reading in the liturgy is 5:8: 'You also be patient. Establish your hearts, for the coming of the Lord [note the Vulgate: *adventus Domini*] is at hand.' This is the classic Advent theme of waiting-yet-closeness, which is also the mystery of Christian hope. It is this meaning, the Latin text uses the word *adventus* twice, that is significant today. Within the letter James is concerned to affirm both the closeness of the coming and the need to engage with the world and work in it and continue working in it; he fears that people who hear the 'the coming is near' will simply abandon care for the world and the good

works of Christians. This might seem a far-fetched fear, but it is worth noting that many American fundamentalists today declare that it is not worthwhile worrying about the ecological crisis of global warming or the destruction of the environment precisely because they believe the Second Coming or 'The Rapture' is just around the corner!

Gospel: Mt 11:2-11
This passage, a well-formed unit within the gospel, is one of the densest in the whole of Matthew or Luke (who has a slightly different version in 7:18-28). The reason for this density lies in the historical relationship that this passage allows us to reconstruct between John the Baptist and Jesus, and to conclude that there was an encounter between Jesus and John's followers whose memory is preserved in this passage beneath a theological overlay that is part of the universal kerygma which allied, and indeed related by blood, John and Jesus.

That there was any personal knowledge of Jesus by John is most unlikely; Jesus was clearly very influenced by John and was probably originally one of his disciples. However, Jesus left John and radically departed from his teaching: the kingdom was coming, but it would not be the great crunch for all but the elect that John preached, but a kingdom of the Father's forgiveness that was being taught and established in table-fellowships when Jesus gathered and ate with his disciples. The new Israel was not the remnant that would survive by way of joining a special band marked off by 'a plunge of repentance', but would be established by a new token group, The Twelve, who would act as a focus for the regathering of Israel from being scattered over the hills: and the tax-collectors, prostitutes, and sinners of all sorts would be gathered in and given a share in this end-time.

At some point, John must have feared that his ministry was ending and yet the End was not coming: so what of this new movement of Jesus of Nazareth? It is in this context that the questioners went to Jesus, and Jesus replies by asking them to look at his works. He is separate from John, but John is not criticised: perhaps the younger teacher still recognises the wisdom of his master even if he has gone his own way.

This complex relationship between Jesus and John was further complicated because it appears that among the followers of Jesus there was a sizable proportion that were originally John's disciples – and indeed many of these never really abandoned their first master's apocalyptic leanings and hence the ill-fitting legacy of apocalypticism in Christianity. So how were these various groups to be accommodated? The solution found in all the gospels is that John was the final prophet preparing the way for Jesus. However, there were still these other little bits of memory and teaching (such as today's gospel) which allow us to see behind the theological positioning of John relative to the Christ.

HOMILY NOTES

1. The time of wishing 'Happy Christmas' is already here: the adverts are full of holly and 'Christmas Cheer'; the diary is full of Christmas related events; and 'getting ready' is an urgent state of being. So what if you are one of those people who find the whole thing a drag? Find Christmas a time of stress? Just cannot wait for the spring light? Or think it is all overplayed? It probably means that you suffer in silence as it appears to be 'not the done thing' to be 'down on Christmas'. Alternatively, one can just feel guilty and stressed that one is 'not feeling as one ought to feel'. Then there is the question of the family, the in-laws, or the tensions of all the extra people in the house. Preachers can often so idealise 'the family', that they ignore the real pain of many of their hearers and this, in effect, alienates them from the gospel's message.

2. The simple fact is that many people hate Christmas, wish it would pass quickly, dismiss it as only important if there are children to be entertained, or a time of loneliness. This is a significant group in any community; they are not to be likened to Scrooge in Dickens' *A Christmas Carol*; and their feelings should find expression at some point in the liturgy. Preaching is about helping people grow in wisdom and holi-

ness, not simply the broadcasting of 'our message' over and over in the manner of religion channels on television. So how does one engage with the people for whom the whole Christmas thing is painful?

3. Step 1: Acknowledge that that these attitudes exist and are worthy of being taken seriously. No one should feel that they could be dismissed as 'party poopers' or for 'not getting into the spirit of the thing'. Christmas is a time of heightened emotions, complex memories, and a series of stress inducing deadlines due to the various tasks that have to be done before such and such a moment.

4. Step 2: Even if Christmas is a pain for you, human beings celebrate collective memories of all sorts of things and this is a basic element in every religion and culture. Such special times are as old as humanity, as the stones of Newgrange and Stonehenge bear mute witness. You may find it 'a pain' but without such common memories we would not be bound together as a society. Moreover, without 'high days' the passing of time would have a grim monotony. We are creatures that need special times and ordinary time. Here is part of the genius of the gospel with its cycle of festivals rooted simultaneously in the cycles of nature (Christmas is linked to midwinter, the original pasch was a spring-time agricultural feast) and the revelation of God's love in the incarnation and paschal mystery. We may not be 'in tune' with Christmas merriment, but without an annual cycle we would be diminished as human beings and as Christians. It is worth recalling the proverb 'A change is as good as a rest': Christmas marks a change from the ordinary – even if it is only because it annoys us so – and any change is an opportunity to take stock of our lives and ways of life. If Christmas really does 'turn you off,' then it can be a call to self-reflection and growth in self-knowledge.

5. Step 3. During the 1960s, when the calendar was being reformed, there were many publications suggesting that either Christmas should be abandoned as distracting from the an-

nual Christian feast (Easter) or arguing that since the
December date had been so overlaid with cultural celebrations that the Christian feast was apparently an 'add-on' and
these writers urged that the feast be moved to another date
during the year. Neither suggestion was acted upon – luckily
both suggestions were so daft that they did not stand a
chance of getting through – but it does raise an interesting
question for us as people who are celebrating Christmas as a
feast and not simply as the time of the winter party. Let us
imagine that the feast of the nativity were moved to, for example, 1 September; what would we be celebrating? This is a
useful question as it can help us separate out the Christian
recollection from the mistletoe-bedecked merriment; and so
can help people who do not like Christmas to separate the
feast which is a key part of memory as believers from the
merriment and the stress. So what really would we celebrate
on 1 September if in a future revision of the calendar the
nativity of the Christ were so moved? You should point out,
by the way, that such a change is fully within the competence
of the Church – for we sometimes think that there is
Christmas existing in itself quite apart from the Christmas
communities that celebrate it: a classic case of confusing effect with cause.

6. That final question, if we moved Christmas Day from 25
   December to 1 September, may help those who dislike
   Christmas to hear their experience reflected in the homily,
   but it is useful question to pose to every member of the gath-
   ering to help them clarify her/his mind on what we as
   Christians are recalling.

Third Sunday of Advent (Year B)

Note
See note on this Sunday at Year A.

Introduction to the Celebration
Today is the day of John the Baptist. He was the last of the prophets whose mission was to bear witness to the Lord when he came among his people. He prepared the way for the Anointed One and pointed him out. Today John is the model for every one of us: we are called be prophets in our world; we are called to bear witness to the Christ; in the wilderness of human greed, injustice, and falsehood we are called to make straight the way of the Lord.

Rite of Penance
For those times when we have failed to imitate the prophet Isaiah in testifying to you, Lord have mercy.
For those times when we have failed to imitate John the Baptist in preparing a way for you, Christ have mercy.
For those times when we have failed to imitate Mary in placing our faith in you, Lord have mercy.

Headings for Readings
First Reading
This prophecy outlines the vocation of the Lord's anointed One, the Christ; and it provides a pattern for our vocations as his witnesses.

Second Reading
Paul gives us a summary of the Christian lifestyle as we await the return of the Christ.

Gospel

Today we hear John's account of the task the Father gave John the Baptist in preparing the way for his Son.

Prayer of the Faithful
President

Friends, this is a time of seeking and waiting: seeking for the presence of Jesus Christ in our lives; seeking out his way in the world we are building each day; seeking the justice and peace that his coming can bring to the world. So let us pray for ourselves and others that our celebration of Advent may renew our quest for the Lord.

Reader(s)

1. For all Christians, that we may seek the Christ in our lives. Lord hear us.

2. For all people of good will, that they may seek the truth. Lord hear us.

3. For all whom we elect to serve in public office, that they may work for the common good. Lord hear us.

4. For all called to the pastoral ministry, that they may make Christ visible in their care. Lord hear us.

5. For all in this church here in ..., that we may be witnesses to Christ in this neighbourhood. Lord hear us.

6. For this community, that we will wait for the Lord's coming at Christmas with rejoicing. Lord hear us.

7. For this family of God, that we will prepare for Christmas with constant prayer. Lord hear us.

8. For this gathering at the Lord's table, that we will be free from strife in all our dealings with one another as we prepare for Christmas. Lord hear us.

9. For all who suffer, that they may know Christ's care, Lord hear us.

10. For all the dead, that they may encounter Christ as the merciful judge, Lord hear us.

President

Father, we celebrate your Son's coming and we long for him to come again. Meanwhile, grant that our celebration of Christmas may not only renew us in body, mind, and spirit; but witness to your Son before our world. We ask this through Christ our Lord. Amen.

Eucharistic Prayer
Even if this Sunday is not 17 December when Preface of Advent II would be used in any case, given the focus of today's gospel on John the Baptist the choice of Preface II of Advent is to be recommended. The reason for this is that that Preface views the ministry of John the Baptist from a johannine perspective.

Invitation to the Our Father
Christ's coming opens for us the way to the Father and so we can say:

Sign of Peace
We bring Christ to birth in our world when we work for peace: let us start that work by declaring peace to those gathered beside us at this holy table.

Invitation to Communion
John the Baptist cried out 'Behold the Lamb of God who takes away the sin of the world'; now we too hear those words, happy are we who are called to his supper.

Communion Reflection
Have a structured silence: 'Amid all the bustle of getting ready for Christmas, let us pray in silence now that each of us will encounter the Christ in the coming festival.' End the silence with the 'Let us pray' of the Prayer after Communion.

Conclusion
Solemn Blessing 1 for Advent (*Missal*, p 367).

Final Note
Bear in mind that this is often the last Sunday on which the 'normal' community is present. People have not gone away yet for Christmas holidays, visitors (either Christians in the locality who rarely participate in the Eucharist; or from elsewhere) have not arrived; it is therefore useful to acknowledge this and wish everyone present that as a community, even if dispersed, all should have a happy Christmas.

COMMENTARY

First Reading: Is 61:1-2, 10-11
Most exegetes see Is 60:1-62:12 forming a unit within Third-Isaiah painting a vision of the glorious new Zion when God's rule is established. Within this unit 61:1-3 is a description of the anointing of the prophet of this glorious time (which is why it was chosen for today). However, what we have is only a verse and a half of this section as the latter part of verse 2 goes on to speak of the Lord's vengeance and so has been cut along with the third verse. Then to give the reading some length, another two verses from a different section (that portraying the glories of the new Zion: 61:4-62:9) of Third-Isaiah have been added. Thus the reading we have today only has integrity within its liturgical context where it presents the qualities that the Anointed One must have and to which his forerunner must bear witness.

Second Reading: 1 Thess 5:16-24
In the lectionary of the 1570 Missal – following a much earlier arrangement – this Sunday had as its epistle Phil 4:4-7 with its powerful opening line: *Gaudete in Domino semper, iterum dico: Gaudete* (Rejoice in the Lord always, again I say: Rejoice) which both gave this Sunday its name, inspired umpteen carols, and pink vestments! However, the command to rejoice is found in several places in Paul, and this is one of them. 1 Thess 5:16 opens in Latin: *Gaudete semper, et sine intercessione orate* as the community waits for the coming (*in aduentu*) of Jesus. It is this line, coupled with the notion that this is Gaudete Sunday, that explains the choice of this reading.

It is part of Paul's encouragement in this his first letter: the community is to wait for the coming return of the Lord, they are not
to be fearful, and they are to wait for the Lord in prayer. Placed
in the context of the liturgy, the reading strikes a note that could
be seen as a summary of Advent:
• the community should be rejoicing;
• it should be without quarrels;
• it should be waiting in prayer;
• because it is living 'in the advent' of the Christ
• whose coming it will celebrated at Christmas.

   This reading may appear a simple piece of Pauline instruc-
tion, but its liturgical reading touches on all the key points of the
nature of liturgical time and how we read 'the scriptures' within it.

Gospel: Jn 1:6-8, 19-28
As with the synoptics, it is part of John's telling of the story of
the church that Jesus's coming was heralded by John the Baptist;
and indeed that the two movements (John's and Jesus's) should
be seen as linked as prelude and main-event. This theme appears several points in the gospel: first here in the account of the
period before the first miracles; then the discussion among
John's disciples about purification (3:25-27); then the question
about the testimony of John (5:33-36); and, lastly, when John – in
contrast to Jesus – is remembered as having done no 'sign'
(10:40-41). In every case the key point is that John denies that he
is the messiah and points to another: Jesus. It is as if John the
Baptist had no teaching except to say: there is the one. In John's
gospel, John the Baptist is a witness, a pointer, and a living sign
in the barest form: he only is in so far as he points beyond himself.

   John the Baptist's message is, therefore, all that you seek you
must seek for in Jesus; and Jesus is, in turn, the one who bears
witness to the Father. In today's reading, a combination of the
two earliest references to John the Baptist, we have the kernel of
this gospel's view of him: 'He was not the light, but came to bear
witness to the light' (1:8); or 'He confessed, he did not deny, but

confessed, "I am not the Christ"' (1:20), and his moving attention directly to Jesus without any question of hesitation. This is a
very different picture of John the Baptist, and a very different
approach to his ministry, to that found in the synoptics, and it is
worth not confusing the two: here there is no mention of John
the Baptist having a message of his own, or his preparing the
people for a cataclysm, or having disciples of his own, or having
any queries as to the identity and message of Jesus. From John
the gospel-writer's perspective, the Baptist has become the
model sacramental person, and thus can be seen as the model
disciple of Jesus.

HOMILY NOTES

1. The last century has been littered by people who have
   claimed to have all the answers to the great human questions
   and who are only too willing share their 'wisdom' with
   everyone else. There have been the great dictators: Lenin,
   Hitler, Stalin, Mussolini, Mao – all knew what the world
   needed and left a trail of destruction in their wake. Then
   there was a veritable army of lesser despots who knew the
   answers for everyone and were prepared to put up with any
   amount of suffering to impose their expert solutions. Then
   there are the experts in personal affairs: how to get this right,
   or to do that properly, or how to be successful or slim or
   happy in ten lessons. All you have to do is buy their book or
   video and follow the instructions. At this time of year there
   are even a slew of books on how to have the perfect
   Christmas, or Christmas party, or perfect Christmas cooking!
   All these experts have something in common: look to me and
   I will solve your problems. And, of course, there is no shortage of religious experts of every make and shape who have a
   sure-fire, quick and simple route to happiness and bliss.

2. Faced with such experts, many of us instinctively recoil for
   there is something deep inside us that says it cannot be a simple as that or there would not be such bother or that life is always more complex than the clarity provided in the various

expert solutions. On the other hand, many of us faced with the complexity of the world and its problems long for a simple solution that will deliver security, clarity, and some happiness. So the experts are never without disciples (or people at least willing to listen to them or buy their books): and for many of the 'experts', that is success enough.

3. John the Baptist is not such an expert. John the gospel-writer decisively moves the focus from him to the Anointed One. The Baptist's vocation is to point away from himself to the Lamb. He is the witness to the truth, not its possessor. He is the way-maker, not the way. Faced with both those who would discredit him as a another religious fraud, or those who would adopt him as their saviour and leader, he makes the same response: 'I am not the Christ ... but among you stands one whom you do not know ... who comes after me, the thong of whose sandal I am not worthy to untie.'

4. Here lies the style of the witness of everyone who recognises the Christ: we point away from ourselves and towards the One who is to come, the One who brings the universe to its completion.

5. But does this mean that we present 'Jesus as the answer to everything'? This is certainly a mode of witness that many Christians are eager to adopt. Jesus has the answer to every one of life's problems. Jesus will make you happy. Jesus will make you secure. Jesus will give you the answers to all your questions from where the universe came from to what is the best way to vote. Or as the old school joke has it: whenever a religion teacher asks you a question, the safest answer to give is 'Jesus'. The 'Jesus is the Answer' of advertising hoardings is not the Jesus we hear proclaimed in John's gospel.

6. For John the gospel-writer Jesus is the way and that begins in a wilderness and while it does end in triumph, that triumph is the cry 'It is completed' upon the cross. As John pointed beyond himself and bore witness to the Christ, the Christ points beyond himself and bears witness to the Father (Jn 5:33-36). The Anointed One does not invite us to adopt a set

of answers, much less sure-success remedies to life's problems, but to embark on his way, to adopt his style, and to
begin that journey from the midst of whatever wilderness we
inhabit.

7. His way is the way of justice, gentleness, peace, and integrity.
   The Anointed One, the Christ, fulfills the prophecy of Isaiah,
   and commends it to his followers as their way. For the spirit
   of the Lord has been given to us, we have been anointed so
   that we are made part of the whole Christ:

   > The Lord has sent me to bring good news to the poor,
   > To bind up hearts that are broken,
   > To proclaim liberty to captives
   > and freedom to those in prison,
   > To proclaim a year of favour from the Lord.

Third Sunday of Advent (Year C)

Note

See note on this Sunday at Year A – this is the one year in the 1969 lectionary cycle when the Epistle 'Gaudete in Domino semper' is read: it was this reading that gave this Sunday its old name. However, it is still only an antiquarian point and probably best ignored!

Introduction to the Celebration

The Lord is near to us: this is a basic Christian belief. It is this belief that makes our Sunday gathering each week so special: Jesus is among us as an assembly, we hear his voice, we share his banquet. But the Lord is also one who is not-yet-here: we have to wait for him, we have to be patient in prayer, we have to be diligent in preparing a way for him to enter our world anew.

Rite of Penance

Lord Jesus, when you came into the world you proclaimed the Father's gentleness, Lord have mercy.
Lord Jesus, when you came into the world you proclaimed the Father's forgiveness, Christ have mercy.
Lord Jesus, when you came into the world you proclaimed the Father's love, Lord have mercy.

Headings for Readings
First Reading
To a people who feel oppressed, the Lord's message through the prophet is to wait patiently for the day of festival is coming.

Second Reading
We Christians rejoice in the nearness of the Lord; but we must also be patient people of hope praying for him to come again and seeking to make him present by the way we live our lives.

Gospel

If we want the Lord to enter our world – a claim we make by preparing for Christmas as Christians: then we must act with justice towards all, we must act with economic integrity, we must act with forgiveness. This was the message of John the Baptist before Christ's first coming and it still holds for Christ's coming among us today.

Prayer of the Faithful

President

Fellow disciples, we are assembled in Jesus as the priestly people; so now, standing before the Father, let us intercede for our own needs as a church, for the whole people of God, for all who are in need, and for the whole creation.

Reader(s)

1. Preparing for the coming of the Christ, let us pray that our minds and hearts will be moved to serve this local church more fruitfully. Lord hear us.

2. Preparing for the coming of the Christ, let us pray that our minds and hearts will be moved to seek how we can help the whole Christian Body. Lord hear us.

3. Preparing for the coming of the Christ, let us pray that our minds and hearts will be moved to work for peace in our society and the world. Lord hear us.

4. Preparing for the coming of the Christ, let us pray that our minds and hearts will be moved to have the courage to proclaim the gospel. Lord hear us.

5. Preparing for the coming of the Christ, let us pray that our minds and hearts will be moved to help and comfort anyone in need. Lord hear us.

6. Preparing for the coming of the Christ, let us pray that our minds and hearts will be moved to care for the creation. Lord hear us.

7. Preparing for the coming of the Christ, let us pray that our minds and hearts will be moved to prepare the way of the Lord in all our deeds. Lord hear us.

President
Father, your Son's first coming showed your love for the world, his coming today is our joy, and his final coming is our source of hope. Sustain us we pray on our journey for we make our prayer as disciples of Jesus Christ, your Son our Lord. Amen.

Eucharistic Prayer
See Year A.

Invitation to the Our Father
As we wait in joyful hope for the coming of our Saviour, Jesus Christ, we pray:

Sign of Peace
The Christ is coming among us bringing us the Father's reconciliation and peace. Let us join in this movement as we exchange a token of peace with one another.

Invitation to Communion
Behold the One who has come and will come again. Happy are we to have him come among us in this banquet.

Communion Reflection
'Rejoice in the Lord always; again I will say, Rejoice.'
Lord, let us rejoice in you now in our thanksgiving.
Lord, let us rejoice in you during the coming festival.
'Let all men know your forbearance.'
Lord, may our peace and patience bear witness to you.
Lord, we thank for sharing your peace with us at your table.
'The Lord is at hand.'
Lord, we thank you for your closeness.
Lord, we thank you for your coming into our world in Palestine.
Lord, we thank you for your coming into our assembly at this holy meal.
Lord, we thank you for your promise to come again.

Conclusion
Solemn Blessing 1 for Advent (*Missal*, p 367).

Bear in mind that this is often the last Sunday on which the 'normal' community is present. People have not gone away yet for Christmas holidays, visitors (either Christians in the locality who rarely participate in the Eucharist; or from elsewhere) have not arrived; it is therefore useful to acknowledge this and wish everyone present that as a community, even if dispersed, all should have a happy Christmas.

COMMENTARY

First Reading: Zeph 3:14-18
Zephaniah ends with joyful boasts of what will happen on the day of the Lord's vengeance, his vindication of his people, his coming. Then everyone in Zion will be summoned to rejoice: then the Lord 'has taken away the judgements against you, he has cast out your enemies' and is set up in the midst of the people as king. This is one image of the messianic times when God visits his people and establishes his king. Within the context of Advent there are two themes running through this reading: first, that there was a time when people looked forward to when the Lord would stand among them – and the nature of that hoped-for coming as an avenger is quietly ignored; second, both this reading and Is 12:2-6 pick up on the notion of rejoicing at the coming of the Lord, being joyful as he is near, being glad at his presence in the midst of his people. As such, these two readings are actually linked to today's second reading, rather than the gospel.

What has apparently happened is that the lectionary compilers were so taken by this day as 'Gaudete Sunday' and so with Phil 4:4-7 that this determined three of the readings, but then took a gospel (appropriately chosen as this is Year C – Luke – and this is one of the John the Baptist Sundays) which takes our thoughts in a very different direction.

Psalm: Is 12:2-6

For most of the Sundays of Advent, Isaiah supplies the first reading: today having had a variation from Isaiah as the reading, we now have the unusual substitution of a psalm with Isaiah. The link with the first reading is Is 12:6: 'Shout, and sing for joy, O inhabitants of Zion, for great in your midst is the Holy One of Israel.' This whole text is the concluding song of the second collection of oracles concerning Judah and Israel (9:7-12:6) from which many readings for the Sundays of Advent are taken.

Second Reading: Phil 4:4-7

In many ways this is a 'classic' Advent reading – it was the Epistle for today in the 1570 lectionary – because of its cry 'The Lord is near.' And, as generations of Christians have heard this, this is because Christmas is near! Hence, rejoice and rejoice again. However, in the context of the letter it is part of the conclusion and Paul's encouragement of the community in Philippi to be joyful and have peace of mind: the Lord is near to them, as he is to every church. Thus, leaving Christmas aside, this text's message that the Lord is near is equivalent to Mt 18:20: 'For where two or three are gathered in my name, there am I in the midst of them.'

Gospel: Lk 3:10-18

The figure of John the Baptist is seen as central to today's liturgy and so we have this rarely read section from Luke. In all four gospels the work and preaching of the Baptist is seen as the divinely appointed preparation for the ministry of the Christ: Mt 3:1-12; Mk 1:1-8; Lk 3:1-19; and Jn 1:6-8. The presence of this precise theme preaching/preparing in all four gospels (distinct from any other material they have on John the Baptist) shows that this was a fundamental element in the kerygma: part of hearing the good news of the Paschal Mystery is that the Baptist has prepared the way. It is to maintain continuity with this structural element of the preaching that it is part of our liturgy to recall, indeed celebrate, the ministry of the Baptist on the Second and Third Sundays of Advent in all three years of the lectionary cycle. If we are going to celebrate the beginning of the Christ-event in the festivals of the Nativity, Epiphany, and Baptism, then we must have celebrated the work of the Baptist before-hand.

Now that we have established the kerygmatic context of this gospel reading, we can look at the precise text in greater detail. Luke's account of the preaching of the Baptist is by far the longest, and most of today's passage is found only in Luke. The whole passage has as its central theme that the arrival of the Christ is at hand: he is already on earth and ready to pronounce judgement. The time of decision is not in some future time, but has started already for his 'winnowing fork' is in his hand. However, as part of the reaction to the presence of the Messiah – provoking this reaction from his hearers is the Baptist's work of preparing the way – Luke has an ethical component: verses 10-14 which are wholly without parallel in the gospel tradition.

If the axe is laid to the tree (v 9), then the people who want to prepare, 'the multitudes,' must now ask: 'What then shall we do?' The replies cover (1) everyone – they must care for the poor: if the time of the Messiah is come there can be no one in need of clothing or food in the land; (2) civic officials – injustice in society is irreconcilable in these times; and (3) soldiers – there can be no exploitation now. This ethical dimension in Luke's present-ation shows that while the early Christians were holding up the Baptist as a model to the churches, they also considered moral behaviour an essential part of their discipleship. This ethical as-pect of welcoming the Christ in this gospel should be a spring board to some searching questions of each community about its own work in society to create the justice worthy of the coming of the Lord. Such ethical questions about Christian obligations to establish the just society are often forced onto the gospel text, but today it emerges directly as an Advent theme.

HOMILY NOTES

1. During Advent we hear several basic elements of the Christian preaching over and over again in the liturgy:
- 'Prepare a way for the Lord';
- 'The Lord is near';
- 'Repent and believe';
- 'The Lord will come again to judge the living and the dead';
- 'We must be people of hope'.

2. In the run-up to Christmas we hear around us several basic elements of the creed of the consumerist first-world:
- 'We need lots of stuff for the party';
- 'I'm in a hurry to get to the shops';
- 'We're flying to Madagascar for the holidays';
- 'Toys are so expensive – lucky that the credit card does not come in till January';
- 'I am fed up with all the Christmas-hype'.

3. Two groups of five sound bites – and as sound bites we hear and use all ten of them – which are also tokens/symptoms of two radically opposed lifestyles, belief systems, visions of the universe.

4. The Christian vision involves, fundamentally, going out from the individual to the other: other people, society, the world in which we live, God. It involves radically challenging our selfishness and the belief that selfishness is the motor that makes the human world go round. We could imagine it as a picture of myself with arrows pointing outwards, then of our gathering for the Eucharist with arrows pointing outwards, then of our society or the whole body of Christians and arrows pointing outwards from it.

5. The consumerist vision puts me at the centre of the universe and all the arrows point inwards: have I got what I want for my happiness, have I got what I desire, am I satisfied, is there the amount of pleasure that I desire? Others only become involved in that we pool our selfishness so that we can have more fun together. The arrows point inwards and it does not matter whose labour is exploited so that I can have what I

want – that is over the horizon and hidden from me. It is ir-relevant if others do not have enough to eat, have poor health care, suffer in ignorance for want of proper education, that I consume more of the earth's resources than whole villages in the developing world.

6. But can we say that the Lord is near when we may contribute to a society that exploits the poor? Can we claim to be prepar-ing the way of the Lord while children die of malnutrition, while whole societies in sub-Saharan Africa are devastated by AIDS and are without drugs to stem its effects? Can we re-joice in the Lord's coming while we simply find things bor-ing and seek new amusements but at the same time know that there are people in society who are in want?

7. Preparing a way for the Lord is simple, indeed a bit of fun, if it is just putting up the holly, doing the shopping, and maybe popping along to a Carol Service: but it is much more than that.

The Christmas Tree

Since the 1970s it has become common practice to have a Christmas Tree in Catholic church buildings. Exactly when and where the practice began is unknown, but the reason for the practice seems obvious: the Christmas Tree is now a fixed festive icon and so it seemed a natural part of decorating the building for the festival. Unlike many liturgical introductions, the tree has produced relatively little opposition in communities, but equally there seems to have been very little thought given to the practice and the possible meanings that could be derived from it. In most places the tree has become just one more element cluttering up the part of the building that in the pre-1970 liturgy was called the 'sanctuary' and has been decorated as if it were in a domestic sitting room. What follows are some points to ponder on the tree and its place in the liturgical space.

- Do have a tree as it is a wonderfully cheerful way of showing that this is Christmas time. There are objections that this is a custom from 'Germanic paganism' and so is 'alien' to Christian liturgy, but these arguments are specious. The Christian faith believes that God the Spirit is the author of all and any truth, wisdom, and joy wherever it is found, and all expressions of belief find their perfection in the Christ. The church has always taken part of its imaginative mosaic of images from the cultures it meets and every culture can enrich our experience. There is a notion that there is a pure 'Christian' set of images and only these should be used, but this is really a form of fundamentalism: all the truth is to be found in one little heap that was established long ago. Moreover, one has only to read the scriptures and see how the Babylonian New Year festival of Akitu was adapted within the prophetic imagination of Israel to see that borrowing festival ideas from surrounding cultures has a long and very positive history.

- Do not become sidetracked into finding 'the meaning' of the tree: all great symbols can stand on their own and we then draw meanings out of them. One does not have to invest a meaning and then decode the meaning: let the tree just be there in all its beauty – already it is a testimony to the wonder of the creation and the creativity of the human hands that decorated it. It tells us that this is a time of festivity, of rejoicing, and that we are 'party animals'. We, as the church, have much to have a party about, and we are supposed to be a community of rejoicing; so since every other party space at the festival will have a tree, the community's liturgical space should have one.

- Do not place it in the 'sanctuary area' as this causes clutter, distracts from the Eucharist, and gives the impression that that area alone is the interesting area. The area surrounding the table is the most important area in the whole building and it should be kept for just that: being where people can gather to eat. It should not have the crib or the tree or anything else. The whole area used by the assembly, as the place of the baptised priestly people, is the 'sanctuary' so have the table in one place, the crib in another, and the tree in a third place. Recently, I saw a church where the crib was built in front of, and beneath the table, next to it was the ambo (separated by less than a metre); on the other side the chair, a lectern, and two stools; beside it a tree shoved up against a paschal candle; a tabernacle on a pre-1970 altar with all its trimmings; a baptismal font; two credences; a stand for the processional cross; a display stand for hymn-numbers; and a few Poinsettia flower pots on stands. The result was a not a place to celebrate but a stage-set for the congregation reduced to the role of an audience. Clutter of images is based on clutter in the imagination and shows a complete failure to understand a sacramental liturgy. So keep the tree in a completely different part of the building such that people when looking at the table do not see it.

- Do make sure the Tree is big enough for the space. Most

Christmas Trees are less than three metres tall and this is ideal for a domestic room setting. However, such a tree is lost or looks just 'wrong' in a large and high space such as most churches. Moreover, if the tree has to be bigger to suit the space, then so too the decorations have to be bigger so as not to be out of scale with the tree. This means that the decor-ation has to be relatively simple for while a mass of small trinkets may add magic to a domestic tree, on a larger tree that can be seen from several metres away one has to use fewer and more noticeable decorations or it just looks a mess.

• Do not use flashing lights. Flashing lights are deliberately chosen so as to attract our attention from whatever we are looking at as we perceive flashes with our peripheral vision when a steady light source would not be noticed. Since dur-ing the liturgy there should not be anything to distract us from the Word or the table, it is best to avoid such lights.

• Do link the tree with the Jesse Tree: this can be simply done by printing some of the names from Mt 1:6-16 on cards and hanging them on the tree (starting with Jesse on the low branches and having Jesus at the pinnacle). This is the list of names that belong on a Jesse Tree: Jesse; David; Solomon; Rehoboam; Abijah; Asa; Jehoshaphat; Joram; Uzziah; Jotham; Ahaz; Hezekiah; Manasseh; Amos; Josiah; Jechoniah; Shealtiel; Zerubbabel; Abiud; Eliakim; Azor; Zadok; Achim; Eliud; Eleazar; Matthan; Jacob; Joseph; Mary; Jesus. (However, bear in mind that the last time I drew atten-tion to this list, the first comment I heard was 'Why is only one woman mentioned?')

• Do put it up before the Fourth Sunday in Advent as this al-lows for a blessing for the tree, which is one more visible ac-tion that we are preparing for Christmas. A simple blessing could be this: Lord, this Christmas Tree is your gift from the earth and the work of human hands. Bless it and grant us all a time of happiness and rejoicing for we are recalling the birth of your Son, our Lord.'

• Do link the tree with our obligations as servants of the poor and needy. If the tree has been put up during Advent, it allows for a plan for people to bring gifts for the poor to be placed under it. Just as gifts under a domestic tree are for our immediate family, so here the gifts are for the larger family towards which we have obligations. The tree can be a way to remind people that while we as Christians can rejoice because God is with us, our rejoicing is always tinged with a note of disquiet because of the suffering and poverty that is in the world.

- Do not reduce the tree to a catechetical object or over explain it: we gather to celebrate, not to download information!

Fourth Sunday of Advent (Year A)

Introduction to the Celebration

We are beginning the celebration of God coming to us, God being with us, we being brought into the presence of God. This is the great mystery of Christmas: it is the feast of Emmanuel which means 'God is with us.' This is our special celebration this Sunday, but each time we gather here we remember the words of Jesus: 'When two or three are gathered here in my name, I am there among them'. So, let us spend time reminding ourselves that Jesus is among us, we are in his presence in this gathering, and recalling that we are the people who proclaim him as Emmanuel: God is with us.

Rite of Penance

Lord Jesus, you came once in Bethlehem announcing the Father's peace, Lord have mercy.

Lord Jesus, you come among us now announcing the Father's forgiveness, Christ have mercy.

Lord Jesus, you will come again announcing the Father's welcome, Lord have mercy.

Headings for Readings

First Reading

Here we have one of those lines in the prophets which the first preachers of the gospel recognised as pointing to Jesus: Jesus is Emmanuel, God with us.

Second Reading

This passage contains in a nutshell Paul's way of presenting Jesus: he is Lord, the Son of God and the Son of David, he is proclaimed by the Spirit, and through him we are called to be saints.

Gospel

This gospel ascribes to Jesus the name 'Emmanuel' meaning 'God is with us': believing that God is with us, with us now in this Eucharist, with us in our lives, with us until the end of time, is a basic part of our faith.

Prayer of the Faithful
President

Friends, with Christmas almost upon us we must now ask the Father for the grace of a happy and holy Christmas.

Reader(s)

1. For all Christians, that the coming festival may renew us in body, mind, and heart. Lord hear us.

2. For all people of goodwill, that they may have the wisdom to build a world of peace and justice. Lord hear us.

3. For all who are going to travel in the coming days, that they may have a safe journey. Lord hear us.

4. For ourselves, that we will have a peaceful and joyful Christmas and discover new depths of the mystery of Jesus during these days. Lord hear us.

5. For all of us, that we may meet Christ at the end beckoning us to the Father. Lord hear us.

President

Father, we are about to rejoice and celebrate your Son's birth in Bethlehem of Judea, As we do so, hear the prayers we make to you for we make them as the Body of Christ, your Son, our Lord. Amen.

Eucharistic Prayer
Preface of Advent II (P2).

Invitation to the Our Father

We are about to recall on Christmas Day the coming of the Son of God into our world; and because we are the people who have welcomed him into our lives, we can now pray:

Sign of Peace
We are looking forward to the coming of the Prince of Peace. Let us celebrate his peace and offer a sign of peace to one another.

Invitation to Communion
When the Lord Jesus came among us he gathered his followers around him at table showing them how to give thanks to the Father. Happy are we whom he has now gathered around this table.

Communion Reflection
This is our good news about the Son of God.
He was descended from David according to the flesh,
And he was designated Son of God in power,
According to the Spirit of holiness,
By his resurrection from the dead.
The good news is about Jesus Christ our Lord,
Through whom we have received grace
And have been sent to proclaim the obedience of faith
among all the nations for the glory of his name.
We are one of these nations,
and by his call we belong to Jesus Christ.
Adapted from Rom 1:3-6.

Conclusion
Prayer over the People 24 (*Missal*, p 383) is very suitable for the last days of Advent.

COMMENTARY

First Reading: Is 7:10-14
In today's first reading and gospel we have a classic example of the most common rationale that determined the order of readings in the 1969 lectionary. The starting point is today's gospel, Matthew's account of the events (1:18-24) just prior to the actual time of the nativity (2:1-12). Given that (1) this is the Year of Matthew, and (2) that today is just prior to the celebration of the

nativity, this is the perfect choice. Now since this gospel reading quotes Is 7:14, then that is the perfect choice of reading in a sequence of prophesy-fulfillment. Since Matthew is explicitly using that notion of prophesy-fulfillment, it is eminently in keeping with the gospel for the liturgy today to do likewise: a model example of the churches' fidelity to the evangelist's kerygma.

What this text means within the assembly today could not be clearer: it is the interpretation found in today's gospel. But that leaves us with the question about what it may have meant within the original preaching of Isaiah. King Ahaz had, against the counsel of Isaiah concluded an alliance with the Assyrians as their vassal as the best way to preserve his throne. Now Isaiah encounters him again and offers a new 'sign' that Yahweh is looking after the people, this is the passage that runs from 7:10-17. The 'sign' is that a 'young woman' (*ha alma*) – there is a Hebrew word, *betula*, for virgin but it is not found here – either has conceived or is about to conceive a son who will be king. This obviously refers to Ahaz's young wife and by giving the child the name Immanuel it will be the sign – as are other names suggested by Isaiah – that the person is a sign of Yahweh's continuing support and care. The message is that the long-term future of the dynasty is secure, so Ahaz should put his trust in God and not in alliances. By stopping at v 14, rather than at the unit's natural end at v 17, the reading forms the ideal jumping off-point for the way the text is used in the gospel; however, if one reads it to v 17 it becomes far more obvious that Isaiah was thinking of a child who was to be born within the life time of Ahaz rather than in the more distant future. This editing is a very good example of how the text when read within a Bible or studied in scripture-study group can be very different to the use of a particular text within the liturgy.

Textual Note: There is also in today's reading the famous, or infamous, question of what text should we read: Isaiah according to the Hebrew which mentions that a 'young woman' has conceived or will conceive, or the text of the Septuagint which translated (or mistranslated) *ha alma* as *parthenos* (i.e. a woman who has had no sexual experience) and which to Christian eyes 'predicts' the virgin birth. It was this Greek translation that the gospel writer was using. The problem has been known about since the fifth century, but became a heated debate in the nineteenth century where it was seen as the crux of three problems: first, explaining the Hebrew text away was seen as essential to the 'defence of the virgin birth of Jesus' (mainly a Protestant concern) for there was the belief that the 'Hebrew text was the truth'; second, that the cult of the virgin Mary was part of the divine plan (mainly a Catholic concern); or third, that the gospel's presentation of Jesus was essentially a morass of confusions and fables (a point mainly made by rationalist enemies of Christianity). The homily is not the place to engage in this sort of technical apologetics, but it may come up as a spontaneous question, and a way of replying that is both concise and honest is needed. My reply to this question takes this form: When we say that we believe that Jesus is God having become a human being, or say that Jesus is Emmanuel 'God with us' we are uttering the mystery that is at the centre of the whole of our faith, not expressing a belief in some notion of divinely written books. Moreover, in religious discourse, words are an attempt to grasp a reality that is beyond words; it is not a case that the reality is the product of words.

However, this passage does bring to focus a problem with our English lectionary. When it was being put together there was not a special translation made for liturgical purposes, rather a choice was made of existing translations made primarily for printing in Bibles (originally both the Jerusalem Bible and the Revised Standard Version, then in the second edition of the lectionary appeared only in the Jerusalem Bible version) not lectionaries. In Bibles the usual modern procedure has been to translate the Hebrew where there is a Hebrew text and only in its absence to translate from the Septuagint. However, this is not a good procedure for the liturgy where the Old Testament is being read in conjunction with early Christian texts such as the gospels, for the simple reason that the scriptures of the early church was the Septuagint and one can often only hear the scriptural echoes in the early Christian texts if one is listening to a translation based on the Septuagint rather that the Hebrew. Today is a perfect example of this problem. We should note that in both the Vulgate, and the Neo-Vulgate of 1979, despite awareness that the Hebrew has *alma* not *betula*, we find Is 7:14 rendered *ecce virgo concipiet* following the Septuagint. One can therefore simply replace 7:14 with the corresponding line from the gospel text.

Lastly, when the Jerusalem Bible appeared in 1966 the translators were proud of the ambiguity of 'the maiden is with child' as it allowed them 'to have their cake and eat it'; however, since then it has been the subject of ridicule as an example of less-than-honest translating (and indeed it was dropped in favour of 'young woman is with child' in the New Jerusalem Bible of 1985). It is a pity that this deliberate fudge should still have a place in the liturgy.

Second Reading: Rom 1:1-7
The opening of the letter to the Romans is as close as Paul ever came to summarising the faith he preached in four sentences (vv 3-6) and at the same time identifying himself and his authority (vv 1-2) while sending greeting to his readers (v 7). The passage manages to place Christ as the culmination of history and at the centre of a worldwide church, while at the same time seeing Christ as empowered by the Spirit and all occurring to the glory of the Father.

Gospel: Mt 1:18-24
This is Matthew's account of the origins and divine identity of Jesus which is seen as being the fulfillment of the divine promise in Isaiah. There are two central elements in this reading: first, the birth of Jesus is the fulfillment of the divine promise to be with this people and give them a leader who will lead them into life; second, that deliverer, named Jesus [i.e. a name meaning sav-

iour], is truly the one who is entitled to the name Emmanuel for he is God with us.

Textual Note: Just as there is a famous textual problem concerning the virgin birth in the first reading, so there is one also in this gospel. The textual unit is 1:18-25 which is then followed immediately by the nativity account. However, v 25 ('but [Joseph] knew her not until she had borne a son; and he called his name Jesus') has been omitted for doctrinal reasons as it is the verse appealed to by all those who accept the virginal conception and birth of Jesus but reject the notion that Mary was 'ever virgin' or that the brothers and sisters of Jesus were not his siblings. So, lest the 'until' (*heós*) raise doubts about the cult of Mary as 'ever virgin', the phrase has been expunged. When v 25 is read in the liturgy (at the Christmas Vigil Mass) it is rendered so obliquely by the Jerusalem Bible as to make the problem invisible.

HOMILY NOTES

1. The name 'Immanuel' or 'Emmanuel' (the spelling differences are related to Hebrew and Greek forms respectively) is only found on two occasions in the books the first Christians looked upon as 'The Scriptures': in Is 7:14 and 8:8 where it is a name that can be applied to Ahaz's son and to the whole people and which is interpreted in Is 8:10 as 'God is with us.' Matthew, in using it at the beginning of his gospel (and he is the only evangelist who uses the term or quotes Is 7:14), and explicitly explaining its meaning, is forming a frame to his entire gospel whose final words are: 'I am with you always, to the close of the age.' So we can see his gospel within the boundaries set by 1:23 and 28:20 – it is the story of the presence of God with his people. Now this perspective on the Christ-event is a theme at the very heart of Advent/ Christmas. From this perspective, to accept the gospel is to believe that God is with us.

2. But what does it mean to believe that 'God is with us'? That we actually believe this – as distinct from giving it verbal recognition – we should not take for granted. Our world

tends to push 'God' out to the frontiers of our ways of thinking and imagining life and the universe. From the way most
people use the word 'god' it is clear that they are thinking of
a distant, impersonal force. For other people – those who
dabble in the New Age Movement – the word 'god' often sig-
nifies a projection of our needs for an unknown other that
can be trifled with but is not seen as a person who has made
himself known through revelation. There are many who call
themselves Christians who think of 'god' as far from them,
but also think that 'it's good to have a religious dimension' to
their lives: 'god' is just a code word standing for 'all noble
human desires'. All these fall very far short of the living person who lives within the Good News, and which is what
gives life in every generation to its message.

Then, for Christians, there are the objects, systems, and
beliefs that are seen as more present, more pressing, and
more 'real' than God: money, power, and sex are still the
great headings under which we can range the various forms
of idolatry where a created object is put in the place of the
creator. And, on that note it is worth pointing out that there is
a special form of idolatry to which clergy are prone: imagining the reality of the divine as less important than the
panoply of religion – an idolatry that manifests itself when
people are more sensitive to the forms and regulation of the
structures than to the gentle breath of God or the demands of
justice, mercy, and doing what is right.

3. To live our lives in the light of 'God is with us' is the vocation
of each Christian, but it is also the vocation of a lifetime.

4. How can the whole topic of believing 'God is with us' then be
brought before us in a homily? One the one hand, the whole
liturgy of Advent and Christmas is an attempt to bring this
mystery before us; but on the other hand, one can hear the
words but this is not some simple piece of information to be
learned; it is something that we have to grasp with our
minds, our emotions, and our wills. One way is to lead a
meditation on a series of questions.

5. Do we believe we encounter the presence of God in our gathering? Jesus said: 'For where two or three are gathered in my name, there am I in the midst of them' (Mt 18:20).

Do we believe we encounter the presence of God in combating hunger and human want? Jesus said: 'for I was hungry and you gave me food, I was thirsty and you gave me drink, I was a stranger and you welcomed me' (Mt 25:35).

Do we believe we encounter the presence of God in combating poverty and injustice? Jesus said: 'I was naked and you clothed me, I was sick and you visited me, I was in prison and you came to me' (Mt 25:36).

Do we believe we encounter the presence of God in love, in goodness, in creativity? We believe that God is the source of our light and goodness. As Jesus said: 'Let your light so shine before all, that they may see your good works and give glory to your Father who is in heaven' (Mt 5:16).

Do we believe that we can encounter the presence of God in prayer, and become aware that God is personal and hears us? Jesus said: 'And whatever you ask in prayer, you will receive, if you have faith' (Mt 21:22).

6. In each case I have taken the quotation from a single gospel – Matthew – to show how this concern with believing in the presence of God, God being with us, runs right through his gospel; but the same point could be illustrated from any number of places. It is a basic conviction of Christians that God is known and close and seeks to encounter us.

7. Over the next few days we will hear 'Emmanuel' in the liturgy in its prayers and hymns and carols. We may hear this gospel passage read several times. Each time we hear the name 'Emmanuel' we have to remind ourselves that we are challenged to believe that 'God is with us.' It is the Christian conviction about this that inspires the whole celebration of Christmas.

Fourth Sunday of Advent (Year B)

Introduction to the Celebration

Christmas is just about here, but we all know that there are still lots of things to be done. One of these things is for us as a community of the followers of Jesus to appreciate more fully that it is only in the life he brings to us and shares with us that we can be truly at rest and happy and at peace. So today at our sacred gathering there is a prayer running through all we say and do: 'Lord, come into our hearts this Christmas as our Lord, our Leader, and our Light.'

Rite of Penance

Lord, we await your coming as our reconciliation, Lord have mercy.

Lord, we await your coming as our light in darkness, Christ have mercy.

Lord, we await your coming as our prince of peace, Lord have mercy.

Headings for Readings

First Reading

For generations the promise made to the House of David was seen as God's promise to be with his people; we see Jesus as the fulfillment of this promise: God now dwells among his people.

A More Formal Introduction

Today we read the Prophecy of Nathan. This is the great charter of the House of David: God's promise that he, and not David, would ensure the survival of the dynasty. It is the prophesy that in years to come, when David will have lain long in his tomb, one of his descendents will reign, and the Lord will be a father to this king, and this king a son to the Lord. This prophecy is at the heart of the hopes of the people of Israel for a messiah, a Christ.

It is in the light of this prophecy that people addressed Jesus as 'Son of David' and we read of him at Christmas time as being of the 'house and lineage of David'.

Second Reading
Here St Paul tells us that when Jesus was born it was the revealing by the Father of a mystery kept secret for endless ages.

Gospel
In a few days [or tomorrow] it will be Christmas, so today we recall the events just before the birth of Jesus. God fulfills his promise made long ago: Jesus will be the Son of the Most High and will sit on the throne of his ancestor David.

Prayer of the Faithful
President
Friends, as we wait for the Lord's coming into our lives this Christmas it is our duty to pray to the Father for our needs in this church, for the needs of the whole church of God, for the needs of all in want, and the needs of all humanity. So let us pray:
Reader(s)
1. Waiting for the Lord's coming we pray for all Christians: may we be renewed in Christ. Lord hear us.
2. Waiting for the Lord's coming we pray for all peoples: may we enjoy the gift of peace. Lord hear us.
3. Waiting for the Lord's coming we pray for all searchers: may they find the truth. Lord hear us.
4. Waiting for the Lord's coming we pray for all who dwell in darkness: may they receive light. Lord hear us.
5. Waiting for the Lord's coming we pray for all in the shadow of death: may they inherit life. Lord hear us.
President
Father, your Son's coming brought us freedom, peace, light, truth, and life. Hear our pleas for these gifts in our lives today and grant them in Christ Jesus our Lord. Amen.

Eucharistic Prayer
Preface of Advent II (P2).

Invitation to the Our Father
As we wait for the coming of our saviour Jesus Christ, with him we pray:

Sign of Peace
As we get ready to welcome the Prince of Peace, let us declare our willingness to build peace with one another.

Invitation to Communion
The Lord, the Son of David, who is coming among us, bids us to come to him. Happy are we who share in this supper.

Communion Reflection
Use the O antiphons as a litany. They can be found in the Lectionary, pp 95-6, in sequence, laid out as Gospel Acclamations, begin each one as 'O wisdom,' etc. A suitable response would be: 'Come Lord, and save your people.'

Conclusion
Prayer over the People 24 (*Missal*, p 383) is very suitable for the last days of Advent.

COMMENTARY

First Reading: 2 Sam 7:1-5, 8-12, 14, 16
As presented in today's reading this is a well-edited form of 2 Sam 7:1-17 which is the prophesy of Nathan. One of the key points in this, as a prophecy, is that it is God, not David, that builds this house and ensures its continuance. This text expressed the basis of Messianism in Israel, and it is appealed to in any number of places in other writings that form our Old Testament. Moreover, when the first followers of Jesus presented him as 'house and lineage of David' (Lk 2:4) they were building, in effect, on this passage. It is worth noting that Jesus is referred

to as belonging to the family of David over twenty times in the gospels. Equally, when the liturgy at this time of year refers to Jesus as 'O root of Jesse' or 'O key of David' or reads the genealogies, the ultimate locus of those appeals is this text.

This is an Advent reading *par excellence*, and perfect for this Sunday. However, because it is a first reading it can be eclipsed within the liturgy. Therefore creative thought is needed to show that this text has a key place in our memory as Christians because we call Jesus the 'Son of David'. At the very least there should be a special briefing of the lector and a special introduction of this prophecy by the president. Today's psalm is another expression of the sort of hope found in the prophecy, and so an ideal response to it.

Second Reading: Rom 16:25-7
These final verses of Romans – Paul's most carefully structured letter as these are preserved – is usually described as the doxology of the letter. We read it with a particular emphasis, but one wholly consistent with its thought, on this Sunday in the liturgy. The appearance of Jesus (which we are about to celebrate) was the moment of revelation of the great mystery. However, while it was a mystery kept secret, it was predicted in prophecy (which is what we have been recalling during Advent). Prophecy told the people to look forward to the Christ, the Christ is the great mystery of God. What was once hidden is now clear; and because it is now revealed, it must be preached.

Gospel: Lk 1:26-38
This is the annunciation story, and is read today as setting the scene for Christmas day. However, this gives it a special significance which should be respected: all too often when this pericope appears preachers race off to explore either a favourite marian theme (e.g. Mary's 'Fiat') or else generalise it as a homily on the notion of the incarnation. The first reading provided the particular key to how this text is to be approached today (as distinct from on other occasions in the liturgical year): the angel is

sent to a virgin betrothed to a man of the House of David (Lk 1:26) – and that Luke considered Joseph to be of the House of David is made explicit in his genealogy (Lk 3:23 and 31). Now we are reading of the final moment encompassed by the prophecy: God is fulfilling his promise and just as it was God not David that would build the house, so it is God not Joseph who will provide the Son of David.

Note how this Davidic theme runs through the whole reading:

• Mary is betrothed to the House of David.

• This Son of David is the Son of the Most High – the Lord can call him uniquely 'his son' and this Son can uniquely call on the Lord as 'his Father'.

• The Lord will give him the throne of his ancestor, David.

• He will rule over Jacob's House (one of David's ancestors; cf Lk 3:34).

• The Spirit will overshadow Mary, and so this Son of David 'will be holy and will be called Son of God'.

Jesus, in short, is God's perfect fulfillment of his promise beyond the widest dreams of those who trusted in the Prophecy of Nathan.

HOMILY NOTES

1. Part of the way that Christians have always attempted to celebrate and communicate the mystery of the Lord has been to apply passages and titles to him from the time of the covenant of preparation: the time of the Old Testament. The liturgy abounds with such titles at this time, but most Christians miss them as they are found in the daily eucharistic liturgy and in the Liturgy of the Hours. Often when they do come up we pass on so quickly that we miss them, yet these titles express some of our most basic hopes.

2. The most famous set of Advent titles are the 'Great O Antiphons' that accompany the Magnificat at Evening Prayer between the 17 and 23 December. Exactly how old they are is disputed (some date them to the second century),

but by around 800 preachers were already using the acrostic for remembering their order to make a point in preaching. The acrostic works like this: take the first letter of each in reverse order and it spells two words thus:

O Sapientia	17 December
O Adonai	18 December
O Radix	19 December
O Clavis	20 December
O Oriens	21 December
O Radix	22 December
O Emmauel	23 December

The words *ero cras* mean 'I am coming tomorrow' (literally: 'I will be [here] tomorrow').

3. How can one use them? First, they can be put in the newsletter so that people have a text they might read in the coming days (they can be found in the Lectionary, pp 95-6, as Alleluia verses for each day and in the Breviary in their original function as Magnificat antiphons). Second, the homily today can just be a comment or two of these titles.

4. Jesus the Anointed One of the Father is:
   Our wisdom who is more than all human cunning;
   Our leader who is like the morning star and calls us from sleep;
   The one promised by the Father who frees us from darkness;
   The one who shows us the way that leads to peace;
   And he is the giver of light and happiness to suffering humanity.
   He is God living among his people.

5. Jesus Christ whom we follow and who we are about to welcome again this Christmas is all of these, and more.

6. One of the ways that we expand our religious understanding is by expanding the range of names we use to name the divine. Here is a lovely set of names all addressing Christ using a different Old Testament range of images; it was by applying such images that the first Christology was created. Using them today – and having the Prophecy of Nathan as the first

reading is a cue for bringing them to the foreground today – can deepen our appreciation of the mystery we are celebrating.

Note

This Sunday has another marian theme running through it – although in most circumstances it probably would only add noise to draw attention to it – which is the celebration of the moment of the Annunciation such as is celebrated in the recitation of the Angelus. Not only is the gospel reading that of the Annunciation, but the collect for today is the famous *Gratiam tuam* known to generations of English-speaking Catholics as 'Pour forth we beseech thee, O Lord, thy grace ...' and now rendered: 'Lord, fill our hearts with your love ...'. If this is a theme that you want to explore, then one way of doing so is to recall that Christians – following the example of the Jews of the Second Temple – have always seen regular collective times of prayer as a way of both sanctifying the day and of praying as a whole body even if individuals are scattered. In the early church this led to the practice of reciting the Our Father at dawn, noon, and sunset; while in more recent times it has been expressed in the recitation of the Angelus.

Fourth Sunday of Advent (Year C)

Introduction to the Celebration

Christmas is upon us: yet are we ready? Christmas we are told is a time for fun, a time for peace, and time for rejoicing. Yet for many of us it is a time of stress and extra work to get done everything that needs to be done. A time when we are fearful that the children won't be disappointed or that there won't be tension in relationships or there won't be a breakdown in the ceasefire with the in-laws. And on top of all this there is a feeling of guilt for feeling like this when we should be rejoicing. So we can look on our meal this morning as time-out from all this stress. Jesus comes to us because he loves us, not because we have worked to bring him here or are ready for him. He comes among us now and offers us rest and forgiveness and peace. He invites us to share his table, the table he has prepared for us, and to rejoice and relax at that table, for it is the table of his love.

Rite of Penance

Lord Jesus, you come to bring light into our darkness, Lord have mercy.

Lord Jesus, you come to bring healing into our distress, Christ have mercy.

Lord Jesus, you come to bring wholeness into our fractured lives, Lord have mercy.

Headings for Readings
First Reading

The prince to be born in the tiny village of Bethlehem will stand and feed his flock, the whole of Israel; and extend his dominion to the very ends of the earth.

Second Reading

The Son of God came among us as a human being to do the will of the Father: 'O God, here I am, I am come to do your will.'

148

Gospel

Mary is our model of faith: she believed there would be a fulfillment of what was spoken to her by the Lord.

Prayer of the Faithful

President

Sisters and Brothers, Christmas is almost upon us yet we know we still have many preparations to make, and we know that as a community we still have a long way to go to be fitting welcomers of the Lord Jesus. So now let us pray to our Father in heaven for our needs as a church, for the whole church of God, and for all people of good will.

Reader(s)

1. For this community. That we may give a welcome to Christ Jesus in our hearts this Christmas, Lord hear us.

2. For all who are busy getting ready for this festival. That we may not become distracted with all our rushing around, Lord hear us.

3. For the whole People of God. That this festival may renew us and help us to refocus on Jesus as Lord. Lord hear us.

4. For all people of good will. That this festival may be a time of peace and hope. Lord hear us.

5. For all with special needs. That God will move our hearts to help them at this time of festivity. Lord hear us.

6. For all who are seeking reconciliation. That God the Father may be revealed to them in Christ Jesus, Lord hear us.

5. For all who are going to travel at this time, especially members of this community who are going away for Christmas. That their journeys may be safe and that they may find welcome and peace at their destinations. Lord hear us.

President

Father, we long to celebrate the coming of your Son as our brother, as we wait and watch, hear our prayers for we make them through Christ our Lord. Amen.

Eucharistic Prayer
Preface of Advent II (P2) sets the tone for this whole day in the liturgy.

Invitation to the Our Father
While we wait for the Lord to come again, we pray:

Sign of Peace
We are waiting to welcome the Lord, but there is no greater welcome for the Lord in our lives than when our hearts have sought peace with everyone around us. Let us express our desire for peace to our neighbours.

Invitation to Communion
The Lord is coming among us, he is our reconciliation with the Father and with one another, and he bids us to come to this table.

Communion Reflection
Lord Jesus, all the prophets proclaimed your future coming.
The virgin mother bore you in her womb
with love beyond all telling.
John the Baptist was your herald
and made you known when at last you came.
In your love you have filled us with joy
as we prepare to celebrate your birth,
So that when you come you may find us
watching in prayer, our hearts filled with wonder and praise.
Adapted from Preface of Advent II.

Conclusion
Prayer over the People 24 (*Missal*, p 383) is very suitable for the last days of Advent.

COMMENTARY

First Reading: Mic 5:1-4

This text is read as part of the Advent liturgy as it is directly referred to in Matthew's gospel as part of the messianic preparation. Herod was told: 'In Bethlehem of Judea; for so it has been
written by the prophet: "And you, Bethlehem, in the land of
Judah, are by no means least among the rulers of Judah; for from
you shall come a ruler who is to shepherd my people Israel"' (Mt
2:5-6). And by the later first century it was taken for granted that
part of Jesus's messianic fulfillment was to be seen in that he
came from Bethlehem of Judea. That this a common theme in
Matthew and Luke is not surprising since both see having infancy
narratives as part of their respective presentations of the gospel,
but we should note that it was also more widespread within the
kerygma, as witness Jn 7:42: 'Has not the scripture said that the
Christ is descended from David, and comes from Bethlehem, the
village where David was?' So we can reconstruct how this text
from Micah was used in the early church with a high level of
precision. In answer to the question how do we know that Jesus
is the fulfillment of the Davidic promises of a new king and
shepherd of Israel? Well, he was born in the exact place that
scripture says he should have been born! Moreover, we should
note the importance of the shepherd of Israel who is the son of
David as one of the designations of Jesus in the liturgy from the
time in which the gospels were being composed as we can witness in the *Didache*.

Micah identifies Bethlehem as the place of the new David as
this was already seen as the home of Jesse, David's father (e.g. 1
Sam 17:12), and so the new ruler of the twelve tribes must have
the same background (remember that within his world that
genealogy is identical with original homestead and with inner
identity – this is a way of thinking now wholly foreign to us except for the way royalty is said to belong to the 'royal house of
Somewhere'). This new David would have power very similar
to that which was possessed by the leader of the superpower of
the day: the pharaoh. Like pharaoh he is imagined as a shepherd

of his people, and like him the extent of his power is defined by geographical markers except that in the case of the new David it is the very ends of the earth itself rather that some places on the earth that are the markers (contrast Jos 1:4).

The gospels take up the shepherd theme but, by combining it with the other prophetic images of gathering the scattered and lost, transform it into a redemptive motif such as we see in the Good Shepherd parable (Jn 10:11). Likewise, we see the dominion reaching to the ends of the earth being transformed by Luke as the gospel being preached to the ends of the earth. But perhaps the most significant transformation is that the new Davidic king would rule over the twelve brothers/ tribes which became the group of The Twelve immediately around Jesus. Since that institution of The Twelve goes back to Jesus's own time (and indeed seems to have only survived as a memory after Jesus because by the time of the gospels The Twelve are being equated with apostles and bishops), in all likelihood the use of texts like Micah go back to the usage of Jesus himself.

Given the importance of this reading it is a pity that it does not accompany the reading of Mt 2; however, that is impossible because this reading is quintessentially an Advent reading (hence it is here), but Matthew's journey of the Magi is seen as one of the events that fall after the Nativity (and is read on the feast of the Epiphany).

Second Reading: Heb 10:5-10
This passage is used in the liturgy today because the author of the letter puts its quoted 'prophecy' (Ps 39:7-9) into the mouth of the Christ at the moment 'of his coming into the world'. In terms of its content the passage has no connection with the themes of Advent, being concerned with the cross being the one, perfect, priestly sacrifice. The nature of that sacrifice being further clarified as not being the suffering or death that the cross involved, but the perfect sacrifice of obedience to the Father's will which is seen in Jesus's total self-offering.

This is a very important text in clarifying the nature of Christian sacrifice and correcting the false notion that the sacrifice of the cross consists in its bloodiness. This theme of the link between slaughter and sacrifice is so often invoked in modern warfare when people say about dead soldiers 'they made the ultimate sacrifice' and then this non-Christian use of religious language is then referred to the Christ with the result that his sacrifice is reduced and our image of God brutalised. The author of Hebrews was reacting to this tendency already present in the late first/early second century period, but alas this message is so far from the spirit of this Sunday that it really cannot be explored today.

Gospel: Lk 1:39-44

Luke's linking of the ministry of John the Baptist with that of Jesus reached its high-point in this section: they were cousins. And it is this overarching need to connect the two prophets that stands behind this incident in the gospel. This move by Luke is wholly his own. While all four bring the two ministries into alignment as precursor-fulfillment at the baptism in the Jordan, only Luke makes them relatives with knowledge of one another from even before their infancies. However, despite being found in only one of the four, it is the lukan story that has become the standard explanation of the relationship for subsequent Christian tradition.

HOMILY NOTES

1. It is often hard to preach on this Sunday as it can be so close to the festival that one can sense the distraction in the minds of people: there are other things happening and we are all in a bit of a rush. So one needs a relatively snappy but staccato way to break into people's imaginations and overcome their distractions.

2. One way to do this is to focus on the first reading and use it to imagine what we believe about Jesus the Christ. Put another way, preach the text through our consciousness of the gospel

in the manner these prophetic texts have been used in the liturgy since, at least, the time of Matthew's preaching.

3. What do we want to recall about Jesus the Christ as we move closer to Christmas?

4. 'But you, O Bethlehem Ephrathah, who are little to be among the clans of Judah, from you shall come forth for me one who is to be ruler in Israel, whose origin is from of old, from ancient days' (Mic 5:2).

- The Son of God, the Word through whom all things were made, visible and invisible, has been born in a tiny village in Palestine.
- We are spoken to by one who is a human being with us, who has been born a human being for our sake: for us and our salvation he came down from heaven.
- Jesus is the ruler in Israel, the fulfillment of the promises that God would deliver his people from slavery.
- Jesus is our ruler and leader, and the king who will come again to judge the living and the dead.

5. 'And he shall stand and feed his flock in the strength of the Lord, in the majesty of the name of the Lord his God. And they shall dwell secure, for now he shall be great to the ends of the earth' (Mic 5:4).

- Jesus is the Good Shepherd.
- Jesus gathers up all who are scattered and wandering lost on the hillsides.
- Jesus rejoices when those who are lost are found: there is more rejoicing in heaven when one sinner repents than over ninety nine others who have no need of repentance.
- Jesus is the one who feeds his people: we are gathered at his table to share in his banquet.
- Jesus reveals the majesty of the Father to us and he glorifies the Father's name.
- Jesus's kingdom has no end, and we are charged to bring his gospel to the very ends of the earth.

6. We prepare for the nativity of Jesus, but the most important nativity is his birth in our lives when we take him as our

priest, our prophet, and our king. Unless he is born within us, in our world, then our celebration of his birth in Bethlehem long ago is an empty sham.

The Crib

The crib is one of the most popular religious symbols of
Christmas, and its preparation and use is a definite part of the
community's Christmas liturgy. However, the building of the
crib, what it communicates, and where it is located do not often
figure on the agenda of those planning the liturgy, and the crib
itself often gives the impression of being thrown up in a hurry,
with little thought about its significance or potential for liturgical celebration.

Exegetical Considerations
Let us start with the basic crib images:
1. Joseph and Mary with an infant laying in a little cot of straw:
'the manger' – 'manger' has a quasi-sacral status in translating
he phatné in Lk 2:7, 12, and 16, presumably as it is fixed in the
memory by such carols as 'Away in the manger', but many people today when asked what is a 'manger' only know that it was
where the infant Jesus was laid: a manger is a feeding trough for
livestock.

2. This is often located near a building in something like a
barn; or else in a cave-like structure.

3. Nearby there are an ox/cow and an ass.

4. Around are some shepherds – usually three in number –
and perhaps a sheep or two.

5. Then there are three other figures, depicted as kings, each
bearing a gift.

6. Above this is a star.

8. Then, perhaps, there are a few winged figures and a ban-
ner with something like 'Gloria in excelsis Deo' written on it.

9. Possibly a backdrop with palm trees and sand to suggest
Palestine.

We are so familiar with this from Christmas cards, nativity
plays, and just looking at cribs that we fail to note how sophistic-

ated a reading of our memory of the coming of the Christ is contained in this image. Familiarity has, in the case of the crib scene,
bred a contempt for the whole idea as if it were just there for the
children or a seasonal decoration.

The scene is a combination of the two nativity accounts presented as a complementary whole: the Christian memory at
once recognising that the different gospel accounts are parts of
the one good news of Christ. From Mt 2:1-12 we get the location
of Bethlehem, the coming of the wise men from 'the East' and
the star. The word used by Matthew is *magoi* (*magi* in Latin) and
the meaning of this term was clear in his world: it meant astrologers; and the home of astrology was believed to exist 'in the
East' in Babylon. Within the gospel, the story is intended to show
the coming together of prophesy within Israel (the books con-
sulted at Mt 2:4-6 by 'the chief priests and scribes of the people'
and the wider revelation seen in the most obvious of religious
objects: the heavens.) Natural wisdom could show these men
that something momentous was afoot, and then it was given a
name through the revelation of Israel. Within popular culture
the astrologer was the epitome of the wise man – a bit like the
proverbial village schoolmaster – and it would only be much
later that Christians began to condemn it as a practice. For
Matthew (in a similar way to Paul in the opening chapters of
Romans) the heavens provide a universally accessible window
on the handiwork of the creator; these men were attentive to the
structure of history (we see Matthew's interest in this in the
genealogy) and so noticed the 'new star' – within Matthew's
view of the universe a 'new star' is tantamount to a start of a
new creation – and so the magoi investigate it: that leads them to
Israel and they are then able to find the child in Bethlehem.

Christian tradition, well established by the fifth century, also
saw in these visitors the fulfilment of a prophesy in the psalms
(remembering that they read every verse in the psalms as having reference to the Christ). In Ps 72 (71 in the LXX/Vulgate
numbers), vv 10-15, they found this:

May the kings of Tarshish and of the isles render him tribute,

may the kings of Sheba and Seba bring gifts.
May all kings fall down before him, all nations give him service.
For he delivers the needy when they call, the poor and those who have no helper.
He has pity on the weak and the needy, and saves the lives of the needy.
From oppression and violence he redeems their life; and precious is their blood in his sight.
Long may he live! May gold of Sheba be given to him.

When Christians read these words they seemed virtually identical to the account of events in Matthew, it was a fulfilment of the prophesy of David in the psalms. So the *magoi* were also kings, and became three in number as the King of Tarshish, the King of Sheba, and the King of Seba. The scene from Matthew illuminated the psalter, and *vice versa*. The presence of this image – and the statues of the kings should be in the crib from the start, not put in on 6 January, as it is a single narrative within our ecclesial memory – is a testimony to the way we have read scripture to draw insight into the mystery of the incarnation. Moreover, we should not underestimate the power of this image when actual kings were local rulers: earthly power was to be laid before an infant in a feeding trough. This was part of the Christian notion of the 'restructuring' of all authority/power brought about by the incarnation.

A similar use of the Old Testament produced the ox and the ass: 'The ox knows its owner, and the donkey its master's crib; but Israel does not know, my people do not understand' (Is 1:3). When Christian imagination heard of the trough in which Jesus was laid, it immediately went on to ask what sort of animals would have been there to use that trough. Isaiah supplied the answer. However, this simple mechanism of prophesy/fulfilment can turn the narrative into mechanical set of 'proof texts' such as are used by biblical fundamentalists. Better to simply note that as with the kings, Christians have always sought to understand Jesus within the context of the older covenant.

From Luke's account we get the shepherds, the angels, and the stable on the assumption that if there was no room in the inn then the trough must have been in the stables. From Luke also we get the story of the shepherds going to visit the crib, and from the presence of shepherds get a few sheep in the crib. The presence of three shepherds in many cribs seems to have been an attempt to balance the *magoi*, and as we have seen there were three of them as there were three kings mentioned in Ps 72. Recently I read somewhere in a work on the Christmas liturgy a dismissal of Luke's account as 'bucolic romanticism' – but this misses the very point Luke seems determined to make: that Jesus, while hailed by the angels, enters into the very confusion and mess of ordinary human life – no room, a trough, and a few night watchmen. This gives us the cue that the crib scene can show the whole human world spinning on in its cares unaware of the Christ: yet it is into the whole of the world that the Christ has entered.

Lastly, in many cribs the covering is not a stable or barn but a cave. This might just seem an insignificant detail which is but a testimony to the whims of artists. However, the notion that Jesus was born in a cave outside Bethlehem can actually be tracked back to that strange second-century text known today as the *Protoevangelium of James*. In that text, chs 17-18, Joseph is an old man heading off with his sons from a previous marriage to Bethlehem for the census, and he is embarrassed for a very young Mary and wonders how she and her son conceived by the Holy Spirit can be registered. Fearful both of the embarrassment and the bureaucrats if he enters Bethlehem with Mary, he finds a cave on its outskirts and leaves Mary there in the care of his sons while he goes off to find a midwife and a solution to his registration queries! The cave image shows just how complex is our memory as the church, and indeed that as early as the second century Christians were clamouring for more incidental details of the birth of Jesus and the lives of those close to him. However, it is best not to use a cave as the structure of a crib scene: not only does it not fit as well with the two gospel accounts as a stable, but a cave is a landscape item that belongs outside the human realm (the very reason it was picked in the *Protoevangelium of James*), and the very core of Luke's message is that it is into our human time and into our human society the Lord has entered as the individual Jesus, the son of Mary. The stable is the very image of our human constructed, but earthy, world.

The crib image is not a simple scene: it is a witness to the complex way that the church has read the scriptures down the centuries as a single message testifying to the revelation of God in Jesus – an idea first expressed by Luke in his Emmaus scene: 'Then beginning with Moses and all the prophets, he interpreted to them the things about himself in all the scriptures' (24:27). At no point is the memory tied to some notion of factual reconstruction of 'what it was like back then'; rather the historical fact of the birth is interpreted within the larger context of belief seeking to make sense of a mystery larger than factual history.

Ideal landscape

The crib is not a museum re-construction of what it was like in Palestine two millennia ago, nor is it a teaching model or diagram such as one might find in a Bible atlas. The crib represents one place in our world – Bethlehem, but it is also every place because it is Christ's birth everywhere that his people are present today that is being celebrated. The crib is an ideal landscape – just look at the medieval representations one sees on some Christmas cards which place the crib scene in the local valley or plane with the local architecture of the day around about it – at once specific and general: this is the space and time of the liturgy, not that of the history lecture. We are celebrating Jesus here and now and there and then. The crib must have quaintness because our culture loves verisimilitude, but it must also touch our world. One of the most successful cribs I have seen had the standard stable scene as its foreground, but its backdrop did not open on to sands and palms but a busy main street with bakers, butchers and what not, and a circus scene behind that again, all busy with tiny figures. If we cannot imagine the divine plan encompassing that streetscape, then we have replaced a belief in the incarnation with a Gnostic notion of a religious realm that fails to touch the everyday world.

Location

The area around the Eucharistic table has in many places been transformed from being 'the sanctuary' of the pre-1970 rite (essentially the place apart belonging to the ministers marked off by rails and gates) to become in many church buildings the stage area: everything takes places there as this is where 'people can see.' So we have the table, near it the ambo, then a chair, often a lectern, often the baptismal font (and at this time of year maybe an Advent Wreath and a Christmas Tree – two other objects that can be moved elsewhere), and a few other odds and ends. We seem to have forgotten that we stopped 'saying Mass with backs to the people' not because it was thought to be a good idea for people to see what the priest was doing, but so that the table could be placed in such a way that the people could gather around it! The effect of making 'the sanctuary' a performance stage is that the rest of the church ceases to function as a liturgical space becoming simply 'the seating area', and so in many places the crib is also placed near the altar – and indeed in some places it is located in front of, even between the legs of, the Eucharistic table.

This increasingly common practice manifests a seriously confused view of both the Eucharist and the memory-object of the crib. The Eucharistic table is the very heart of the liturgical space, and it is a table to be gathered around and to be eaten from: it is not the focal point on a stage, and it is certainly not the backdrop for other objects which distract from it. Even if many buildings have only pre-1970 furniture imperfectly adapted to the present rite, adding anything to this assemblage that further ingrains the idea that the table is an object to be viewed, apart from the gathered people, is regrettable. On that table we celebrate the coming of the Christ among us as we gather to eat his body and drink his blood: pictures of his coming, such as a crib, are only a confusion. 'Interact with one symbol at a time' is a basic law of ritual. Secondly, the crib is there to provoke memory and wonder: it must have a close-up beauty that invites our imagination to enter 'its space'. This cannot be achieved if it is tacked onto, or located under a table. This symbol requires a space of its own – just for itself – so that we can go there and look and see and remember and feel without distractions. The sacred Table of the Lord deserves its own space that it should never have to share with anything else. At Christmas, the crib likewise deserves its own space where it can perform its function for the community.

The best space is one that (1) allows a procession from that crib to the president's chair; that (2) is apart from the area of all who are celebrating the Eucharist; that (3) gives enough space to the crib allowing movement around it (not just traffic, but space for liturgical activity and individual devotion); and ideally (4) whose location can easily be known by everyone entering the building. But the bottom line is that if it has to be near the Lord's Table, then it must be as far away and as unobtrusive as possible during the Eucharist.

Interaction

The crib must not only be something seen, it must strive to have the quality of all great symbols that invite us to not only remember but to grow in understanding, affection, and which move us to a sense of identification and willingness to make the symbol part of us. Such symbols usually have the quality of being synaesthectic: they involve several of our senses simultaneously. Ashes on Ash Wednesday is a good example: we hear the words, we see the ashes, we may be able to see and smell the burning palms, we feel them on our foreheads, there is a sense of 'getting something' individually, we have to move and kneel to get them, we are conscious of them on our foreheads afterwards. There is no Christmas equivalent within the liturgy except the practice of a midnight Mass where the very unusualness of the hour deeply impacts on people, but 'a visit to the crib' can go a long way towards being a synaesthetic experience.

First, the crib must be in a space that can be interacted with – it is not simple a model scenario that can be viewed. Imagine those models of battles that one sees in museums or architects' models of new buildings behind glass: you are just intended to look, yet even in these they make them free of the wall so that they can be seen from all sides and walked around. The crib must be in a space that allows one to walk around it, see it from several sides, see into it like poking one's head inside a door to see what the inside of a room is like. In the National Museum of Ireland there is sometimes on display a magnificent baroque crib with umpteen figures but it is safely behind thick glass and it is just below reading height for the average sized visitor. This is the perfect museum environment: you are intended to view the object and marvel at this crib as a work of art – not to marvel at the Christ-event! The crib in a church must be the very opposite: the crib-builder is not the object of admiration but the narrative. So it must be open to view, people must be able to get up close to it, must be able to feel that it has three-dimensions. So it should be approachable on as many sides as possible. It can always have, at least, two sides by making it jut out in a V-from a wall: the fact that people see one another through the crib brings them into its space (this is the basic idea behind theatre in the round).

Second, it should not invite a stare from standing height: that makes it just an object to be viewed passively. It should encourage the visitor to bend down to look in, to kneel down to see inside it. This is linked to its lighting: the inside of the stable should have that softer and lower level of light that bespeaks domestic intimacy.

Third, it is a place of public prayer: it should encourage people to stay for a few moments and pray. There should be places to kneel and places to sit – but not set in such a way that they act as a *de facto* barrier around the crib space. That space must be unbounded from the space of the visitor, and within that space should be some *prie-dieux* and a few chairs.

Fourth, there should be something to do at the crib. The great action at all such places of devotion is the ability to light a candle. It involves all the senses and draws people from merely words and images into the living world of light and touch and fire. It makes the crib a shrine. In some places this candelabrum has been replaced with a collection box for a 'worthy cause' such as the homeless at Christmas. One should not exclude the other: before a symbol of the incarnation, religious wonder should move us to offer a gift (like the objects in the kings' hands) in adoration such as a candle which allows a very sense-perceptible interaction with the memory, but also a practical concern for the world into which the Word entered in the form of an equally sense-perceptible gift to the poor.

Lastly, building a crib is creating a shrine, not making a 3-D teaching aid (even if it can perform that function): so think of it like the grotto in Lourdes rather than an explanatory model in an exhibition.

Blessing

Here is a possible rite of blessing:

Form a procession with incense, cross, lights, and proceed to the crib while a carol is sung.

Bringing the choir in the procession, with lanterns like those of street carol singers, can be very effective.

If the liturgy begins with this procession and carol – rather than a 'warm-up' session of carols – it make the event far more dramatic. The Christmas liturgy must begin with something sharp and noteworthy, not with someone leading a battery of hymns/carols.

Someone brings the statue of the infant in the procession. At the crib, the presiding priest begins:

Dear Friends,

The joyful moment to recall the birth of our Saviour Jesus Christ has now come: so we have gathered here this evening/ night/ dawn/ day to rejoice with the angels and proclaim the coming of the reign of peace to all humanity. During the time of Advent we have been recalling God's

plan of salvation when he prepared his chosen people to receive his Son; we have been renewing our commitment during those weeks to being his disciples; now we rejoice in the
great mystery: for to us is born this day in the city of David a
Saviour, who is Christ the Lord.
Let us reflect in silence on the holiness of this feast.

Gospel Reading (see the note on the *Gospel Passages for Christmas*,
pp 174)
At the Vigil and Day Masses
The Lord be with you.
And also with you.

A reading from the holy gospel according to Luke.
In those days a decree went out from Caesar Augustus that all
the world should be enrolled. This was the first enrollment,
when Quirinius was governor of Syria. And all went to be enrolled, each to his own city. And Joseph also went up from
Galilee, from the city of Nazareth, to Judea, to the city of David,
which is called Bethlehem, because he was of the house and lineage of David, to be enrolled with Mary, his betrothed, who was
with child. And while they were there, the time came for her to
be delivered. And she gave birth to her first-born son and
wrapped him in swaddling cloths, and laid him in a manger, because there was no place for them in the inn. And in that region
there were shepherds out in the field, keeping watch over their
flock by night. And an angel of the Lord appeared to them, and
the glory of the Lord shone around them, and they were filled
with fear. And the angel said to them, 'Be not afraid; for behold,
I bring you good news of a great joy which will come to all the
people; for to you is born this day in the city of David a Saviour,
who is Christ the Lord. And this will be a sign for you: you will
find a babe wrapped in swaddling cloths and lying in a manger.'
And suddenly there was with the angel a multitude of the heavenly host praising God and saying, 'Glory to God in the highest,
and on earth peace among men with whom he is pleased!' When

the angels went away from them into heaven, the shepherds said to one another, 'Let us go over to Bethlehem and see this thing that has happened, which the Lord has made known to us.' And they went with haste, and found Mary and Joseph, and the babe lying in a manger. And when they saw it they made known the saying which had been told them concerning this child; and all who heard it wondered at what the shepherds told them. But Mary kept all these things, pondering them in her heart. And the shepherds returned, glorifying and praising God for all they had heard and seen, as it had been told them. This is the gospel of the Lord. (Lk 2:1-20 RSV)

At Midnight Mass use the shorter form of the Joannine prologue (Jn 1:1-5, 9-14) as found in the Lectionary, vol I, pp 112-3.
At the Dawn Mass read only Lk 2:1-14: stop at 'Glory to God in the highest, and on earth peace among men with whom he is pleased!'

Place the infant in the crib and incense it by walking around the crib.
   Let us pray.
   God our Father,
   when the fullness of time had come, you sent your Son, born of a woman, born under the law, in order to redeem those who were under the law, so that we might receive adoption as children.
   And because we are your children, you have sent the Spirit of your Son into our hearts, crying, 'Abba! Father!'
   So look upon us now and bless + this crib and make it holy.
   Grant that when we come here we may be filled with awe at this new and radiant vision of your glory which it recalls for us.
   We make this prayer through Christ our Lord. Amen.

Now let us join in singing/saying the prayer of the angels before the newborn Christ.

The Gloria is sung/said while the procession moves away from the crib. When the priest reaches his chair he continues with the appropriate opening prayer.

Visitors to Church at Christmas

Most Christian liturgy was originally formulated and imagined in highly integrated cultures that shared common background, experiences, values, and religious outlooks. So the whole community could be expected to have one cultural background and most to have been members of that denomination from infancy. Moreover, the liturgies were produced in a culture where travel was exceptional and usually only for short highly defined periods such as 'the summer holidays'. Just recall how few people took an annual 'foreign holiday' in 1970 when our Missal appeared. Today, and especially at Christmas, one can expect a wide variety of people within the congregation reflecting not only our multi-cultural societies, but the ease of travel to various places for every holiday period, and also a breakdown of traditional denominational boundaries. Whereas even a generation ago one could expect to find only Catholics at the Eucharist in a Catholic Church and only Anglicans at Holy Communion in an Anglican Church, today people will often go to 'the one that's nearest' or go with their spouses to just one liturgy, or even just tag along with whatever service the people they are staying with for the holidays are attending. One should be careful not to try to describe the limits of this cultural/religious intermixing: there may well be non-believers in the congregation at Christmas who simply want the 'religion bit' as part of taking part in the 'traditional festivities' because they want 'to get into the spirit of the thing' in much the same way that even those who are not football fans wear national badges when their country's team is playing in the World Cup. This religious multiformity/pluralism is welcomed and abhorred in equal measures by church leaders, but it is a fact nonetheless and it is responding to this fact that is my focus here.

An obvious, and quite frequently chosen, response is to decry this as the bizarre relativism of the modern world, the pick-

and-mix attitude to religion that is tantamount to a denial of supernatural revelation, and then, with Canon Law in close-support, to patrol the boundaries of orthodoxy. This takes the form of announcements that 'this is a Catholic service' and visitors should know their place and 'only those who are Catholics should come up for communion' and any other person should who wants something should 'come up for a blessing' and mark themselves out as such by folding their arms or some similar sign. Alas, I have heard on Christmas morning a priest who pointed out that any Catholics who were there only for this Mass (i.e. Christmas and Easter Catholics), and had not been to Confession to confess the mortal sin of missing Mass on Sundays, should not come to communion. And I have even heard a priest who reminded people who were in irregular unions that they too were in a state of sin and 'they should not approach the altar'. This reaction may be canonically justifiable, but that does not mean that it is an acceptable way for a president of a eucharistic assembly to behave. All actions and statements at a Eucharist can only be judged in terms of what is being celebrated – the Eucharist – within the overall vision of the Christian kerygma. Moreover, it is a matter of Christian ethics that one must not cause hurt or pain when acting in the name of the all-holy God. Put simply, before any statement is made on behalf of the assembly by its president, that priest must judge what it would feel like to be the recipient of that message. This is an ethical demand quite superior to any notion based on the desire to win converts which reasons that one should not send out a 'bad signal' about the unwelcoming attitudes of the church – although that is another valid consideration.

Having a balanced approach to this phenomenon of our times means we should bear in mind the following considerations.

First, the Eucharist is the family gathering of the Christians and has all the intimacy of a family meal around a table – this is its basic form from the praxis of Jesus and the house churches of the early Christians where the Eucharist developed its still recognisable shape. As such an intimate affair it is not surprising that it does not consider itself 'open to all comers': you already have to belong before you eat with the family. However, over the centuries we have build churches that have lost all such sense of close community and, *de facto*, Catholics come to a Mass as they know that there they can fulfil their desire 'to get Mass' or 'get Mass and communion'. This is far from an ideal attitude, but it is the actual mess in which we live. As such, we leave the doors open for all comers. So we cannot blame people who have just walked in off the street for being there. They are there because we put the times of services up outside and leave the doors open: it is, *de facto*, an invitation to all who read the notice to come in.

However, once people are within the community at the Eucharist, then another logic takes over: now they are at the meal and around the table [fact], so the internal logic of the meal governs behaviour. If someone is in your dining room at meal times, is s/he just asked to leave or does the human ritual of being at a meal not insist that a place is found, and the food stretched to cover the extra person? Most of us learned this basic sacramental logic as children when our mothers told us that there was not enough of a particular food to feed both the guests and us at our table, and hence we had rules of thumb like 'family hold back.' This applies equally to the Eucharistic meal: if people come in, then we must make them welcome in the name of the Christ for this is his, not simply our, meal. And the Christ ate with all those who were prepared to welcome him to their table even to the shock of the religious authorities, and we cannot imagine him being less welcoming in return. So if they are there, the strangers must be included.

Second, putting in tests of orthodoxy or orthopraxis supposes that there is a perfect Christian and that 'getting communion' is somehow a reward for such up-right behaviour. If you asked any group of Catholics what their beliefs are on controversial areas of doctrine between the various denominations you might find that there are very few who would pass the Denzinger test.

The place in which each of us stands before God is a matter known only in the depths of the conscience, except that all of us stand in need of the divine mercy. To make statements in the midst of the holy mystery that our place in relation to God is a matter that can be known by the application of a few rules of practice (e.g. 'Unless you have been to confession ...') is to brutalise that most intimate and sacred of relationships, and to do so in the context of the Lord's banquet is a species of blasphemy.

And on a practical note once you start using tests for orthodoxy and orthopraxis as an excluding device then you have to decide where to stop! Do you stop at people not in canonical communion with the See of Rome? Do you ask if they will sign a declaration of orthodoxy? Have they to be at Mass every Sunday or else to have been to confession and confessed that particular sin? What of all the families in the community – the vast majority – who just happen to have no more than two children? When one gets into that situation one has ceased to imagine the Eucharist as the Lord's loving banquet in which thanks is offered to the Father, and one has reverted to the medieval vision of the Eucharist, rejected by the Second Vatican Council, of it being a sacred commodity to be got and of an event to be 'attended' so as to have a tick on one's spiritual scorecard.

Third, the obverse of what is often called 'pick-and mix' spirituality is the fact that we live in an age where ordinary people are searching for God (even if they may not call their search by that name) like never before. Our culture is one where the mere fact that answers are handed down from the past is seen to be defective for that very reason. Moreover, one of the most common elements in most spiritual quests today is for a sense of belonging to community. We as the Christian community make the bold claim that this quest meets its perfect fulfilment in the community of the Christ, hence it is appropriate that we should wish anyone who comes among us to sense that feeling of community and sense the welcome that is there for every man and woman. One of the things that distinguishes a Catholic community which sees itself as a church, from a sect that sees itself as an

elect, is that the former wishes to do everything to draw the
boundaries so as to include people, the latter defines itself by excluding people. If we are seeking to proclaim the good news in
our time then one of the messages we must transmit is that we
are a welcoming community and within the church, and the particular church assembled at the Eucharist with open doors, there
is a community that can fill the modern human being's desire for
community in the face of consumerist individualism.

So are there rules of thumb regarding visitors at the
Eucharist at Christmas?

- Acknowledge that there are visitors there, and that many of
  them are non-Catholics. Such an acknowledgement can
  make people feel at ease that they are known about and welcomed as such. They do not feel they have to pretend not to
  be who they are and hide their identity.
- Make everyone feel positively welcome: wherever you come
  from, you are here now, and let us all thank the Father together.
- Give people the benefit of the doubt (as God gives us), so assume people are people of good will. They are not there out
  of bad motives or as spies from some 'society for relativist
  thought'. The message to the shepherds was to all people of
  good will – so assume that and do not then chastise people
  because they do not have the right canonical credentials.
- Assuming that there are people present who have little understanding of what is going on, be that bit more explanatory.
  This is a basic work of the kerygma and many Catholics may
  benefit as well.
- Do not make excluding announcements about who can and
  cannot 'receive communion'. People know the rules (it is one
  bit of Canon Law the media pick up on) and so presume their
  good will, leave it to their consciences, and to God.
- Do not make announcements that suppose that 'being at
  Mass' and 'getting communion' are separable realities (this
  possibility of separating them is itself a surviving product of
  a defective praxis by the church in the early middle ages): the

Eucharist is a meal as that is what Jesus wanted, and part of a meal is eating!

- Do not get worried about people being there out of curiosity; but pray that what begins as curiosity may grow to faith. (It was curiosity that drew the shepherds to go over to Bethlehem according to Luke.)
- We are always called to act with charity: so we must not cause insult or pain. We must remember that God loves everyone – it is he, after all, who keeps everyone in existence.
- Show that we are people of joy, not killjoys.
- Remember: 'a bruised reed he will not break, and a dimly burning wick he will not quench' (Is 42:3 and Mt 12:20).
- Remember: 'And the Pharisees and the scribes murmured, saying, "This man receives sinners and eats with them"' (Lk 15:2).
- Remember we do not act at the liturgy in our own name, nor as local agents/ representatives of Canon Law, but in the name of the Lord 'who desires all men to be saved and to come to the knowledge of the truth' (1 Tim 2:4) – and no human being likes being excluded or told how defective they are. When we make people feel that way we push them farther from the good news we are here to preach.

The Gospel Readings on Christmas Day

Every Christmas there is one liturgical problem that seems to crop up again either in conversation or in guides for the liturgy: what about the gospels at the Vigil and Day-time Masses? At the moment there are four gospels laid out in the Lectionary for the feast:

Christmas Eve – Vigil Mass:	Mt 1:1-25 (or a shorter form 1:18-25).
Christmas Day – Midnight Mass:	Lk 2:1-14.
Christmas Day – Dawn Mass:	Lk 2: 15-20.
Christmas Day – Daytime Mass:	Jn 1:1-18 (or a shorter form 1:1-5, 9-14)

The Pastoral Problem

1. With very few exceptions, people only go to one celebration of the Eucharist in the whole 24-hour period of Christmas Eve-Christmas Day.

2. In recent decades the celebration on Christmas Eve has become ever more popular: in many communities that Eucharist is better attended than either the Midnight celebration or any celebration in the morning.

3. The dawn celebration has often been dropped – its old rationale of people who wanted an early celebration at which they could 'go to communion' [having fasted from midnight] having disappeared.

4. Most people expect to hear 'the Christmas story' at the celebration they attend – Lk 2:1-20 comes closest to being the expression of that story within the canonical gospels; and most priests believe that this is the most appropriate gospel to be read, and it is the gospel they want to use as a launching pad for their homily.

5. Many, both priests and people, have a low regard for the matthaean genealogy; and even the concluding part (the shorter

form in the Lectionary) does not bring up the Christmas 'scene'. Many priests argue that it is a poor basis for a homily.

6. Many priests believe that the johannine prologue 'does nothing for their people' and there is a dislike about using it in preaching.

7. At no Mass is the whole account in Luke read (it being divided between the Midnight and Dawn Masses).

8. In many places this has led to either using the midnight or dawn readings at all the Masses, so the internal echoes between readings and prayers are lost; or if the whole of those Masses are used for the Vigil and Day Masses, their time clues are lost.

The Theological Problem

The mystery of the incarnation is greater than any one gospel passage, and indeed greater than all of them combined. There is a danger that we reduce this mystery to 'the simple story' – which in effect means we falsify it. The church's memory is full of riches and it is part of the preacher's duty to be the wise scribe 'who brings out of his treasure what is new and what is old' (Mt 13:52). The mystery of the incarnation we celebrate at Christmas is larger than the memory of the event of the birth in Bethlehem: hence the importance of Jn 1 and Matthew's genealogy. The person of the Christ is not simply the image of the baby in the manger but of him 'through whom all was made' (Jn 1 and the Creed). The event in Bethlehem is also a covenant between God and his people, and this is part of the larger plan of divine history, revelation, and prophecy: themes in the forefront of the matthaean genealogy.

The task is to enrich the imaginations of the communities, not to reduce them to what are seen as 'the bottom line'. Whenever such reductions have occurred they have eventually led to a complete corruption of 'the simple truths' they were meant to convey. Anything that is reduced to its bare bones supposes that those minima are the bare bones, but equally forgets that a skeleton may be simple but it is also a lot less than a human being.

Another Solution

People's desire to 'hear the story of the day' is a legitimate desire given that our liturgy does pick on this day to celebrate the nativity. It has been *de facto* a principle of the liturgy since feast days appeared – in the fourth century at the latest – that we read the gospels linked with them. Equally, as those charged with handing on the tradition in its fullness there must be care not to collapse the church's memory by using only one account in the liturgy.

A solution that meets both legitimate needs works like this for the four celebrations:

1. At the Vigil

Have the procession to the crib and there read the whole lukan account (2:1-20) – see notes on The Crib, pp 156 – which will be further highlighted by being read next to the stable scene.

Then read at the time of the gospel the whole matthaean genealogy. Its conclusion (1:18-25) should not be used on its own as it only makes full sense as the fulfilment of the divine plan laid down in earlier covenants/ 'ages.' If the genealogy provokes questions, so much the better, the questioners can be directed to joining an adult education group in the new year now that they have discovered a question.

In fact, the lukan crib story and the matthaean genealogy form a wonderful pair of readings in one liturgy, showing two very different ways to narrate the coming of the Christ.

2. At Midnight Mass

Use the shorter form of the Joannine prologue (Jn 1:1-5, 9-14) as found in the Lectionary, vol I, pp 112-3 as the text at the crib. Then use the given gospel as the Eucharist's gospel reading.

This is not a perfect solution as it still does not use the whole of the 'expected' lukan account – so there is a strong case for extending the gospel and reading all 20 verses. The Lectionary's decision to stop at v 14 was presumably based on the need to have a separate gospel for the Dawn Mass and vv 15-20 seems to fit that better. However, since probably only the priest will be at both celebrations, a little duplication is not a problem.

Use the shorter form of John at the crib: the passages omitted are the interpolations concerning John the Baptist and only complicate the prologue on this day.

Again, the juxtaposition of John and Luke in one liturgy draws up for people just how we need many different starting points in our wonder and wondering at the mystery.

3. *At the Dawn Mass*

Read Lk 2:1-14 at the crib (stopping at 'Glory to God in the highest, and on earth peace among men with whom he is pleased!'). Then read the Mass's gospel at the time for the gospel which is its continuation.

4. *At the Day Mass*

Read the whole lukan story at the crib, and the shorter form of the prologue as the Mass's gospel – and, again, benefit for the combination.

Christmas

'Next to the yearly celebration of the paschal mystery, the church holds most sacred the memorial of Christ's birth and early manifestations. This is the purpose of the Christmas season.'

'The Christmas season runs from Evening Prayer I of Christmas until the Sunday after Epiphany or after 6 January, inclusive.'
General Norms for the Liturgical Year and Calendar, nn 32, 33.

Nativity of Our Lord: Vigil Mass

Note

This celebration often has the character of being less than 'the full works' for Christmas, being seen as a replacement or substitute for those who cannot go to Mass when Christmas has 'really begun' at midnight. However, such feelings fail to take account that for those who are celebrating the Vigil Mass this is their only religious celebration for the feast. So this celebration must have all that is expected of Christmas Mass, such as the blessing of the crib, even if the celebrant has to repeat it all again later on at midnight.

CELEBRANT'S GUIDE

Introduction to the Celebration
See the texts for the blessing of the crib, p 156.

Headings for Readings
First Reading
In this reading the prophet looks forward to a time of joy when the Lord will come to his people: then there will be a festival as joyful as any wedding feast. It is this joyful coming of the Lord that we have gathered here this evening to celebrate.

Second Reading
Here is a little early Christian sermon that summarises how we Christians view the time that prepared the way for the coming of Jesus.

Gospel
This evening's gospel is quite strange to our ears: all those strange names of the ancestors of Jesus. This gospel reminds us that Jesus did not just appear 'out of the blue': his coming was promised by God, his way was prepared by God, and his coming marks the beginning of a new chapter in the history of God's people.

Prayer of the Faithful
President

My sisters and brothers, this is our great feast: God has become one with us, so that we can become one again with God. So united with our new born saviour, Jesus the Son of God and the Son of Mary, let us pray to his Father and our Father.

Reader(s)

1. For all who call on the name of Christ; that this festival may renew their faith, hope, and love. Lord hear us.

2. For all people of good will; that we, and all human beings, will choose the way that leads to peace. Lord hear us.

3. For all who are poor; that human hearts will be moved to share humanity's riches with them just as the Father has shared the riches of his love with us in Jesus Christ, Lord hear us.

4. For all who are believers in God; that the coming year will see faith building up our world rather than dividing it. Lord hear us.

5. For all who are in darkness: of faith, of hope, of love; that the light of Christ may bring light, joy, and peace. Lord hear us.

6. For our own church gathered here for the Lord's banquet; that our celebrations may be truly merry, free from discord, a time to be reunited with those we love, and a time of peace and happiness. Lord hear us.

7. For all who are visitors here with us [this evening] [tonight] [today] that they may feel truly welcome, that if they are here out of curiosity that it may grow to faith, and that everyone may hear the glad tidings of great joy within their lives. Lord hear us.

President

Father, we rejoice that your Son, the Prince of Peace, our saviour, our prophet, and our brother was born this day in Bethlehem of Judea; so hear our prayers for we make them in union with that same Christ, our Lord. Amen.

Eucharistic Prayer

Preface I of Christmas (P3) is probably best (the other two Christmas prefaces contain references to 'dawn' and 'today' which do not quite fit with the time at which the Christmas Eve celebration takes place); Eucharistic Prayer I is probably best as it can be fitted specially to the feast through the special 'Communicantes' (item 83, p 486).

Invitation to the Our Father
My sisters and brothers, when the time had fully come, the Father sent forth his Son, born of the woman Mary, born under the law, to redeem those who were under the law, so that we might receive adoption as sons and daughters. And because we are daughters and sons, God has sent the Spirit of his Son into our hearts, crying, 'Abba! Father!', so now let us pray:

Sign of Peace
We rejoice in the coming of the Prince of Peace; we rejoice in the presence among us of the Word made flesh; let us exchange glad tidings of peace and joy with one another.

Invitation to Communion
He came among us as a child in Bethlehem, now he comes among us in this sacred banquet: behold the Lamb of God, behold the Christ, Emmanuel, God with us, happy are we who share now in his supper.

Communion Reflection
The liturgy can seem too busy at Christmas, and by this time there can be a palpable anxiety to 'finish up' and move on. In such an atmosphere a communion reflection just feels like something dragging it out rather than a chance to produce. However, part of belonging to the community of faith is recognising that we need to be called to quiet reflection if we are to appreciate the mystery in which we exist. One way is to create a formal 'minute's silence' for reflection. So formally introduce it:
Today is filled with the hubbub of the festival, but let us spend 60 seconds recalling that this is Christ's Mass: the celebration of the Son of God becoming our brother by becoming the Son of Mary.

Then watch your watch and 60 seconds later, conclude:

> Grant Lord that this Christ's Mass we have just celebrated may set the tone for all our celebrating this Christmas. Amen.

Conclusion
Solemn Blessing 2 for Christmas (*Missal*, p 368).

COMMENTARY

First Reading: Is 62:1-5
This reading from a unit within Trito-Isaiah where the glorious new Zion, i.e. Zion after the Lord has returned to her and spoken again to her, is spoken of in terms of a marriage between Yahweh and the land/people. Once the Lord begins to speak again, the people is forgiven and is secure from its enemies. The thinking behind this passage is very similar to that in Hosea: the Lord is the faithful spouse, adulterous Israel is forgiven and called to be a faithful wife once more.

This imagery of the relationship of God and his people in being that of marriage (and one where the wife is the unfaithful one), and where the closeness of God is his willingness once again to speak, is not without problems in Christian usage, especially at Christmas. Moreover, the imagery that sees the woman (Israel) as the fickle one raises problems of the male perspective of the author.

Second Reading: Acts 13:16-17, 22-25
This is a carefully and well-edited sermon put into the mouth of Paul by Luke and it captures the author's theology of history perfectly. Moreover, it gives us a focused insight into how the early church saw its existence as the direct continuity of the life of Israel (as seen also in the genealogies in Matthew and Luke). God has been caring for his people since they were first formed as a people and leading them in a definite direction to that moment when the Christ, his Son, would be born. This reading and today's gospel can be seen as commentaries on one another: nearly contemporary texts expressing the same aspect of early Christian faith and self-understanding.

Gospel: Mt 1:1-25 (Shorter form: Mt 1: 18-25)

1. The short form of this gospel is superficially attractive: the Christmas Story at Christmas time shorn of distractions; the list of names seems to be built for boredom and for embarrassment as 'the names are tongue-twisters.' However, the matthaean nativity scene only makes sense as the final moment of the orderly progression of God's providence.

2. The revised lectionary has a misprint in its opening. It says 'A reading from the holy gospel ...' whereas it should read 'The beginning of the holy gospel ...'.

3. Genealogies are ways of showing identity and explaining the role of one's past in one's present. It was with these that the early church explained its relationship to the whole history of Israel and to its scriptures (what later generations of Christians would call the 'Old Testament'). Moreover, the past explained the present for history was not an aimless succession of events but the work of God preparing the way for the coming of the Christ. And just as Abraham, David, and the time of the deportation marked the beginning of new eras in the history of the relationship with God, new covenants, so too the birth of Jesus marks a new beginning, a new age, a new era. It is in the light of that belief that Christians have read the whole of the law and the prophets as being their own pre-history (cf Lk 24:27), have dated events using AD dating (i.e. years since the beginning of the era of the Christ), and have referred to Jesus as the new dawn and the new light (see, for example, Preface of Christmas III).

HOMILY NOTES

1. The homily today always seems to be inadequate: the festival is bubbling over with symbols of the season (holly, ivy, Santa, and whatnot) and with people's heightened emotions on the big day. Moreover, the mystery that one has to speak about is so much more than anything capable of being put into words that anything actually said seems paltry and trite. Yet the day still needs a word. The day needs to have its focus drawn to the mind as well as to the senses. And, there

may be many there in the assembly today who will never hear the word from one end of the year to the other, and to them alone is owed the duty of preaching. The task is to take the theme of God-with-us and present it in such a way that (1) the homily can be followed using a framework already familiar to the audience; (2) that seems appropriately seasonal; and (3) that has a certain lightness suited to holiday time.

2. Here is a strategy that can produce a short homily that is easy to follow. The individuals who make up the congregation are asked to imagine where they stand in the array of people that are mentioned in the Bethlehem scene.

3. Do you imagine yourself as one of the people inside the inn? For this group the birth of Jesus is an irrelevance: it does not touch them and they show no interest. To them it was just an external knock on the door, and they just kept going on with what they were doing. Then as now, this is the majority of people.

4. Do you place yourself among the shepherds? Here are people who are open to wonder. They can accept good news. They are people who are already part of a faith tradition, they shared the practices, hopes, and fears of the people, but were also ready to respond with faith to the voice of God.

5. Do you imagine yourself as one of the wise ones, the kings, who came from the east? These are people who are dedicated to searching out the great human questions, but they are not just engaged in idle speculation: they set out and searched for the truth. They listened to the promptings of conscience; they did not come empty handed. These are dedicated searchers after the truth and conscientious doers of the good. All their talents they are placing in the service of God-with-us.

6. Do you imagine yourself like Joseph: caring for the welfare of the church, working in the community, taking on special responsibilities towards the Word made flesh. He is helping to make the good news known, and prepared to response to the inner call of vocation.

7. Do you imagine yourself as sharing in the vocation of Mary? She first brought the Anointed One into the world; but it is through us that Jesus enters our world.
8. We are all at the birth scene: each of us is called upon to fulfill all these vocations in varying ways.

Nativity of Our Lord: Midnight Mass

Introduction to the Celebration
See the texts for the blessing of the crib, p 156.

Headings for Readings
First Reading
The prophet looks forward to the time when the Prince of peace will take his place as the successor of King David leading the people of God out of darkness.

Second Reading
With the coming of Jesus, God's love for us has been revealed.

Gospel
The Lord has entered our world, our time, our humanity. The Lord has become the Son of Mary, the brother of each one of us gathered here.

Prayer of the Faithful
See Resources for Christmas Vigil Mass, p 181.

Eucharistic Prayer
Preface I of Christmas (P3) is probably best (the other two Christmas prefaces contain references to 'dawn' and 'today' which do not quite fit with the time at which the Christmas Midnight celebration takes place); Eucharistic Prayer I is probably best as it can be fitted specially to the feast through the special 'Communicantes' (item 83, p 486).

Invitation to the Our Father
My sisters and brothers, when the time had fully come, the Father sent forth his Son, born of the woman Mary, born under the law, to redeem those who were under the law, so that we

might receive adoption as sons and daughters. And because we are daughters and sons, God has sent the Spirit of his Son into our hearts, crying, 'Abba! Father!', so now let us pray:

Sign of Peace
The angels have proclaimed peace on earth and good will to all. Let us offer the gift of peace and good will to each other.

Invitation to Communion
Behold the Lamb of God, behold our brother born for our sake in Bethlehem long ago, present here now as our Lord bidding us to share in the banquet of heaven.

Communion Reflection
See Resources for Christmas Vigil Mass, p 182.

Conclusion
Solemn Blessing 2 for Christmas (*Missal*, p 368).

COMMENTARY

First Reading: Is 9:1-7
This is an imaginative portrait of the rule of the perfect king of Israel: the successor of David will bring about wise and good government, and inaugurate a true state of peace and well-being. The whole passage is summed up in the phrase 'the Prince of Peace' – and the introduction of this passage, so familiar in the English-speaking world from its use in Handel's *Messiah*, into the liturgy in 1970 has added a new dimension into how the liturgy views Christmas: it is the feast celebrating the coming of the Father's peace and reconciliation. The passage was chosen as it can be seen to be a prophecy of the message of the angels in Lk 2:14.

Second Reading: Titus 2:11-14
The choice of this reading for this celebration seems strange: a snippet of text that seems to be wholly devoid of Christmas

themes, and indeed without much internal coherence as a reading. The answer to the choice lies in the history of the lectionary.
Initially, those revising the lectionary wished to make as few
changes to the lectionary codified in the Missal of 1570 as possible, and this reading has survived from that lectionary where it
was the epistle for the first Mass of Christmas *in nocte*. That then
leaves the question as to why it was chosen in that lectionary.
The answer lies in a single verse whose link with Christmas can
only be seen when read in Latin: *expectantes beatam spem et adven-
tum gloriae magni Dei et salvatoris nostri Iesu Christi* (Titus 2:13).
This can be rendered loosely as 'as we wait in joyful hope for the
coming [literally: the advent] of the glory of our great God and
saviour Jesus Christ' – we are familiar with the expression as it is
used in the new prayer written for the Missal of 1970 to conclude
the Our Father in the Communion Rite. Having been attracted by
that single verse, 2:13, it was necessary to read the additional verses before and after it to form a coherent paragraph for the reading.

The meaning of these verses can only be studied in the context of a much larger portion of the Letter to Titus, and that
exegesis has no bearing on the use of the text in the liturgy at
midnight Mass. This is a very obvious case where the lectionary
is still in need of fine tuning; and, given that the selection of the
passage ultimately turns on a pun in Latin, where the differences between Latin and the original (*epiphaneia*) and the vernac-
ulars needs to be taken into account.

Gospel: Lk 2:1-14 (or 2:1-20)
As it stands this is the gospel from the midnight Mass of the lectionary of 1570 and it is curtailed at v 14, as it was assumed that
the remainder of the nativity story would be read at the second
Mass (our 'Mass at Dawn'). However, clergy apart, people only
attend either the midnight or the dawn Mass, so cutting off the
last five verses destroys what is a single unified story both in the
gospel text and in Christian imagination. People expect to hear
the whole story, Luke intended it as one story, and so the best
policy is to read 2:1-20.

The nativity story as presented by Luke fits snugly within his theology of history: we have come to the crucial moment that history has been preparing for, the whole world is on the move, and so too is the family into which the Christ is to be born. The world of Roman history (the census) and the world of Israel's history (going to the city of King David at Bethlehem) come together with the divine history when the angels appear and proclaim the message of universal peace.

HOMILY NOTES

See notes for the Christmas Vigil Mass, p 184.

Nativity of Our Lord: Dawn Mass

Introduction to the Celebration
See the texts for the blessing of the crib, p 156.

Headings for Readings
First Reading
The prophet gives us a new set of names to tell us who we are having welcomed the Lord's Anointed: we are 'a holy people' and 'the Lord's redeemed'.

Second Reading
In Jesus we see the goodness of God revealed to us.

Gospel
The shepherds are the first to hear the good news: the Christ has been born and bids us come to him.

Prayer of the Faithful
See Resources for Christmas Vigil Mass, p 181.

Eucharistic Prayer
Preface III of Christmas (P5) is probably best as it contains a reference to 'dawn', but the other two Christmas prefaces fit equally well. Eucharistic Prayer I is probably best as it can be fitted specially to the feast through the special 'Communicantes' (item 83, p 486).

Invitation to the Our Father
My sisters and brothers, when the time had fully come, the Father sent forth his Son, born of the woman Mary, born under the law, to redeem those who were under the law, so that we might receive adoption as sons and daughters. And because we

are daughters and sons, God has sent the Spirit of his Son into our hearts, crying, 'Abba! Father!', so now let us pray:

Sign of Peace
Christ's coming has brought joy and peace among us. Let us express that joy and peace to one another.

Invitation to Communion
We have gathered at the table of the Lord, rejoicing that he has come among us, let us rejoice that we are his friends at this holy feast.

Communion Reflection
See Resources for Christmas Vigil Mass, p 182.

Conclusion
Solemn Blessing 2 for Christmas (*Missal*, p 368).

COMMENTARY

First Reading: Is 62:11-12
Trito-Isaiah declares that on the day of the Lord the people will be changed and be given a new set of identities: the will move from being 'a people' to be a 'the consecrated people'; 'the Lord's redeemed'; 'the sought-after'; and 'the city not-forsaken'. It was with titles such as these that many early Christians sought to identify themselves as the successors to the earlier covenant; see, for example, 1 Pet 2:9: 'But you are a chosen race, a royal priesthood, a holy nation, God's own people, that you may declare the wonderful deeds of him who called you out of darkness into his marvellous light.'

Second Reading: Titus 3:4-7
As with the choice of Titus 2:11-14 at Midnight Mass, the rationale for this reading lies in its having been the reading at 'the second Mass' in the 1570 lectionary. Its choice there as a Christmas reading was determined by its opening verse in

Latin: *apparuit benignitas et humanitas salvatoris nostri Dei*. No matter how this verse is rendered in any modern language it does not convey that Christmas 'flavour' it has in Latin, and the other verses (added so that it forms a coherent paragraph) take the mind far from today's celebration.

Exegesis of the passage is irrelevant to its use in the liturgy today where its selection is simply accidental upon the way Latin uses verbs.

Gospel: Lk 2:15-20
See the notes for the gospel at Midnight Mass, p 189.
If you have not had a ceremony at the crib and there read Lk 2:1-14, then you should consider using the whole Lukan pericope (2:1-20) at this Mass. Luke wrote the story to be read as a piece; he did not envisage that it would be broken into two artificial sections in the Roman rite so that two separate Masses could be celebrated by the same body of clergy in two different Roman churches.

HOMILY NOTES

See notes for the Christmas Vigil Mass, p 184.

Nativity of Our Lord: Day Mass

Introduction to the Celebration
See the texts for the blessing of the crib, p 156.

Headings for Readings
First Reading
The good news has come, Jesus is born in Bethlehem, and this news reaches out to the very end so the earth. Salvation has come to every nation under heaven

Second Reading
God speaks to us in many ways, but in Jesus we have someone still more wonderful: God has entered our humanity and so we can stand in the presence of God.

Gospel
Jesus is the light of the world: he has come and shines his light into the darkness of our world.

Prayer of the Faithful
See Resources for Christmas Vigil Mass, p 181.

Eucharistic Prayer
Preface II of Christmas (P4) is probably best as it contains a reference to 'today', but the other two Christmas prefaces fit equally well. Eucharistic Prayer I is probably best as it can be fitted specially to the feast through the special 'Communicantes' (item 83, p 486).

Invitation to the Our Father
My sisters and brothers, when the time had fully come, the Father sent forth his Son, born of the woman Mary, born under the law, to redeem those who were under the law, so that we

might receive adoption as sons and daughters. And because we are daughters and sons, God has sent the Spirit of his Son into our hearts, crying, 'Abba! Father!', so now let us pray:

Sign of Peace
The Prince of Peace has come; let us wish each other the peace of Christ, and declare ourselves to be Christ's peacemakers.

Invitation to Communion
Behold the Prince of Peace who bids us to share his table now and beckons us to join him in the banquet of heaven.

Communion Reflection
See Resources for Christmas Vigil Mass, p 182.

Conclusion
Solemn Blessing 2 for Christmas (*Missal*, p 368).

COMMENTARY

First Reading: Is 52:7-10
This is one of a number of passages in the Old Testament that look forward to a time when the Lord's consolation will pass outwards from Israel to every nation, and from Jerusalem outwards in ever widening circles until it reaches the ends of the earth. This text is paradigmatic for how Christians have understood the revelation of the good news in Jesus since at least the time of Luke, who uses this passage as the key structure for the life of the church in the time after the ascension.

Second Reading: Heb 1:1-6
This passage is another inheritance from the 1570 lectionary (where 1:1-12 was read), but it fits the theme of today very well. There are and have been many revelations of God, but Christian faith sees in Jesus a definitive and unique revelation of God. Jesus is the unique First-born Son of the Father, even the angels fall down in worship, and, implies the author, so must we.

Gospel: Jn 1:1-18 (shorter form: Jn 1:1-5, 9-14)
See 'The Gospel Readings on Christmas Day', p 174; and the notes on the gospel for the Second Sunday of Christmas, p 238.

HOMILY NOTES

1. The homily today has to be simple, snappy, and seasonal. The reason for this is obvious: there are many in the gathering who are not frequent diners at the eucharistic table, and for virtually everyone there are lots of other things going through their minds such as what's going to happen at lunch, keeping an eye on children with new toys, or how not to get annoyed with the in-laws.

2. So the homily has to have the inclusiveness of a 'Thought for the Day' on the radio, yet adequately identify the Christian solemnity we are celebrating. One way to do this is to focus on the Christ as the Prince of Peace.

3. Look at the coming of the Son of God: not in a show of force but in simplicity and poverty.

4. The majesty of God makes itself felt by sharing human weakness, limitation and suffering, not by making humans feel his majesty and power.

5. Fear and threats are marks of human relations at every level; the message of the angels to the shepherds is peace on earth, good will to men and women.

6. We celebrate the Prince of Peace. Are we willing to adopt the way of peace ourselves?

7. We seek security and justice. Are we brave enough to be peacemakers?

8. We are celebrating God sharing his life with us in Jesus; we have gathered for the Lord to share his table with us; are we willing to share our lives and tables and riches with others: for that is how peace and justice are established?

Sunday in the Octave of Christmas (Year A): The Feast of the Holy Family

Introduction to the Celebration

In these days between Christmas Day and New Year's Day we as the People of God spend time reflecting on just what the Christmas mystery tells us about God. We reflect that his Son has come among us: born as an infant at a particular moment in time, in a particular place, in a particular culture – this is Jesus our brother. Like each of us he had a unique set of relationships: with Mary, with Joseph, with the other people who lived around him. But with us, his followers, he established another unique relationship by making each of us a child of God. Let us call to mind how we have behaved as daughters and sons of the Father and how we may have injured our brothers and sisters.

Rite of Penance

Option c. iii (*Missal*, p 392-3) is appropriate.

Headings for Readings
First Reading

Here is the ideal of family life as presented in one of the books of ancient Jewish wisdom: parents and children honouring and respecting each other, and this lifestyle being pleasing to God and a way to holiness.

Second Reading

Here is the ideal of family life as presented in one of the earliest Christian books: gentleness to one another in the family and larger community is a way of pleasing the Father.

Gospel

We now read the story of the Flight into Egypt: from the very

197

first days of his life there were those for whom the coming of the Christ was not the joyful message of salvation but bad news: yet even in these difficulties God's plan of salvation was not thwarted.

Prayer of the Faithful
President
Today we continue to celebrate the coming of the Word of God as our brother, Jesus the Anointed One. This coming has changed our world and makes demands on us as his disciples: now as children of the Father let us ask for our needs.
Reader(s)
1. Recalling the birth of Jesus, that we as his sisters and brothers may be the People of Peace. Lord hear us.
2. Recalling the birth of Jesus, that we as his sisters and brothers may respect human life and dignity. Lord hear us.
3. Recalling the birth of Jesus, that we as his sisters and brothers may live happily within our families. Lord hear us.
4. Recalling the birth of Jesus, that we as his sisters and brothers may grow in our understanding of our vocations. Lord hear us.
5. Recalling the birth of Jesus, that we as his sisters and brothers may work to aid all who are refugees or displaced by famine or warfare. Lord hear us.
6. Recalling the birth of Jesus, that we as his sisters and brothers may have the gentleness in our lives that witnesses the Father's love. Lord hear us.
7. Recalling the birth of Jesus, that we as his sisters and brothers may have sympathy for all whose families are in crisis. Lord hear us.
8. Recalling the birth of Jesus, that we as his sisters and brothers may bring him to birth anew in the coming year. Lord hear us.
President
Father, your love is beyond all our thoughts; in these days we try to glimpse it in the wonder of your Word made flesh. Hear the prayers we now make to you for we make them through that Christ, your Son, our Lord. Amen.

Eucharistic Prayer
Preface of Christmas II (P4) probably fits today best; Eucharistic
Prayer I is preferable as it has the special Christmas form of 'In
union with the whole church ...'

Invitation to the Our Father
When the Son came among us as one of us, he revealed the
Father and established that relationship with the Father that en-
ables us to now pray:

Sign of Peace
Gathered as the family of the Lord in our act of thanksgiving,
called to be gentle towards one another, we offer a sign of peace
to each other.

Invitation to Communion
He has come among us and shared our trials. Behold the Lamb
of God who takes away the sins of the world, happy are we to be
thankful with him at his supper.

Communion Reflection
Liturgy always runs the risk of being too wordy. Have a structured silence when the last member of the community has
shared the loaf and cup by saying: 'Let us now sit quietly and
spend time in reflection.' Break the silence by introducing the
Post Communion Prayer with 'Let us now stand and pray'.

Conclusion
Solemn Blessing 2 for Christmas (*Missal*, p 368).

Except in years when Christmas Day falls on Sunday, this may
be the last time that the majority of the community gather in
prayer before the New Year will have begun; hence the informal
words at the end of the Eucharist should include good wishes
for a happy new year.

COMMENTARY

First Reading: Ecclesiasticus 3:2-6, 12-14

This is a piece of proverbial wisdom on the importance of maintaining the right order of discipline, power, and authority within an extended family towards the patriarch. It belongs to the families within the upper echelons of a society where the family functions in a way that (a few royal or great landowning dynasties apart) we think more appropriate to corporations today. Unless the patriarch rule, then disorder will break out among the various sons and their branches of the family; this will lead to chaos, and the ultimate defeat of the family. As the text is edited in the lectionary, this sense of family is somewhat obscured as the reference to the sons serving their father as a master is omitted, as is the reference to father's blessing being essential to the good order within the family's undertakings.

We might think of this as a reading that only makes sense within the context of the Ancient Near East, but that would fail to recognise that most traditional societies in Europe until just a few centuries ago would have recognised this pattern of family as being at the heart of government (this model never applied to the households of the tradesmen, the peasants, the poor, or the slaves). A good example would be the way that early Christian Ireland was ruled by great families with numerous sub-branches (e.g. the Uí Neill/ O'Neill's [literally: the descendants of Neil] who ruled much of the northern part of Ireland for centuries) who were expected to act together when threatened and to owe allegiance to the current head of the family. In such a society, and it is that kind of society that produced Europe's royal houses, this reading is true, peace-making wisdom, which probably explains why virtually every line of this passage can be found in early medieval law codes from Europe. However, it makes little sense in the context of the current nuclear family of mother, father, 1.8 children, and a mortgage. Equally, given that one of the few things we know of Jesus's family was that he came from the artisan class (Mk 6:3), it makes little sense for his family either.

This book is now universally known as 'Sirach' and was so named in the first English lectionary of 1971, so it is regrettable that the old, and confusing, Vulgate name has re-appeared in the current lectionary.

Second Reading: Col 3:12-21
The church of Colossae was not founded by Paul, nor visited by him, yet it clearly wanted to have close relations with nearby Pauline churches and one way of establishing such links was to read letters from such churches at their assembly: hence this letter. It was written (probably in the later first century) by someone who knew Paul's work, his style, and his theology, and then who attributed this letter to his master. The letter has a more rotund style than those by Paul himself – a characteristic that can be seen in today's reading.

The stance of the whole letter is founded in its Christology – Christ has brought about the end times now and we live in them through the mystery of baptism – and this is what drives this passage. You, the church of Colossae, have put on a new nature in baptism: you have become the Christian church and as such you form the household of God. Given your new dignity, the individual households (husbands, wives, children, slaves) must behave as befits the great new family they belong to in Christ. Here is a vision of how one early Christian theologian saw the link to the new status of the whole body of Christians, the household / family of God, and thereby presented an image to explain practical relations within the households that made up his community.

Two points should be noted. First, the author is not making the statements on behaviour as a set of ethical norms for 'the good family' as if a part of the Christian services to the world is to promote 'family values' – rather it is a behaviour that flows out of baptism and the new relationship in Christ to the Father. Second, we should note that this reading does not seek to create values, but to take the values of the world it inherits and give

them Christian value; we see this in the verse following the lec-
tion today (v 22) which is about how Christian slaves should
obey their Christian masters. By stopping before this verse
(which is an intrinsic part of the unit of text in the letter) the creators of the lectionary have given the whole passage an artificial
quality of 'timelessness' which fails to take account of the fact
that all theology, this letter included, is written in a context with
its limitations as well as its good points. The world of the family
of the later first-century Greek city-state is a long way from most
modern contexts, and to simply take over bits and pieces on
practical matters as relevant is the essence of fundamentalism.

Gospel: Mt 2:13-15, 19-23
This is another part of the complex matthaean infancy narrative.
The first section (2:13-15) follows on immediately after the visit
of the magi to the infant; the latter section follows after the tale
of Herod ordering the death of all the infants under two years
around Bethlehem on the basis of the prophecy in Jer 31:15/ Mt
2:18. The two sections as edited here fit well together as they
deal with the incident (found only in Matthew) known as 'the
flight into Egypt'. This incident is chosen today as it is the reference here at 2:14 to Joseph, Mary, and the child that forms the
standard image of 'the holy family'.

The incident in Matthew seems to be based around his desire
to see fulfilled in Jesus as many scriptural prophecies as possible. We have already noted the one from Jer 31 that allowed
Herod to know where Jesus would be born and hence order a
massacre, but we have now two more. By moving the family to
Egypt, he can now have fulfilled: 'When Israel was a child, I
loved him, and out of Egypt I called my son' (Hosea 11:1). Then
he is able to explain why a descendent of David comes from
Nazareth rather than Judea, and in the process fulfill yet another
prophecy: 'He shall be called a Nazarene.' There is only one
problem here: the source of this quotation cannot be found in the
Old Testament despite the fact that exegetes since Origen have
had sleepless nights looking for it. Indeed, one of the ways of

finding out whether or not a writer on Matthew's gospel is a fundamentalist with a belief in literal inerrancy or immediate inspiration is to see how she/he gets worked up about successfully finding this prophecy.

In the liturgical context it is worth noting that the Christmas liturgy is not interested in the linear story of the life of Jesus as found in the infancy narratives. This feast is always before Epiphany, usually before the circumcision, always before the presentation in the temple, sometimes before the feast of the Holy Innocents. We are recalling a mystery, not running a pageant. Hence, preachers should be careful in comments as if all these memorials ran in parallel between our calendar and their 'logical' sequence derived from a harmony of the two infancy narratives.

HOMILY NOTES

1. Preaching immediately after Christmas seems to be just the straw that breaks the camel's back: we have worked hard to prepare for Christmas Day, now there is a sense of a lull. This is perfectly natural because after a moment of stressed solemn time, there is the necessary moment of quiet. This time between Christmas and New Year is the time when in the liturgy we have the octave: the time for letting the mystery of Christmas slowly sink in. And this reflective, letting it sink in slowly quality must dominate the homily today. Moreover, many people are still away who are normally in the congregation, while there may still be visitors from elsewhere. So it does not feel like a normal Sunday morning.

2. Moreover, there are other problems with preaching on this feast. First, it can draw out a mawkish piety: the lovely ideal family which will seem so far distant as to be irrelevant to many in the community whose relationships are far from ideal or for whom the Christmas period has been one of extra stress. Musing on families in a general way or speculating on a Galilean peasant family's life two millennia ago may seem appropriate to the preacher but, especially if the preacher is a

celibate, such musings just make for non-communication. Any breakdown in communication is especially sad today for in this period after Christmas there is the heightened awareness, by everyone taking part, of what is happening in the liturgy. This is the result of us still being in the wake of the great feast and the holiday period. Second, there is the moralist's approach: this is really the day for speaking about the 'Christian ideal' of family life. What can then follow is a potted mix of injunctions and abstract ideals where theology (laced with canon law) is allowed free rein in lieu of a psychology of relationships or a sociological analysis of contemporary society. Whether or not this is well received, rejected, or ignored is beside the point: such speculation has no place in today's liturgy for it supplants the purpose of the feast for an ulterior motive. The liturgy of Christmas is about our wonder at the incarnation and a loving reflection on its implications for us as Christians, and no other aim, even one so worthy as promoting the Christian notion of marriage, should deflect us. The Son of God made flesh, not as an abstract being labelled 'human', but as an individual with a specific history, Jesus the son of Mary and with Joseph as his father in their specific setting of a small town where Joseph worked as an artisan – this is the wonder we must recall today.

3. The old dictum 'God became man in Jesus Christ' obscured the basic issue at the heart of this feast: God the Son did not become a 'man' or 'human' as we think of these as abstract categories – he became another unique individual with a history and a distinct identity. Just as you and I are unique, unrepeatable and distinct in our specific backgrounds and cultures and experiences, so too was Jesus. This is a celebration of the depths of the humanity of our Lord. But as Christians we also believe that we all share something that is equally deep with one another: each of us is a daughter or son of the Father. We are the children of God and we share this with Jesus as a member of his family. This is a conviction

of faith in the loving reality of God that makes us brothers and sisters to one another and to Jesus. This is not some abstract notion of sharing in a common human nature. We may, as a matter of our philosophical perspective, hold that there is a common humanity and a common human nature which allows us to share experiences and joys and sufferings, but to call each other brothers and sisters in Christ is not simply to have a religious 'take' on human nature. To be brothers and sisters in Christ is to be distinct and unique creations with distinct vocations within the care of God, and to have the commonality of the love of the Father calling us as his people united in his Son – a union achieved in the mystery we recall at Christmas. Put bluntly, the secular world may promote the notion of 'universal human brotherhood' (*fraternité*) – and as responsible people in the world we should support this ideal as a way of overcoming wars, exploitation, oppression, and bringing help to anyone who suffers. But our Christian vision of the links that bind each individual to every other individual is both more rich – in that it stresses each's uniqueness – and more profound: we are brothers and sisters because each is a daughter or son of the Father, and it is through the Word that we are given this dignity.

4. So how do we communicate this new set of relationships that is established through the specific history of Jesus? For most of us the crib in the church is just there: one of the Christmas trimmings which might be referred to for the 'children's sake' on Christmas Day but precious little afterward. Yet (see 'The Crib, pp 156) this assembly is a wonderful collage of our basic memory of the entry of the Word into the creation. This is a day on which the crib can be exploited in the homily. People do not have to be actually looking at the crib while you speak – in fact it is better if they cannot see it during the homily (people using PowerPoint should have realised by now that if you leave the images on all the time the people stop listening to you and get caught up with what they see), everyone can remember what a crib looks like while you preach, and they can visit it afterwards.

5. Just reflect on the contradictions contained in the crib. First, we have a private family moment – the birth of Jesus – without the larger family nearby and with no hint that it has impact on those immediately around; yet we are told that this event is heralded by angels to shepherds as of momentous significance to humanity. Second, the inn is full, they have come on the wrong day at the wrong hour – and so has the baby – for the equivalent of the 'No vacancies' sign is out and they have not 'booked ahead'. The reference to the 'no room in the inn' (Lk 2:7) indicates a serious lack of planning, yet we see Luke quoting the whole history of humanity, back to Adam to show God's planning, the prophets and John the Baptist preparing the way, and this birth being proclaimed as 'the fall and rising of many in Israel' (Lk 2:34). God's planning is praised for its loving providence, yet events occur in a way that was determined by how many got to the inn that evening before them.

6. So what do these contradictions mean? They show us that the mystery of God and our re-creation in the Christ is greater than our human minds. We are caught up in a mystery of love, but it does not bring ready answers and simply success. These contradictions make us reassess any preconceived ideas we might have about a 'god' or about religion. The Father does not act like a bullying super-power for whom we are playthings or puppets, but reveals himself in his Son coming among us as one of us. We live in the mystery of the revelation of God in the particularities of a human life: the vast plan for the incarnation, yet there was no room that night in the inn! Christianity is a religion of the absolute reign of God, but that takes the small person seriously and leans towards the powerless.

7. If more members of your assembly are drawn to just go and look at the crib than usual, i.e. to reflect on the church's memory of the coming of the Christ, then this is one of the times when you can check out if your communication has got through.

Appendix:
Perceptions of the Holy Family and Early Christian Sources

Today we celebrate the feast of 'the Holy Family of Jesus, Mary and Joseph'. This is the adequate focus for the feast as the mystery we are celebrating is the coming of the Son in Jesus; we are not making the whole family life of Jesus the centre of attention. It is necessary to draw this distinction as one of the effects of Catholics today having a greater awareness of biblical materials is that many no longer imagine the family of Jesus as just these three, and they assume that Mary had other children with Joseph as the father, later on after the birth of Jesus. The older image was that of Jesus as an 'only child' such that Mary would not only be his virgin mother and he her first born (all that Luke's gospel claims), but that Mary was 'ever virgin' (i.e. she remained a virgin after the birth of Jesus (the *virginitas post partum)* and so would be the model for the state of perpetual virginity as the highest religious state. When the notion of virginity as a religious ideal began to appear within Christianity in the early fourth century, it became necessary to 'write out' the four brothers and, at least, two sisters of Jesus recorded in the gospels from the common memory. This was done most famously by Jerome who argued that in the Greek of the New Testament 'brothers' and 'sisters' must be have been used to translate some more obscure Aramaic term that meant 'cousins'. Why 'must' it have been so? Even Jerome admitted that he had no linguistic evidence for this surmise. Jerome's certainty that Jesus did not have younger brothers and sisters was derived from the impossibility than any woman could become so close to perfect holiness that we could address her as Mother of God without her being perpetually a virgin. For Mary to have had other children was to Jerome religiously unthinkable due to the dignity he accorded to virginity relative to marriage. However, recent years have seen even Catholic scholars simply accepting as a matter of historical fact that Jesus grew up in a family of seven (see John P. Meier, *A*

Marginal Jew III: Companions and Competitors (New York 2001), p 616). Meanwhile special pleading in the manner of Jerome has become a fringe activity, the last scholarly attempt being by John McHugh (*The Mother of Jesus in the New Testament*, London 1975, pp 200-254), but see the gentle unravelling of his work by Raymond Brown (*Biblical Exegesis and Church Doctrine*, London 1985, pp 69-74).

This parting of the ways between exegetical, historical scholarship and the liturgical memory as celebrated today must be handled carefully. On the one hand, it is inappropriate to simply adopt 'the bull in the china shop' approach and dismiss this feast – even if it is a new feast (introduced in 1893 and given its present position in 1969) and while we might hope that it would be quietly dropped in the next revision of the calendar or moved to 30 December except when that day falls on Sunday – for the notion of Mary being 'ever virgin' is deeply within the tradition (just look at the number of places in the liturgy, e.g. in Eucharistic Prayer I: 'we honour Mary, the ever-virgin mother' (*gloriosae semper Virginis Mariae*) where we refer to the perpetual virginity). Moreover, it is even more deeply held by eastern Christians where exegesis is still pursued as a corollary of the liturgical tradition. Although it must be said that it is often thrown up by western non-Catholic Christians as an example of willingly declaring a matter of faith something that we admit is contrary to historical fact.

On the other hand, the question 'Did Jesus have real brothers?' is one that does come up from the Catholic in the street today (yet when I ask older priests when they were first asked this question they say that it is only in the last couple of decades), and it is sometimes a major crisis for Catholics engaged in theological studies who are still familiar with traditional marian doctrine. In the front of such questions we must answer honestly and avoid unworthy fudges by the device of introducing hypothetical doubts: e.g. 'this is uncertain so we cannot really know!' The matter is certain not only from the canonical texts that refer to Jesus's siblings (most famously: '"Is not this the carpenter, the son of Mary and brother of James and Joses and Judas and Simon, and are not his sisters here with us?"' (Mk 6:3), but we have the evidence of Eusebius who preserves memories of the role of his brothers in the early episcopate. To such questioners an answer must be given that is in accord with the evidence we possess. Belief in the virgin birth of Jesus is something that has been part of the Christian memory at least as far back as the time of Luke the evangelist and this is what has inspired the creeds, and hence our addressing Mary as the Blessed Virgin, the Mother of God. However, the early generations of Christians knew that Jesus was one of a family of at least seven (we only know there were 'sisters' in the plural: exactly how many daughters Joseph and Mary had we do not know) and that they do not appear to have had any hesitation in asserting that after her first-born, Mary bore Joseph at least another six children of whom we know the names of the males – and indeed from the very 'old fashioned' Jewish names they gave the five boys we can infer it was a very pious family. Later, when the cult of virginity as the ideal religious state for both men and women began to become an important matter in Christian practice, it became inconceivable that Mary could be the 'all holy Mother of God' and also to have been a normal wife to Joseph and mother to their children. Hence the development of the notion of the perpetual virginity, stories of Joseph being an old man at the time he accepted Mary, and the image of the Holy Family as just Jesus, Mary and Joseph as portrayed in so many paintings down the centuries. Equally, there is an opposite movement today among some feminist Catholic theologians who wish to rejoice in Mary having all the worries and troubles of being the mother of a large family and all the difficulties of making ends meet which that must have involved. This is equally to be rejected as simply speculation from silence: we must simply note that the gospel record preserves no details of the family life of Jesus except that seven children survived to adulthood.

However, today the focus is not on the 'biological' family of Jesus right through his life, but on the Word made flesh within the particularities of history from the moment of his birth. So if one concentrates on the wonder of the particularity of the incarnation, and avoids patches of local colour which refer to the household arrangements in Nazareth, then the larger theological 'hot potato' should not arise.

Sunday in the Octave of Christmas (Year B): The Feast of the Holy Family

Introduction to the Celebration

Today we continue to meditate in our assembly on the mystery of the incarnation, and to focus our thoughts we reflect that the Word made flesh was born into a human family, in a particular culture, and so knows all our limitations from, as it were, the inside. It is because Jesus knows us through and through that he can sympathise with us in our weakness and we can have confidence in calling on him for his mercy.

Rite of Penance

Option c. vii (*Missal*, p 394-5) is appropriate.

Headings for Readings

First Reading

We are gathered here as a family of faith because we all have a common father in faith: Abraham.

Second Reading

Abraham is the father of our family of faith because he obeyed God in faith. Since the earliest times we have seen our father Abraham as our model of obedience to the will of the heavenly Father.

Gospel

The temple is the place of prayer of the family of Abraham: when Jesus is presented in the temple, he is accepting his religious inheritance and being joined to it.

Prayer of the Faithful
President

Sisters and brothers, at this time of year we recall the scene at the birth in Bethlehem: Jesus wrapped up and lying in the manger watched over by his loving parents, Joseph and Mary. But we also recall that he is our priest, our prophet, and our king. So, in union with Jesus, now seated at the right hand of the Father, let us pray for our needs, the needs of the church, and the needs of humanity.

Reader(s)

1. That within the family of Christians there may be concord, unity, and a common desire to serve the Lord. Lord in your mercy, hear our prayer.

2. That within the family of this community there may be harmony, joy, and communal support. Lord in your mercy, hear our prayer.

3. That within our own families there may be happiness, understanding, and mutual fidelity. Lord in your mercy, hear our prayer.

4. That every family that is under strain at the moment may get the support it needs to restore peace and joy. Lord in your mercy, hear our prayer.

5. That all the religions that look to our father Abraham as their father may grow in mutual understanding as members of a family. Lord in your mercy, hear our prayer.

6. That the family of humankind may learn the ways that lead to understanding, peace, and justice. Lord in your mercy, hear our prayer.

President

Father, we are rejoicing this day that your eternal Son has entered our human world to share our human lot, hear our prayers for we seek to follow your Son so as to share the heavenly life he has with you, and the Holy Spirit, God, for ever and ever. Amen.

Eucharistic Prayer
Preface of Christmas II (P4) probably fits today best. There is really no alternative to Eucharistic Prayer I today for two reasons: first, it contains the reference to 'the sacrifice of Abraham, our father in faith' which is linked to the first reading; and second, this Eucharistic Prayer has the special Christmas form of 'In union with the whole church …'

Invitation to the Our Father
Through baptism we became the holy household of God, and so we can say our family prayer:

Sign of Peace
Rejoicing at the birth of the infant prince of peace, let us offer a sign of peace to each other as members of God's family.

Invitation to Communion
Behold the Lamb of God, behold him who entered our human existence as an infant, and who now bids us to share his table as his holy family.

Communion Reflection
Lord, we believe in you: increase our faith.
We trust in you; strengthen our trust.
We love you: let us love you more and more.
We are sorry for our sins: deepen our sorrow.

We worship you as our first beginning,
We long for you as our last end,
We praise you as our constant helper,
And call on you as our loving protector.

Guide us by your wisdom,
Correct us with your justice,
Comfort us with your mercy,
And protect us with your power. Amen.

Adapted from the first three verses of 'the universal prayer' (of Clement XI), Missal, pp 1021-2.

Conclusion
Solemn Blessing 2 for Christmas (*Missal*, p 368).

Except in years when Christmas Day falls on Sunday, this may be the last time that the majority of the community gather in prayer before the New Year will have begun; hence the informal words at the end of the Eucharist should include good wishes for a happy new year.

COMMENTARY

First Reading: Gen 15:1-6, 21:1-3
This reading from Genesis is offered as an optional alternative to the reading from Sirach given for Year A; this reading is much better suited to today than Sirach and so to be preferred.

This is one of the foundation texts of Israel: the story of Abram / Abraham becoming the father of Isaac and so the father of descendents as numerous as the stars of heaven: this is the fruit of the covenant with Abraham that then underpins the people's identity as a distinct people with a specific sacred destiny. This concern with Abraham as the father of a great family continued within Christianity and we see it becoming the basis for seeing gentile Christians as the spiritual descendents of Abraham in Paul (Rom and Gal) and in the Letter to the Hebrews. To be a child of Abraham is to be an inheritor of the covenant, and a beneficiary of the divine promises made to him. This continued in the liturgy where the anaphora of the Latin church – what we refer to now as Eucharistic Prayer I – refers to 'the sacrifice of Abraham, our father in faith'. Abraham's sacrifice is a model by which we can understand the sacrifice of Jesus to the Father on the cross, and our offerings as the Father's people now gathered at the Eucharistic Table.

The story of Abraham is a myth of origins related to the question of why all the people should pull together and see themselves having a common identity; the answer is that they are all one extended family. This is, in effect, the basic myth of religious unity among the people and helped to form the notion of Israel –

the people of God bonded together in covenant which is seen as being made between God and an extended family. To be a descendent is a key to religious identity and cohesion within that religion. The early Christians continued this theme of unity through descent – quite apart from Paul's approach – in the desire to link Jesus to Abraham in both of the genealogies (Mt 1:2 and Lk 3:34): in other words, to understand Jesus is to understand the place of Abraham. This is confirmed in the prayer put on Jesus's lips in Lk 16:24 – to be a holy person in the New Israel is to call on Abraham as father and intercessor. While in Jn (8:56) this link between Jesus and Abraham is spelled out in that Abraham is rejoicing to see the Day of the Christ: the father is still with his people and rejoicing at their blessing in seeing the Day of the Lord in Jesus. We today find this notion that religious unity is a function of family – a result of having common ancestors – strange as we see unity as ideological (i.e. accepting the same religious doctrines). We seem far happier at ticking boxes about 'beliefs' – abstract propositions – than reading the genealogies; but such ideological notions of religion are comparatively modern and seem to be far less successful at helping people see commonality than the older family-ancestor approach.

However, this text from Genesis and the older genealogical approach to religious diversity may still have an important role to play in modern society where Judaism, Islam, and Christianity all invoke the same ancestor myth of being children of Abraham, and so of belonging to 'the Abrahamic family'. This approach to inter-religious dialogue and growth in mutual respect and tolerance may have a lot to recommend it, not least in that such myths work by stressing common elements and the need for peace within a family (one of the key reasons that led to their original growth), while discussions of religious propositions (as the history of denominational disputes within western Christianity amply demonstrates) usually proceeds by distinguishing one proposition from another, and so noting not common elements but differences.

Second Reading: Heb 11:8, 11-12, 17-19.

If Genesis is chosen as the first reading, then this is the perfect accompaniment as it shows how the Genesis text – and the tradition of faith within which that text was valued – was developed within early Christianity. The author of Hebrews imagines the incarnation as having taken place for the sake of the family of Abraham – this is the group to which the Christ is sent (2:16). Abraham is then the model which shows God's faithfulness (6: 13-15); the one who shows respect to Melchizedek and so the dignity of Jesus the Melchizedek-like priest (7:1-9), and now, finally, he is the model of obedience both of the Son to the Father and of these Christian children of Abraham to God.

Only within the family context of being the descendents of Abraham can the internal logic of the entire letter be understood.

Gospel: Lk 2:22-40 (shorter form: Lk 2:22, 39-40).

This text forms a unit of text within Luke's infancy narrative, so to read the shorted form is to mutilate the text.

For Luke the temple is the religious centre of the people of God thus he has the preaching of the gospel emanating from it ([the disciples] were continually in the temple blessing God 24:53) to the ends of the earth, and earlier at the death of Jesus its curtain was torn in two (23:45). So Jesus has to enter it as soon as possible after his birth. In entering the temple he is simultaneously inheriting its identity as his own, and claiming the temple as his own. The temple is the place where he is truly and publicly recognised, and the place in which his identity is established as the glory of Israel (the temple is the abode of the divine glory) and the light to the nations (for the temple is set in the midst of the nations (Ezek 5:5 and Acts 1:8).

HOMILY NOTES

1. The story of the presentation in the temple is one of the events of the infancy narratives from which Luke wishes us to draw information for our understanding of the true and full identity of Jesus.

2. The task is, therefore, to go through the gospel text and draw out the series of images Luke wishes to convey, and through them build up a mosaic of the identity of the Lord.

3. Here is a list working through today's gospel text:

   He was born within the context of the Law of Moses.

   He was born under the Law.

   He is the one whom the righteous and devout awaited.

   He is the desire of the prophets who sought the consolation of Israel.

   He is God's salvation prepared in the presence of all peoples.

   He is a light to all nations.

   He is the glory of the people of God.

   He is set for the fall and rising of many in Israel.

   He is a sign that is spoken against.

   He is the one whom the women prophets awaited.

   He is the redemption of Jerusalem.

   He is the one filled with wisdom.

   He is the one on whom the favour of God rests.

4. We celebrate the mystery of God among us: we could go right through the gospels adding titles and descriptions – and yet we would still not have plumbed the depths of the identity of our saviour. Today we think of him especially as the infant in the manger, but he is also the Word through whom all things were made and without him was not anything made that was made. To follow him is life, but we will never grasp his identity for he draws us into the mystery of God.

Sunday in the Octave of Christmas (Year C): The Feast of the Holy Family

Introduction to the Celebration

We gather here each Sunday and call each other sisters and brothers, we exchange the sign of peace as if we are all one family, and we offer thanks and prayers to God the Father as our Father. We can do this because we are a family of faith, adopted as children of God through our brother Jesus the Christ. So today we reflect that Jesus has made us family through his becoming a member of a human family: the holy family of Nazareth.

Rite of Penance

Lord Jesus, you have entered our world with the gift of peace, Lord have mercy.

Lord Jesus, you have shared our joys and suffering as the son of Mary, Christ have mercy.

Lord Jesus, you gather us here in the Holy Spirit as the beloved family of the Father, Lord have mercy.

Headings for Readings

First Reading

Samuel was the Lord's gift to Hannah, so she gave him to the service of the Lord in thanksgiving.

Second Reading

Because Jesus was born within a human family we can now think of ourselves as the children of God.

Gospel

We look to Jesus our Lord as he is the one who is the Wisdom of the Father and he has come among us when he was born within the holy family.

Prayer of the Faithful
Use the Sample Formula for the Christmas Season given on p 998 of the *Missal*; or see Year A or Year B.

Eucharistic Prayer
Preface of Christmas I (P3) or II (P4) probably fit today better than Preface of Christmas III (P5). Eucharistic Prayer I is preferable as it has the special Christmas form of 'In union with the whole church ...'

Invitation to the Our Father
Made sons and daughters of the Father in his Son Jesus, as one family let us now pray to our Father in heaven:

Sign of Peace
We have been made members of God's family through the Son of God being born in a human family; let us exchange peace and greetings with one another as members of this holy family.

Invitation to Communion
We are gathered as a family around a table. Let us greet the Saviour born for us who invites us here to share his sacred banquet.

Communion Reflection
Lord, come into our hearts this Christmas as our Lord, our Leader, and our Light.
Lord, come into our hearts this Christmas reminding us that you came among us as our brother in Palestine.
Lord, come into our hearts this Christmas reminding us that you will come again to judge the living and the dead.
Lord, come into our hearts this Christmas and enable us to bring your peace and care to those in need.
Lord, come into our hearts this Christmas and enable us to bring your light to those in darkness.
Lord, come into our hearts this Christmas and make us your holy people, united in love with all who call on your name.

Lord, come into our hearts this Christmas and transform us into your Body in the world today.
Lord, come into our hearts this Christmas and grant us a joyful celebration of your birth.

Conclusion
Solemn Blessing 2 for Christmas (*Missal*, p 368).

Except in years when Christmas Day falls on Sunday, this may be the last time that the majority of the community gather in prayer before the New Year will have begun; hence the informal words at the end of the Eucharist should include good wishes for a happy new year.

COMMENTARY

First Reading: 1 Sam 1:20-22, 24-28
Given today's gospel, which is fixed for Year C, then the reading of 1 Sam is to be preferred (even if it is presented in the lectionary as only an alternative to the reading from Sirach given for year A). The reason it is to be preferred is that it is the perfect text to go with today's section of Luke. Luke had Hannah in mind in several places in his infancy narrative (e.g. the Song of Hannah is the model for the Magnificat), and here is one of the most obvious of those places. The family of Hannah, Elkanah and Samuel go to the place of sacrifice annually and offer sacrifice there: the family of Mary, Joseph and Jesus go likewise to the temple in Jerusalem to offer sacrifice. Then as Samuel is wholly devoted to the Lord's service, there in Jerusalem it becomes clear that Jesus must be in his 'Father's house.'

Today we read this text from 1 Sam in the liturgy not as part of a patrimony of ancient sacred texts which might have some intrinsic meaning, but we read it through the eyes of the gospel writer. It is that reading that gives it significance for us today.

Second Reading: 1 Jn 3:1-2, 21-24
This is one of the few places in extant early Christian writings

where the followers of Jesus are described in terms of being 'children of God' who are lavished with love by their Father. Its use today shifts the focus from the family of Nazareth imagined as Mary, Joseph and Jesus, to the community as the family of faith. As such it broadens this feast into being a reflection on how our status before the Father is transformed by the birth of Jesus within a family, i.e. the reality of human existence.

Gospel: Lk 2:41-52
The temple is a key place in Luke's gospel (see the notes on the gospel for Year B), and here, as the last event in his infancy narrative, he presents Jesus as the Wisdom of Israel. It is in the midst of the temple – where God is present among his people – that Jesus has to be about his Father's business.

HOMILY NOTES

1. One of the differences between being a follower of the Christ and being a follower of a philosophy or a religious guru is that we are devoted to a person, not to a set of ideas. We are interested in Jesus because he is the truth, not simply because he is the messenger. For Christians the messenger is the message; and the messenger is Jesus. We believe we are brought into the Father's kingdom by the Son, not because we adhere to anything that might be said to be Jesus's religious wisdom. Indeed, when one counts up the verses in the gospels that could be said to be Jesus's teaching, and compare it with the number devoted to his life and the events of his life, it becomes abundantly clear that the kerygma is about the person of Jesus, of which what he taught is just a part. God's ultimate revelation is a person, and not either a set of instructions or a body of philosophy. I am always surprised at the reaction of non-Christians (and indeed of fundamentalist Christians who think of God's revelation as 'the bible') when I ask them to bear in mind that Jesus is the only founder of a major religion who left no writings – and indeed that the only reference we have to his writing anything was with his

finger in sand and we do not know what he wrote! The reaction is usually one of complete shock: how can you found a
great world religion and not write a book of wisdom. The
nearest we come is a collection of sayings written down by
his followers of which we have only an indirect record and
over which we have been arguing as to the form and meaning ever since.

2. If it is the person that is the message, then at no point is this
   more obviously the case than when Jesus was an infant, long
   before he could be a wise, kind rabbi able to lead a band of
   disciples. Such devotion to the infant Saviour has been a feature of Christianity down the centuries. It must have been already present at the time Matthew preached his gospel (last
   decades of the first century) for he has the magi offer gifts to
   the infant and fall down and worship the infant. We see it
   even more plainly in the second century with the
   Protoevangelium of James, and it continues right up to the early
   twentieth century with devotions such as to the Infant of
   Prague or in religious names such as St Thérèse of the Child
   Jesus. It has fallen below the horizon in recent decades for a
   variety of reasons, yet it is in devotion to the infant we see
   some of the basic themes of our christology. Today is one day
   in the liturgical year when this theme of devotion to the child
   Jesus can be explored while being in harmony with the overall theme of day.

3. We worship Jesus because in his humanity – humanity with
   all the vulnerability of a child – we see our saviour. The infant's coming among us is the good news of God being close
   to his people. Jesus is Emmanuel. We as his disciples, with
   our strength and wisdom and riches, must be prepared to lay
   it at his feet.

4. We can romantically idealise childhood or we can see childhood as really only the privation of adulthood. Most societies
   tend towards the latter view; contemporary western society
   tends toward the romanticisation of childhood. Devotion to
   the child Jesus is neither one nor other of these attitudes, but

the recognition in prayer that God came among us in every aspect of our humanity. Jesus is our gateway to the Father, not some set of abstractions or practices that we claim to derive from him.

5. It is easy to visit the crib if we do so to show it off to the children: the children wonder at the magical scene, the parents enjoy their children's wonder. It is much harder for us as adults to recapture the wonder of the crib as a visible expression of the wonder of the incarnation:

> In the wonder of the incarnation,
> your eternal Word has brought to the eyes of faith
> a new and radiant vision of your glory.
> In him we see our God made visible
> And so are caught up in the love
> of the God we cannot see.

6. It is easy to bring the children 'to see the crib'; it is much harder for us to pray there – for the crib to cease to be a simple model and for it to become an icon to focus our worship. Yet unless we can find the means to pray at the crib – a physical reality functioning sacramentally – and there worship the child Jesus, we cannot discover true humility, nor understand the adult Jesus when he said: 'Let the children come to me, do not hinder them; for to such belongs the kingdom of God. Truly, I say to you, whoever does not receive the kingdom of God like a child shall not enter it' (Mk 10:14-5/ Lk 18-16-17).

1 January: Solemnity of Mary, Mother of God (Years A, B, C)

Note

The most basic fact about today is that it is New Year's Day, the public holiday that marks the end of the holiday season, and the beginning of any number of other things from diaries to keeping accounts of various sorts. In everyone's eyes it is a special day. If we think of time as made up of 'stressed' (= special days; special time) and 'unstressed' (= ordinary days; everyday time) periods, then this is a 'stressed' day *par excellence*. It is a day that begins very consciously at midnight on New Year's Eve with parties, fireworks, bells, and street theatre, and is ended by the television news showing how this day, because it is this day, has been celebrated around the world. There are other New Year's days (Jewish New Year, Muslim New Year, Chinese New Year), but this is the calendar day that is most widely celebrated. So if people do celebrate by joining together for the Eucharist – and it is an excellent way for a Christian community to begin the New Year – they will expect that this is the focus of the celebration. However, if we follow the liturgical calendar they will be disappointed: there is no mention of today being New Year's Day in the prayers in the *Missal* – indeed the only mention of New Year's Day is found in the solemn blessings (*Missal*, p 368) where there is one for the 'Beginning of the New Year.' This failure to celebrate with those celebrating New Year is a major fault of the calendar reform of 1970. While it seemed to the reformers that there was no better way to mark this day than to make it a celebration of Mary's greatest title, *Theotokos*, that notion is so far away from most people's imagination that it just creates confusion.

So we have the world, and most Christians, celebrating New Year's Day, but the calendar wants to celebrate a Marian feast; but there is still more confusion: one is also celebrating the octave day of Christmas (i.e. liturgically we can still view today as Christmas Day) and there is usually a desire to celebrate this day as 'a day of prayer for peace' – a theme that is just imposed on top of the liturgy. If one tries to celebrate all of these by combining them, the liturgy becomes a muddle: 'we are here to celebrate X and Y and it is also Z and we will also keep in mind ...' Today there is still a fragrance of celebration in the air that the liturgy must capitalise on, and build upon, and sanctify: people know that something new is happening, there is a frisson of expectation, there is a moment of levity and goodwill; this can be the experience that can shape an attitude to the eucharistic mysteries so that the celebration of ordinary life also becomes a celebration of the incarnate One who has made the whole world holy by his presence.

We might wonder how this occurred, especially when there is a Votive Mass for 'The Beginning of the Civil Year' (*Missal*, p 828) but with this rubric: 'This Mass may not be celebrated on 1 January, the solemnity of Mary the Mother of God.' In the pre-1970 rite this day was the Octave Day and the feast of the Circumcision with the single verse, Lk 2:21, as its gospel. In order to make more of this it became the present Marian feast. However, for those parts of the world where New Year was not on 1 January the reform instituted the votive Mass with its more inclusive theology of sanctifying the experience of people as they celebrate. Alas, more and more places are thereby left without a Mass-text today that links with most people's actual celebrations. This absence indicates a cultural and ritual weakness in the present calendar; and frequently causes a dissonance in celebrations. There is a strong case to approach today by ignoring this day as a Marian feast and as the octave-day of Christmas, and focus on it as New Year's Day, even using the Votive Mass, praying that in the time-period that is beginning those gathered will grow in holiness.

CELEBRANT'S GUIDE

Introduction to the Celebration
This is a great day of joy the world over: a new year has just begun and with it is the hope of new relationships of peace, new

endeavours to make life better for the human family, and resolutions to start afresh in many areas of our individual lives. We as Christians share this joy for our good news is that the Father of mercies is always extending his love and care so that we can return to him and start over afresh. In sending us his Son as a human being born of Mary in Bethlehem he showed the depth of that love: he offered a new era to the whole human race, and now we are celebrating the beginning of the two thousandth and … year of that era. Now let us reflect on all that we want to start afresh in the coming year, let us ask the Father to help us overcome the old ways of sin and death, and to give us his help in our new endeavours.

Rite of Penance

Son of Mary, your birth is our new beginning, Lord have mercy. Prince of Peace, your birth is our reconciliation, Christ have mercy.

Word made flesh, your birth is our hope for the future, Lord have mercy.

Headings for Readings
First Reading

This is the great blessing used by the people of Israel and still used by us today in our liturgy: it prays that God may see and hear our needs and grant us peace.

Second Reading

The Father's plan for the happiness of humanity came to its fulfillment when the Son of God was born of Mary.

Gospel

Exactly eight days ago we celebrated the birth of Jesus; today we celebrate what happened eight days after that: Mary and Joseph took the infant to be circumcised and then publicly named him Jesus.

Prayer of the Faithful

This is a day when still in some places the Eucharist is used as a formula for civic religion, and dignitaries and politicians wish to be seen as taking part in a religious exercise to mark the new year. If this is the case, then it is best if representatives read each petition and the celebrant voices the prayer 'Lord hear us.'

President

Sisters and brothers, on this day of new beginning in our human lives, let us pray for our own needs, those of our neighbours, and those of all our human brothers and sisters.

Reader(s)

1. That in the coming year, the two thousandth and ... year since the all-holy Mother of God gave birth to our saviour in Bethlehem, that we his people may bear witness to his coming and on-going presence in the world. Lord hear us.

2. That during this coming year, the whole church on earth may be united with one another to be the hands, and feet, and mouth of the Word made Flesh of the virgin Mary. Lord hear us.

3. That in the year that is now beginning, the whole church on earth may be united with the church in heaven, with Mary the Mother of God, all the angels and saints, in offering glory to God. Lord hear us.

4. As people the world over begin a new year, let us pray that there will be a new realisation of the need to build peace between communities and countries so that every human being can live life free from violence. Lord hear us.

5. On this New Year's Day, let us pray for all who serve in public office that they will act with integrity and justice. Lord hear us.

6. Facing a new year, let us be conscious of all who are hungry, poor, oppressed and pray that during this year their sufferings will be eased. Lord hear us.

7. At the start of another year, as once again we mark the earth's journey around the sun, let us recall the order in God's creation and pray that we will respect the creation as God's handiwork and not exploit it. Lord hear us.

8. On this day of New Year's resolutions, that God will strengthen our resolve, help us with our good desires, and give us the grace of perseverance. Lord hear us.

9. As another year begins for this community of faith, that we will grow in love for one another, for our neighbours, and for the Lord. Lord hear us.

President

Father, a new time began when the all holy Mother of God gave birth to the Word, the source of all life, in Bethlehem. Because of his sharing our life with us, we can now pray to you for our needs, the needs of the whole church, and of all humankind. As we begin a new period in our journey as your people this day, hear our needs and grant them through that same Christ, our Lord. Amen.

Eucharistic Prayer

Preface of the Blessed Virgin Mary I (P56), (*Missal*, p 459): the insertion formula given in the Missal, p 53, can be tweaked slightly: as we celebrate on this first day of a new year the motherhood of the Blessed Virgin Mary.

Eucharistic Prayer I with the special Christmas form of the prayer 'In union with the whole church ...'

Invitation to the Our Father

Gathered together in Christ, this is the first time this year that we as a community pray the great prayer of all Christians:

Sign of Peace

This is a day of new beginnings, and of leaving the past behind: this means we must be ready to be reconciled and desire to build peace. Knowing that peace is the will of God and that he blesses those who are peacemakers, let us begin this New Year by giving Christ's peace to each other.

Invitation to Communion
Jesus Christ is the same yesterday, today, and forever; behold
him who now invites us to partake of his table

Communion Reflection
This is the octave day of Christmas and for most people the
Christmas season actually ends with this day and the return of
people to work the next day. Hence, this is the last day for
Christmas carols: their simple joyfulness allows them to be a
very seasonal form of thanksgiving. Moreover, carols have two
other advantages: first, they link this day clearly to Christmas;
and second, they are widely known and so can make visitors
feel at home.
For a more reflective option, use the hymn 'Unto us a child is
given' (*Liturgy of the Hours,* vol 1, pp 553*-554*) as a poem.

Conclusion
Solemn Blessing 3 for the Beginning of the New Year (*Missal*, p
368).

COMMENTARY

First Reading: Num 6:22-27
The choice of this reading for today might, at first sight, seem
strange, but it is the perfect accompaniment to Gal 4:4-7. In the
Law only the son of Aaron (i.e. the priestly tribe within the
whole people) could invoke the name of God (i.e. pronounce a
blessing). Now, Paul tells us, every adopted son (the whole people) can call on the name of God (Abba, Father). So now there is
not a priestly tribe within the people, but the whole people are
priestly (i.e. they can call down the Lord's blessing).
    The logic of the selection of readings today works like this:
this is the eighth day after Christmas; therefore we read the
gospel that mentions this eighth day after Christmas (Lk 2:16-
21). That gospel focuses on circumcision as the event of the
eighth day and presents it as significant for our christology;
therefore we read another passage from the New Testament that

spells out one way of understanding that significance (Gal 4:4-7).

That second reading speaks of the new people of God being able, because of their dignity as adopted sons, to call on the name of the Father, hence the choice of the Old Testament reading which gives an account of the paradigmatic case of the people of Israel calling on the name of God through the sons of Aaron when they invoke the blessing of God on the people.

Second Reading: Galatians 4:4-7
This passage aligns perfectly with today's gospel as one theological reflection on the meaning of what is given in narrative form in the gospel. The Son of God becomes the son of Mary and is under the law – i.e. even to the extent of being circumcised (cf Phil 3:4-5) – so that God's plan can be fulfilled. The inner rationale for why God has chosen to act in this way in his plan of salvation is presented by Paul as to make us capable of being adopted by the Father. If his Son has become one of us, then any of us can become an adopted son. And, if a son, then someone who can address God in the manner of a son: Abba, Father.

Bear in mind two points. First, as it stands the reading only mentions 'sons' not daughters; and this causes offence. Paul's rhetoric is elegant: Jesus the Son, we the sons; but if this is referred to then it must take account of the fact that that is a rhetorical style that our culture rejects. Second, abba is not equivalent to 'dad' or 'pop'; it is a familiar form that only a member of the family can use, it is not a casual form. Again our culture – which virtually never expects a child to address a parent using a formal polite form – is at variance with earlier practice, but it is one thing to the a member of God's family, quite another to be familiar with God. So avoid attempting to 'translate' abba as daddy, and simply explain it as 'my father'.

Gospel: Lk 2:16-21
This element of the infancy story is found only in Luke, yet its first section, the shepherds standing around the infant in the

feed trough in wonder, has become one of the great images of Christmas and is celebrated in the crib. However, today's gospel while focusing on the infant also moves the scene onwards to the beginning of the Christ's life within the people of Israel.

We can distinguish four elements in this reading:

1. The reaction of the shepherds to Jesus (vv 16-18 and 20). The shepherds listen to the voice of the angel and thereby do the will of God. They recognise simultaneously one at whom they wonder and so tell the message to others, and also one of their own: another shepherd. The infant is the shepherd who will gather scatted Israel and so bring joy to the people. This notion of the re-gathering shepherd of scattered Israel is one which disappeared from prominence within the history of the church being replaced with the less precise, and less messianic, image of Christ the Good Shepherd; however, we should note that it is widely found in the first century Christian documents (e.g. it is a key component in the eucharistic theology of the *Didache*).

In short, the shepherds realise that this infant can do the task of shepherding: the gathering in of the People of God for the establishment of the kingdom.

2. The reaction of Mary to the events surrounding the birth (v 19). Mary is presented in Luke as a model of faith and believing trust: she does not see the whole plan of God at once nor understand all she is going through; rather she has to ponder, wonder, and try to make sense of the unfolding events as part of God's unfolding providence.

3. The circumcision (v 21). This event shows that Jesus is 'born under the law' and has now entered the ritual and liturgical life of the People. The Lord of the covenant has now accepted being part of the other side of the bargain. In this event, Luke sees Jesus being stamped, literally, as a member of God's People. We should remember that Luke was writing for an audience that was apparently made up mainly of gentile converts, and that circumcision was seen as a disgrace right across the Greco-Roman world – indeed many Jews sought medical aid to attempt to disguise circumcision so that they would not be objects of derision.

Moreover, by the time that Luke wrote the church had already been through its first great crisis (whether to keep circumcision or not as a ritual) and had rejected circumcision – a decision that Luke agreed with fully. So Luke's insertion of this detail shows he wants this recalled not as a simple fact, but for what it tells us about Jesus's relation to the People and to the Father. We should compare what Paul wrote: 'though I myself have reason for confidence in the flesh also. If any other man thinks he has reason for confidence in the flesh, I have more: circumcised on the eighth day, of the people of Israel, of the tribe of Benjamin, a Hebrew born of Hebrews; as to the law a Pharisee …' (Phil 3:4-5). For Jesus to be circumcised on the eighth day shows that in every detail he is part of the People that he has come to save.

4. The naming (v 21). This is a deliberate linking back to the name given at 1:31. The act of naming identifies the infant's vocation and destiny.

HOMILY NOTES

1. Today is a new start for so many things: it is the beginning of a new time, it offers us new opportunities, it is a time of starting afresh, it is a time of new resolution, it is a moment to let go of the past. These are among the most basic themes of all human ritual. There is some sort of new year festival found in every religion: we have only to think of the Akitu new year festival of Babylonians which has left its imprint on the Old Testament, the great stone-age burial mound of Newgrange in Ireland which celebrates an annual solar event and thus marks a new year, or the fact that while in our society many wonder about the appropriateness of Christian ritual for Christmas, no one doubts the need for rituals for new year. The notion of renewal, or starting over seems to be deep within us and we need to celebrate it.

2. This notion of the need to be able to start over, to let by-gones be by-gones is precisely what we celebrate as the redemption Christ has won for us. He comes to us with the offer of his forgiveness, with the possibility of a new start, a re-birth.

This is why the basic Christian ritual is baptism: the past is over, life begins afresh. This is the same renewal that lies at the heart of Christian forgiveness and the Sacrament of Reconciliation: the past is dead, we can begin anew.

3. The birth of Jesus was a fresh start for the whole of humanity: that is why we Christians started counting the years from that time just over two thousand years ago.

4. Just as we want to start over today in so many ways, the Lord offers us the opportunity to start over afresh in lives through his forgiveness. He offers us the loving hand of his friendship at each gathering at his table. He offers us the strength and grace to walk towards the good in our new year's resolutions.

5. For many people on this day, that the past will remain past and that a fresh start can be made is just a deeply held desire that may be simply the assertion of optimism over experience; for Christians the forgiveness and new beginning we all need is the very heart of the good news of Jesus the Christ.

Second Sunday of Christmas (Years A, B, C)

Introduction to the Celebration

Christmas is now something we are beginning to talk about as having happened: 'How did you get over Christmas?' are the opening words of many of our conversations at the moment. But for us Christians we are still trying to plumb some of the depths of what it means to confess that the Word became flesh and dwelt among us. So we have gathered here to offer thanks to the Father through Christ, while in our readings we will be trying to make sense of what it means to say that 'Christ has come among us.'

Rite of Penance

Option c. iii (*Missal*, p 392-3) is appropriate.

Headings for Readings
First Reading

Today's three readings are actually three great hymns. First, we have a hymn singing the praises of the wisdom of God. The divine Wisdom is present in all human history: he has pitched his tent in Jacob; and we Christians believe that that presence has come to its fullness when the Word became flesh in Jesus Christ. In Jesus, the Son of God has pitched his tent in our humanity.

The Psalm

The short response option, 'Alleluia,' is unsuitable as the note being struck in each reading is that the Word has been made flesh and to acknowledge this is itself an act of praise, and so 'the Word was made flesh and lived among us' is the response to use today.

Second Reading

Since the Second Reading can be omitted, it can also be changed.

Rather than the disjointed reading found in the Lectionary, one could substitute the whole of the Ephesian hymn (as found in the *Breviary*): Eph 1:3-10. Another possibility is to drop the second section of the reading, verses 15-18, and just read the verses 3-6 which do have a unity in today's context.

Our second reading is an early Christian hymn praising the Father for sending us his Son through whom each of us can become his daughter or son. This hymn we have sung since the very first days of Christianity.

Gospel

The opening of St John's gospel is another early Christian hymn praising the Word of the Father who has come among us as our brother Jesus: 'The Word was made flesh, he lived among us, and we saw his glory, the glory that is his as the only Son of the Father, full of grace and truth'.

Prayer of the Faithful

Use the Sample Formula for the Christmas Season given on p 998 of the Missal.

Eucharistic Prayer

Preface of Christmas I (P3) is in line with the Wisdom theme of the first reading and the Johannine prologue; these find echoes also in Eucharistic Prayer III.

Invitation to the Our Father

Rejoicing in the glory of the Word made flesh, let us pray in him to the Father:

Sign of Peace

All who have accepted the Word made flesh have been given power to become children of God, let us exchange the kiss of peace as a token of how we now should live.

Invitation to Communion
Behold the Wisdom that abides by the throne of the Father, the
Word made flesh as our food of life, behold the Lamb who takes
away the sins of the world. Happy are we who share in his banquet.

Communion Reflection
Father,
today our hearts are filled with joy as we recognise in Christ the
revelation of your love.
No eye can see his glory as our God, yet now he is seen as one
like us.
In the wonder of the incarnation the eternal Word has brought
to the eyes of faith a new and radiant vision of your glory.
He is your Son before all ages, yet now he is born in time. He has
come to lift up all things to himself, to restore unity to creation,
and to lead us from exile into your heavenly kingdom.
In him we see our God made visible and so are caught up in love
of the God we cannot see.
Today a new light has dawned upon the world: God has become
one with humankind, and humankind has become one again
with God. Amen.
(Adapted from the Christmas Prefaces)

Conclusion
Solemn Blessing 3 for the Beginning of the New Year (*Missal*, p.
368) is appropriate as for most people what is most obvious
about this time is that is the beginning of the new year – and we
should within our Eucharistic assembly formally ask God's
blessings on the coming year.

COMMENTARY

First Reading: Ecclesiasticus [i.e. Sirach] 24:1-4, 12-6
This is one of the hymns that Wisdom sings about her own work
in the creation: she has been there since the beginning, she has
done all things well, and she has been ordered to pitch her tent

in Jacob (Sir 24:8: *en Iakob kataskénoson*) and to be present in the history of Israel. This hymn is hovering in the background of today's gospel – which is the well-focused target of all three readings today – for the Johannine prologue presents the Word as being present among his people (Jn 1:9-10), and then finally 'pitching his tent' in human nature itself in the incarnation: 'the Word became flesh and pitched his tent among us' (Jn 1:14). This parallelism is lost in that we habitually translate 'pitched his tent among us' (*eskénosen en humin*) as 'dwelt among us'.

It was out of this strand of the wisdom literature and thinking of Israel that the early Christian communities drew some of their richest language and images with which to give voice to their encounter with Jesus: and in today's second reading and gospel we have splendid examples where they took over not only the theology and language but even the liturgical form. It is as if such splendid thoughts can only be expressed in the hymnody of liturgy rather than in the brashness of abstract prose.

There is such confusion over the names of this book that it is not very helpful that the Lectionary uses the out-dated Latin 'applied' name 'Ecclesiasticus' when all modern editions of the scriptures (i.e. those which include this book in their canon: Catholics and Orthodox) in English, and all scholarship on this text, use the name 'Sirach.'

Second Reading: Eph 1:3-6, 15-8
This is one of the earliest Christological hymns. Its praise is addressed to the Father as an act of thanksgiving for his greatest act of love: bringing humanity into the life of the Beloved. The Beloved is one of the titles of Jesus in the early church which later slipped into the background (it is used here and in Col 1:13; in Mk 1:11 and parallels: Mt 3:17 and Luke 3:22; in Mk 9:7 and parallel: Mt 17:5; in Mt 12:18; and in Lk 20:13). The Beloved is the one who does the will of the Father, whom the Father rejoices in, and who expressed all that the Father desires for humanity. The Beloved of the Father makes, in turn, his brothers and sisters his beloved ones – hence the usage of the term in the epistles.

This is the perfect reading to accompany the Johannine prologue, and so an ideal reading for today when the focus of the
readings is reflection on the mystery we have been celebrating at
Christmas.

Gospel: Jn 1:1-18 (shorter form: Jn 1:1-5, 9-14)
John the Evangelist, in all probability, took an existing early
Christian hymn – with a shape very like the shorter form of
today's gospel – and adapted it to be the prologue of his whole
narration of the Christ-event. The insertion, vv 6-9, is John's way
of fitting in the ministry of John the Baptist into the whole plan
of the revelation of the Word in Jesus. Even a quick reading of
the gospel shows that these verses do not seem 'to fit' well: there
is a jump from one subject to another, then another jump back
again. So there are good reasons on many occasions for drop-
ping those verses relating to John the Baptist and reading the
shorter form provided in the Lectionary. First, there is the pastoral reason that it makes the passage easier to follow aurally especially for those for whom the passage may not be very familiar. Second, scripture is the church's book not only because the
text only makes sense within the community, but because it
arose out of that community: so reading an early Christian
hymn re-acquaints us with the earliest moments of our community's liturgy, with some of the basic items in our memory.

However, it is a fact that one of the great preachers of our
narrative as Christians, John the Evangelist, added these verses
about John the Baptist, and it is basic to the churches' memory
that each of these great preachers of the narrative (the four
gospel writers) are individually respected – communities did
not just have one gospel: they held on to four despite the fact
that three of them (Mt, Mk, Lk) are remarkably similar – as each
gives a different slant on the mystery of the Christ; and as John's
gospel remarks: the world could not contain all the books needed
to write down all that could be said about Jesus (Jn 21:25).
Hence, there are times when we should read this text exactly as
it has been transmitted to us and look at its particular theologi-

cal vision. Perhaps, today, when the crowds of Christmas have disappeared and the rush and excitement have died down is a good time to offer a slower, deeper reflection on the mystery of the Word made flesh in Jesus. In which case, use the full text of Jn (1:1-18).

1. The Johannine prologue is one of the truly classic Christian texts: generation after generation have found it a way towards helping them reflect on the mystery of the God we profess, the nature of our identity as God's daughters and son, and the mystery of the Logos entering into our hearts through becoming flesh in Jesus of Nazareth. It is used in the middle of the Angelus, in the Nicene Creed, in every book of Christian theology, virtually every one of the Fathers offered an exegesis of it, and, indeed, for centuries it was read at every celebration of the Eucharist in the Roman Rite as 'the Last Gospel'. However, given that it is such an important text, it is also one of those texts which gets 'skipped over' in preaching as 'too difficult', 'too theological' ('theological' being used as an adjective of abuse), or 'too far above the heads of my congregation'. But reflection on the mystery of mysteries is always more difficult than a moral-teaching story. Believers cannot avoid having a theology (even if they do not realise they have one), and stretching the minds of those with us in the Eucharistic assembly is the primary task of preaching.

2. Let us assume that by today the Christmas crowd has disappeared, the rush to get ready for Christmas is over, and now there is some less pressurised time while it is still festive in spirit: now is a good time to offer a reflection on the mystery of the Christ-event that would be too elaborate for Christmas Day. One way to do this is to offer a formal exegesis of the text in three parts. After the gospel is read and the assembly has sat down, announce the plan explicitly: to take this basic text and lead a reflection on it so that everyone in the assembly can be fed by it.

3. The prologue can be broken into four sections:
    a. verses 1-5;
    b. verses 6-8;
    c. verses 9-15; and
    d. verses 16-18.

    When everyone is sitting, including the preacher – standing
    is not a posture which says 'I am leading a meditative explor-
    ation' of a sacred text, someone (other than the preacher)
    reads the first of these sections, then follows the reflection,
    then the pattern is repeated until all eighteen verses have
    been reflected on.

4. Section a: Jn 1:1-5. The gospel begins with the divine realm:
    the Word dwelling eternally in the bosom of the Father. This
    is the mystery that is at the beginning of all that is created: the
    creation that we see and belong to as material beings. God
    also is the source of the invisible creation: all those beings –
    the angels – created by God but which do not belong to the
    universe of our existence. All that exists has being made
    through the Word: we have the stamp of the Word somehow
    in the very depths of our being. We come into existence from
    God, we have the spark of the divine in our existence, and we
    have been made to be united ultimately in the life of God.

    We Christians cannot imagine God simply as the 'alien
    other' as so many humans imagine God: we are made by
    God, we are made through the Word and we find our true
    identity in God. God is not some mighty way-off force, but
    our very source. In him we can find our happiness.

Quotes for reflection:
God is more intimate to us than our most intimate thought
(Augustine).
Humans 'search for God and perhaps grope for him and find
him, though indeed he is not far from each one of us: for "In him
we live and move and have our being"' (Paul preaching as told
in Acts 17:27-8).
We believe in one Lord, Jesus Christ, ... begotten not made, of

one Being with the Father. Through him all things were made.
(The Nicene Creed).

5. Section b: Jn 1:6-8. Having spoken of all creation – the ele-
    ments, the living beings, us humans, the angels – coming
    forth from God through the Word, now we enter the human
    world of history. From speaking about all humanity and all
    time, John now speaks of one human being: John the Baptist.
    God's care is not just for the whole of creation as a generality:
    he enters into the personal lives and histories of each human
    being in their specific situation, culture, with all his or her
    problems and limitations as well as his or her talents and
    possibilities. John was sent from God. His vocation was to
    announce and point out the Anointed One. He was the
    prophet of our great Prophet. He had a task unique to his
    moment and place in human history: 'to bear witness to the
    light, that all might believe through him.' He is our great
    model: each of us has this same task within our own situ-
    ation, our own moment, in our own small world. We are 'not
    the light, but' are called 'to bear witness to the light.'
    Whenever the light is obscured by our wicked deeds, by the
    poor suffering while we enjoy plenty, by our indifference in
    the face of evil, we fail in our basic vocation. In failing to an-
    nounce the Light, we deny him.

Quotes for reflection:
'His future coming was proclaimed by all the prophets … John
the Baptist was his herald and made him known when at last he
came' (Advent Preface II).
'You [Lord] chose John the Baptist from all the prophets to show
the world its redeemer' (Preface of John the Baptist).

6. Section c: Jn 9-15. Now the Word enters the history of the creation as an individual: not in a massive display of force – we
   tend to think of force and power when we think of the divine
   – but in gentleness. He was already in the depths of every-

thing created; now he entered the creation, in a new way, to bring all to perfection. Christ is not a policeman announcing rules alien to us, but gently calling us to come to that perfection of which each of us is capable. 'He came to his own home, and his own people received him not. But to all who received him, who believed in his name, he gave power to become children of God.' This is who we are: the children of God, those who have accepted his life into their own lives in baptism.

The Word has become flesh: this has been the reason for all our celebrations at Christmas; we have beheld his glory, this is why we can be the people of joyfulness. The Word has pitched his tent among us, in all our needs, among our sufferings, in the ordinary ups and down of everyday life.

Quotes for reflection:
'In the wonder of the incarnation your eternal Word has brought to the eyes of faith a new and radiant vision of your glory' (Christmas Preface I).
'Christ is your Son before all ages, yet now he is born in time. He has come to lift up all things to himself, to restore unity to creation, and to lead mankind from exile into your heavenly kingdom' (Christmas Preface II).
'We believe in one Lord, Jesus Christ ... he came down from heaven, by the power of the Holy Spirit he became incarnate from the Virgin Mary and was made man' (The Nicene Creed).

7. Section d: Jn 1: 16-18. So who are we that have gathered here for this Eucharist? What has happened to us to bring us together as a community of sisters and brothers, charged with a common task and with individual distinct vocations? We are those who have received 'from' Christ's 'fullness'. We 'have all received, grace upon grace'. Life with God, life in the divine presence is ours because of Jesus Christ: 'grace and truth came through Jesus Christ.' We are the people to whom the Lord offers strength in weakness, to whom he offers com-

fort for our wounds, healing for our illnesses, sight for our blindness, wisdom for our stupidity, and forgiveness for our sins.

In Jesus we have seen our God made visible: 'No one has ever seen God; the only Son, who is in the bosom of the Father, he has made him known.'

Quotes for reflection:

'Today you fill our hearts with joy as we recognise in Christ the revelation of your love. No eye can see his glory as our God, yet now he is seen as one like us' (Christmas Preface II).

'In him we see our God made visible and so are caught up in love of the God we cannot see' (Christmas Preface I).

'Today ... a new light has dawned upon the world: God has become one with humankind, and humankind has become one again with God. The eternal Word has taken upon himself our human weakness, giving our mortal nature immortal value' (Christmas Preface III – *adapted*).

Epiphany of Our Lord (Years A, B, C)

Note

The word *epiphania* is, as is always pointed out, a Greek word (in Latin dress) that means 'manifestation,' 'showing,' 'public display'. But it is its being a Greek word that is especially important as it reminds us that the origins of this feast lie within the liturgies of the eastern churches. Indeed, it is the only feast in the western calendar that bears a Greek name (e.g. we refer to the Assumption not the *Koimesis*, and to the Transfiguration not the *Metamorphosis*). This fact that it is a Greek feast that has become embedded within the western liturgy is significant as it explains some of the liturgical tensions inherent in the texts of the liturgy today. Originally, in the East, this feast was the counterpart of the western Nativity and embraced the baptism of Christ, the nativity including the arrival of the magi, and 'the first of the signs' at Cana. Once adopted in the west it could not embrace the nativity as this was already celebrated on 25 December, but since it came so soon after Christmas it could be related to the nativity by being the day of the arrival of the magi. So it moved from being the celebration of the mystery of the public appearing of Jesus to Israel and the nations, to being the historicised commemoration of a post-birth event.

We now have a legacy of this transition from the celebration of a mystery to the recollection of an 'event' in that for western Christians it is officially called 'epiphany' but that means little because it is really the 'Feast of The Three Kings' (as it is called in Germany) or the 'Feast of the Star' (as an eighth century Irish calendar names it). Moreover, when the reform of the liturgy took place in the late 1960s the various teams that worked on the Liturgy of the Hours and the Liturgy of the Eucharist do not seem to have spoken to one another. Hence, in the renewed *Breviary* this feast now has almost the same range of meanings as in the eastern churches as can be seen from the Magnificat

Antiphon: 'Three wonders mark this day we celebrate: today the star led the Magi to the Manger; today water was changed into wine at the marriage feast; today Christ desired to be baptised by John in the river Jordan to bring us salvation.' However, those charged with renewing the Eucharistic Liturgy continued to see it as the festival of the magi's arrival in Bethlehem, as can be seen in the Opening Prayer: 'you revealed your Son to the nations by the guidance of a star ...'. Since these resources are intended for use with an ordinary gathering for the Eucharist, it is this commemoration of the visit of the magi that will be the exclusive focus of attention here. Indeed, paying attention to other aspects of this feast can just be simply confusing given its location in the active liturgical memory of most communities. However, this does commit one to approaching the feast using the mechanisms of allegorical interpretation to an extent not often found in the liturgy since the 1960s.

This then leads us to the question about how are these visitors to Bethlehem to be understood: as magi (whatever they are) or kings? Matthew sees them as astrologers (*magoi*) who recognise that this event affects the whole creation and is a message for all nations (see the conclusion of his gospel). These magi have subsequently become philosophers, priests from religions that recognised their own religions' inadequacy, or most commonly since the eighth century, kings based on them fulfilling certain verses in the Psalms and in Isaiah (used in today's liturgy). As kings they attracted names (Caspar, Melchior, Balthasar) and eventually even their relics were found (now in Köln Cathedral) and this became as much their feast, as Christian saints, as a celebration of an event in the Christmas cycle. Moreover, as the festival of the Three Kings it established itself deeply within western culture and still today in Catholic areas of central Europe one sees written on door lintels in white chalk (blessed specially today) '20+C+M+B+05' invoking a blessing on the house as being worthy to be the dwelling visited by C (Caspar), M (Melchior), and B (Balthasar). All this should remind us that we are dealing here with a far more complex liturgical memory within Christian culture than simply what is found in twelve verses of Matthew's gospel.

Introduction to the Celebration
Today we recall the strange and exotic visitors who went to greet the infant Jesus. They remind us that in a myriad of ways the Christ beckons all of us to gather with him and offer thanks to the Father.

Rite of Penance
Lord Jesus, you received the tribute of gold showing us that you are our king; forgive us those times when we have used our resources badly or unjustly, Lord have mercy.
Lord Jesus, you received the gift of incense showing us that you are our priest; forgive us those times when we have failed to offer you our worship or failed to pray, Christ have mercy.
Lord Jesus, you received an offering of sweet myrrh showing us that you are our healing saviour; forgive us those times when we caused suffering or bitterness, Lord have mercy.

Headings for Readings
First Reading
All the nations will seek out the Lord when he comes.

Second Reading
The goodness of God is now manifested to all humanity in Jesus; we Christians live in the Age of the Epiphany.

Gospel
All humanity is invited to discover their deepest desires in the wonder of the Christ.

Prayer of the Faithful
President
Friends, today the nations came and fell down before the Christ, for through him our prayers are brought before the Father; we

too are in the presence of the Lord Jesus, so through him let us make our petitions to the Father.

Reader(s)

1. On this day when the magi fell down and worshipped the Lord's Anointed, may we and all Christians renew our dedication to Christ's service and to prayer. Lord hear us.

2. On this day when our great Prophet was pointed out to the nations through a star, we pray that God may send a light to all who seek meaning in their lives, all who seek the ways of justice, and all who seek to fathom the mystery of existence. Lord hear us.

3. On this day when wise men placed their treasures at the service of the Word made flesh, we pray that each of us in this church will have the generosity to put our talents and treasures at the service of the good news in the coming year. Lord hear us.

4. On this day when our High Priest received the gift of incense, we pray that this community as God's priestly people may engage more deeply in our liturgy with our minds and hearts and bodies during the coming year.

5. On this day when our great Healer and Saviour received the gift of myrrh, we pray that this community may be the bringer of joy and sweetness to all who are suffering or lonely or afraid, and may bring help and comfort to all who are sick or in need of healing. Lord hear us.

6. On this day when our King received the tribute of gold, let us pray that we will have the wisdom to use our economic resources wisely, justly, and in the service of the poor and needy. Lord hear us.

7. On this day when we rejoice in the gathering of all nations around Emmanuel, let us pray that all who have died in the peace of Christ and all the dead whose faith is known to God alone may be gathered together in heaven. Lord hear us.

President

Father, this day is one of joy for us for your Spirit has revealed to us the mystery of your Word made flesh; look on us with love and grant us our needs for we make our prayer through your Son, Jesus Christ, our Lord. Amen.

Preparation of the Gifts

Given the more informal style of much contemporary liturgy, the use of incense at the Eucharist has all but disappeared even on major feasts. However, this is the day when you should make an exception in even the most relaxed of liturgical settings. Given that one of the gifts of the magi was incense it seems a missed opportunity not to offer this gift of precious smelling perfume as part of our worship today. First incense the gifts, and then have the thurifer incense the whole congregation. This incensing shows that we are collectively a priesthood – an image based in the early Christian memory of those who could offer incense in the temple (cf Lk 1:9) – who can stand and offer praise to God. So instead of the formalist incensation of the people from one point in the building (the former practice was for the congregation to receive three separate double-swings from the entrance of the 'sanctuary'), the thurifer should move through the people incensing them and making this a very obvious, and special, part of today's liturgy.

Eucharistic Prayer

Preface of the Epiphany (P6); and use Eucharistic Prayer I because it has a special Communicantes for today.

Invitation to the Our Father

The Christ was manifested to the nations so that people from every place under heaven could call on the Father in prayer, and so we say:

Sign of Peace

The Son of God came with the message of peace to all the nations and peoples; let us pray for the peace of the world as we offer each other the sign of the peace that is amongst us.

Invitation to Communion

Behold the Word made flesh, behold him before whom the wise men came and fell down and worshipped; happy are we who today are in his presence.

Communion Reflection
This is, in effect, the last 'day of Christmas' for this year, so it is the last possible day when a Christmas Carol is appropriate. Some of these works are the jolly vessels of quite rich theology and, indeed, some are appropriate as communion reflections. A case in point for this day is the carol 'The first Noel'; all the verses of which, apart from the first, are focused on the arrival of the wise men.

Conclusion
Solemn Blessing 4 for Epiphany (*Missal*, p 369).

COMMENTARY

First Reading: Is 60:1-6 and Ps 71
This oracle opens the section of Third-Isaiah that describes the glories of the New Zion of the time of redemption. Israel is no longer a puny kingdom that is regularly overrun by its neighbours because it is at the junction of Egypt and Mesopotamia – in effect, a wilderness cross-roads – but is the very centre of the world: now all look to it, and come to it, rather than just trample over it in passing.

It is this passage, with its reference to kings offering tribute of gold and incense, along with today's psalm, both read by the church as prophecies fulfilled in Jesus, that gave rise to the belief that the three magi mentioned in Mt 2, were actually three kings. In reading this passage, today's psalm, and today's gospel in combination – with the result that we see in the statues of the three kings in our cribs – we are engaging in the kind of reading of scripture that has characterised the church's use of scripture throughout most of its history.

Second Reading: Eph 3:2-3, 5-6
Ephesians was most probably written between 70 and 95 AD by someone who was a disciple of Paul; hence it comes from the same period as Matthew's gospel, and reflects the same level of development within the church's theology with regard to the

universal significance of Jesus. The church now preaches the mystery that was hidden in the past, and indeed that mystery is now made manifest to the nations. The church therefore can be said to live, through the work of the Spirit, in the 'Age of the Epiphany'.

In the Jerusalem Bible lectionary the word 'pagans' has been used instead of 'the nations' (*ta ethné*) and so a link to the first reading/psalm, and a key theme of the whole liturgy today, is lost.

Gospel: Mt 2:1-12
This is one more facet of a single reality in the gospel: the infancy narrative which runs from 1:1 to 2:23. When read today as a discreet 'historical event' that unity is disfigured, but such a reading is almost inevitable given the way that this feast has developed in the West. However, when we note how Is 60:1-6 was read in combination with this gospel passage by the church to produce the 'three kings', we should note that this was not arbitrary combination of texts; because when Matthew wrote he implicitly quoted those verses of Isaiah with its images of light coming in darkness, nations turning to this new day, the world's rulers coming and doing homage, bringing with them royal gifts and then the travellers knowing real joy.

However, when reading the passage the point to try to keep in mind is that this is a story to tell us something of the inner identity of Jesus: it is christology rather than interesting reminiscence. And the sort of questions to avoid is those astronomical ones: was it a comet or a star or a conjunction? Such questions may provoke curiosities from astronomers-turned-autodidact-exegetes, but they miss the point of the gospel completely.

HOMILY NOTES

1. This feast cannot escape the links with the colourful exotic figures in the crib and their gifts. However, the task of the preacher is to draw attention to those aspects of the mystery of the incarnation that Matthew wished to highlight by intro-

ducing the story of the eastern visitors into his infancy narrative.

2. In a nutshell, the infancy narratives in both Luke and Matthew should be seen as 'identity cards': they tell us about who Jesus is, before we hear anything about what he did. But they approach the question of identity using the forms of historical narrative rather than abstract theological categories. Once this is stated then each of the episodes within these narratives, such as the visit of the magi, must be seen as expressing various aspects of the mysterious identity of the Anointed One. So what does this story tell us about Jesus and our faith in him?

3. That Jesus was the one for whom Israel waited over the generations of promise was established by Matthew at the very beginning of his gospel in the genealogy. However, there was also a strand of messianic faith that the Christ would not only bring salvation to Israel, but to all 'the nations', the whole of humanity. We find this faith in the oracle in Zechariah: 'Thus says the Lord of hosts: In those days ten men from nations of every language shall take hold of a Jew, grasping his garment and saying, "Let us go with you, for we have heard that God is with you"' (8:23). Now with the arrival of these magi, representatives of the nations, this prophecy is fulfilled and one more aspect of the nature of Jesus is revealed. Jesus is the one who is awaited by all nations.

4. The message of the Christians is that God has sent us his Son in Jesus Christ; today we rejoice that this mystery of God-with-us is not something that is confined to a select few, but something that is for all humanity.

5. Matthew is careful to show that while God reveals the Anointed One's coming by a star, it is also something that comes through the magi's own deep searching. In this Matthew's gospel is very different from Luke's gospel where the angel tells the shepherds who has come and what it means and what to do, and then they do it. In Matthew we have professional searchers who realise that there is a greater

mystery beyond their present conditions and then set out to find it. They follow the evidence, they at first come to the wrong conclusion when they go to Herod's court, and the truth only becomes clear when they find themselves in the presence of Jesus. The Christ, and his gospel, is thus seen as the fulfillment of human longings and of the human search for the truth – not as something imposed on humanity from outside that is destructive of human desires and creativity. Alas, we Christians often present the gospel in just such a negative way.

6. To celebrate this feast is to rejoice that God's love has become available to us and that that love invites a response from us: to offer to Truth himself all our human talents.

Baptism of the Lord (Year A)

Note

This feast's history really begins in 1970 when it was chosen as the last moment of the Christmas cycle. It has no conceptual link with Christmas, except it could be argued that in the eastern rites it is part of Epiphany and so could be seen as an extension of Epiphany (and it is so linked in the current western Liturgy of the Hours). However, that is not how it is presented in the eucharistic liturgy where it is celebrated as a distinct 'event' in the life of Jesus. So how should we approach this feast?

First, it is now approaching mid-January and for everyone in the congregation, the president included, Christmas is long in the past, people have been back at work for weeks, schools have re-opened, people are already thinking of a 'Spring Break', and even chatter about the New Year seems a little dated. So looking back to Christmas or referring to this as the close of Christmas is just adding noise to the communication.

Second, this is about the baptism of the Christ by John, it is not a celebration of baptism as a sacrament or even the concept of baptism within the Paschal Mystery. Such thoughts belong to Easter, and the Easter Vigil in particular, not to this day. So this is not a day for having a baptism during the Eucharist. Such a celebration just confuses the understanding of what is being recalled and fills the understanding with muddle. Indeed, if it is the community's practice to celebrate the baptism of new members of the gathering during the Eucharist, then this is one of those Sundays which should not be used for baptisms.

Third, when we look at the position of the baptism of Jesus with the gospel kerygma we note that it is the public announcement of the beginning of the work of the Messiah. It marks a beginning of a period, not a conclusion. The basic structure can be seen in Mark, after the opening of the gospel comes the work of John which comes to its conclusion in his baptism of Jesus and

the glorious theophany of approbation: 'Thou art my beloved
Son: with thee I am well pleased' (Mk 1:1-11). The other synoptics maintain this structure except that they add the prelude of
the Infancy Narratives; while in Jn 1:29-34 the testimony of John
the Baptist concluded by his reference to the theophany of the
Spirit descending on Jesus like a dove. In all the gospels, this
'event' is then followed by the messianic ministry (what we
often refer to as the 'public life'). So the baptism of the Lord by
John had a distinct place in the preaching of the church, it
marked the 'visible' anointing by the Father in the Spirit for his
work. It is the great beginning.

    Fourth, the baptism of Jesus now has a definite place in the
liturgy of the church, it is now a moment in our common memory
and celebration of the Lord. So it would be appropriate to look
on it as the beginning of Ordinary Time and, in particular, a celebration of Jesus as 'the Messiah,' 'the Anointed One,' 'the
Christ'. So the tone of these notes is that of beginnings, not of
conclusions.

Introduction to the Celebration
Today we celebrate our faith in Jesus: he is the beloved of the
Father, the anointed one, and the one on whom the Spirit rests.
During the coming months we will be recalling each Sunday his
works and preaching as the Chosen One of the Father, but
Christians have always begun the retelling of the gospel of Jesus
by reminding ourselves who Jesus is. The gospels tell us this by
recalling that he was baptised by John the Baptist in the Jordan
and at that moment the Father's voice was heard and the Spirit
appeared in the form of a dove.

    Let us pause and reflect that we are here because we believe
that Jesus is 'the Anointed One,' 'the Christ,' 'the Messiah,' 'the
One who does the Father's will'.

The Asperges
Use Option A (the Rite of Blessing and Sprinkling Holy Water)
and then first form of the opening prayer; if you choose Option

B (a rite of penance) then kyrie-verses can be found in the resources for Year C.

Headings for Readings
First Reading
The Lord's anointed is the servant who does the will of the
Father; he is the chosen one, the one in whom God's soul de-
lights.

Second Reading
Today we celebrate the beginning of Jesus's work as the messiah,
which means he is 'the Anointed One,' 'the Christ'. In this reading we hear that Jesus is the one who is anointed, marked out,
with the Holy Spirit.

Gospel
Jesus is identified as the Christ by earth and heaven: John testi-
fied he is the One whom Israel awaited; the Father's voice testi-
fied that he is the beloved Son.

Prayer of the Faithful
President
Friends, the work of the Messiah was to gather scattered individuals and make them a single people, a people of God, and a
priestly people able to stand in the presence of the Father inter-
ceding for ourselves and all humanity. So now let us stand and,
as a priestly people united with the Christ, ask the Father for our
needs.
Reader(s)
1. That during the coming year when we hear the Word of God
in the liturgy, we will hear it in our hearts. Lord hear us.
2. That during the coming year we will respond to the Lord's call
to care for the poor, the suffering, and the oppressed. Lord hear
us.
3. That during the coming year there will be a new recognition
that the world is God's creation. Lord hear us.

4. That during the coming year those who are leaders in our society will follow the ways of truth and integrity. Lord hear us.

5. That during the coming year we will grow closer together as a community. Lord hear us.

6. That during the coming year we will grow more attentive as a community to ways to bear testimony to the Christ. Lord hear us.

7. That during the coming year we will be given new courage to confess that Jesus is the Christ, the beloved Son of the Father. Lord hear us.

President

Father, you anointed Jesus with the Holy Spirit and with power as our Saviour. Hear our prayers to you and grant what we ask through your beloved Son, our Lord. Amen.

Eucharistic Prayer

Preface of the Baptism of the Lord (P7), (*Missal*, p 410).

Invitation to the Our Father

In union with the beloved Son, let us pray to the Father:

Sign of Peace

When the Lord set out from the Jordan to preach he announced a message of peace and called people to gather in unity around his table as friends. Let us celebrate this unity he proclaimed in a sign of peace.

Invitation to Communion

Behold the Lamb of God, behold him upon whom the Spirit descended like a dove. Blessed are we who are called to have a share in his supper.

Communion Reflection

The hymn given in the *Breviary*, 'When Jesus comes to be baptised' (vol 1, p 371), for Evening Prayer 1 of this feast is appropriate as a reflection today.

Conclusion

Solemn Blessing 3 for the Beginning of the New Year (*Missal*, p 368) is still appropriate – we should within our Eucharistic assembly formally ask God's blessings on the coming year – and we have been celebrating one of the great beginning moments of the Church's kerygma.

COMMENTARY

First Reading: Is 42: 1-4, 6-7

This is taken from the first of the four Songs of the Suffering Servant found in Deutero-Isaiah. Its significance within the text of Isaiah is not relevant to this liturgical use, where it functions to identify in prophecy several of the themes heard in the 'voice from heaven' in the gospel. The servant is the Lord's, i.e. the Father's, 'chosen one,' 'the one who delights' the Father's 'soul,' and 'upon whom he has put' his 'spirit'.

Second Reading: Acts 10:34-38

This is one of the great set-piece speeches in Acts in which Luke presents his view of the fundamental kerygma of the church by expressing it in perfectly formed homilies. This speech is set immediately after the crucial encounter with Cornelius when the difficulties in bringing the gospel to the nations is, for Luke's readers, finally settled. This is the ideal second reading for today for it is the only reference outside the gospels that refers to the relationship between the work of John the Baptist and the beginning of the work of Jesus, in effect, the mystery we celebrate today.

It is clear from the gospels that the baptism by John the Baptist was one of the key fixed points in telling the story of Jesus, indeed it appears to have been the defining point in the narrative. Here we see that narrative retold in summary form and the 'baptism event' retains that marker position at the start of the messianic work. Luke takes the trinitarian format of his account in Lk 3:22, refashions it without the narrative form, and presents it as an interpretation of the name 'Jesus Christ' or

'Jesus the Christ'. Jesus is 'the Anointed One', 'the Christ,' but what does that mean? God [the Father, not mentioned in the Lk 3 but only heard] anoints Jesus with the Spirit. But this now means that Jesus acts in a unique way in the Spirit: that God has set upon him the Spirit and power in a way that is not found among all the others – the Christians – who have received the Spirit. In summary we could say that Luke's preaching here is 'God gets Jesus to act in the Spirit' and that phrase is equivalent to saying 'Jesus is the Christ.'

Gospel: Mt 3:13-17
The simplest form of the baptism event is that found in Mk 1:9-11 and the almost identical Lk 3:21-22. Matthew makes two changes. First, he adds vv 14-15 stressing John the Baptist's hesitancy over baptising Jesus – this insertion may be his caution lest it be unclear that Jesus was not in need of baptism by John. The second significant difference is that here the heavenly voice – which the reader is expected to identify as that of the Father – does not address Jesus as in Mk and Lk, but the assembly: 'This is my beloved Son ...'

However, the key to the scene is not in its details but in its overall impact: the human and divine worlds, heaven and earth, the history of Israel and the eternity of God's inner life all come together in an unforgettable image. This is a mighty event that is fitting to act as the marker of the commencement of the work of the Christ. And so, it is one of the most explicitly theological scenes in the gospel narrative: the Father identifies Jesus as his Son and the Spirit is seen. Here lies the whole of later christology presented not as propositions but as something that the imagination can work with, while still not giving the false notions of 'seeing' God. We see the Christ, the Son acclaimed as such by the voice from heaven which is heard and not seen, while the Spirit is seen 'descending like (*hosei*) a dove'.

Scenes such as this have become victims of two types of exegetical confusion during the twentieth century. The first was the product of a materialist notion of truth. It began with the materialist question 'If I were there that day what would my TV camera have recorded?' Then when the exegete said 'Nothing', it seemed as if the scene was false and so the whole thing was a concoction to be avoided. We have to realise that this scene is sacramental and placed within a narrative precisely so our human imaginations can handle the mystery: to ask the 'TV camera' question is not to get at the Truth but to commit the blasphemy of Wisdom 15 and imply 'god' as referring to another object, a thing, in our universe. The second confusion is that of assuming that 'theology' is an obscurity overlaid on the 'simple message of Jesus'. The confusion runs like this: Jesus was a loving guy who spoke about God and captured hearts; then came the boffins and made everything complicated with notions of the incarnation, the trinity, and what not, but you can by-pass this and get to the 'heart of the matter'. It's a lovely picture and one that still wins adherents, but there is no evidence for such a 'simple time'. By the time that Mark began preaching his gospel – in the sixties – we see in the baptism-event a fully developed Christian doctrine of God, and it is this that we read again today in the liturgy.

HOMILY NOTES

1. This is a good opportunity to give a simple catechetical homily whose aim is to impart some simple linguistic clarity in order to help people reflect on the gospel's image more fruitfully.

2. We use the words 'Jesus Christ' over and over again. Indeed, we use these two words so often side-by-side that we forget that they have any meaning. Sometimes, we almost think that the word 'Christ' is just a surname tacked on as if one needed to distinguish several people called 'Jesus'. Most Christians use the words interchangeably. I have seen history books with the index entry: 'Christ, J.' followed by page numbers. When I asked a student what was the significance that her essay kept varying between using 'Jesus said' and 'Christ said', her answer was that she changed the usage simply to make it sound less repetitive! So this is a phrase whose significance we cannot take for granted.

3. But our confession of faith is that 'Jesus is the Christ.' The word *christos* means the marked one, the one who has been smeared with oil. But why use this as a description of Jesus? The people of Israel looked forward to the new David, the new King who would institute the Day of the Lord and his victory. David had been marked out as the chosen one of the Lord: 'Then Samuel took the horn of oil, and anointed him in the midst of his brothers; and the Spirit of the Lord came mightily upon David from that day forward' (1 Sam 16:13). 'To be marked out with oil' is the same as 'being the Anointed One' or, if one uses Hebrew, 'the Messiah' or, if one uses Greek, 'the Christ' or to say 'he is the Chosen One of the Father.'

4. Jesus was not literally anointed with oil to mark him out as 'the Anointed One,' but in the gospels he is shown as being marked out by the Father's voice and by the descent of the Spirit upon him. To say 'Jesus is the Christ' is to say he is the one who is uniquely the Son of the Father, and uniquely the bearer of the Spirit.

5. To say 'Jesus is the Christ' is to utter a basic creed which only makes sense when we imagine that statement within the scene we have just read in the gospel. To say 'You, O Jesus are the Christ' is to offer praise through the beloved Son to the Father in the Holy Spirit.

Baptism of the Lord (Year B)

Note
See Year A.

Introduction to the Celebration
Today marks the beginning of the public life and ministry of Jesus Christ as he set out to do the Father's will and announce the arrival of the kingdom of God. And the moment of the beginning of the messianic work of Jesus is marked by the moment of his baptism in the Jordan. He is acclaimed on earth by the prophet John and links himself to John by being baptised by him. He is acclaimed from heaven by the voice of the Father and the presence of the Spirit. As the people who have heard his preaching and accepted his call, who have confessed him as the Christ, and set out to follow his way, let us pause and consider the words addressed to Jesus: 'Thou art my beloved Son, with thee I am well pleased.'

The Asperges
Use Option A (the Rite of Blessing and Sprinkling with Holy Water) and then the first form of the opening prayer; if you choose Option B (a Rite of Penance) then kyrie-verses can be found in the resources for Year C.

Headings for Readings
First Reading
This is a prophecy of the new world that will be ushered in when the Messiah, the Holy One of Israel, comes among God's people; we believe that this time of the Lord began with the baptism of Jesus in the Jordan.

Second Reading
One can use the option for Year B, but Acts 10:34-38 (the reading for Year A) is to be preferred because it is the only passage in the New Testament outside the gospels that mentions today's feast.

However, if you use the Year B option:

In this reading we hear an answer to the question what does it mean to call Jesus 'the Christ': Jesus is the one sent by the Father and he sends the Holy Spirit into our lives.

Gospel
The Father addresses Jesus: 'You are my Son, the Beloved; my favour rests on you.'

Prayer of the Faithful
President
My friends, today we recall that Jesus is the Christ, the beloved Son of the Father, and because he has come and shared our humanity we can stand now with him and ask the Father for all we need.
Reader(s)
1. On this day when Jesus began his ministry we pray that his body, the church, will be faithful to the gospel he entrusted to it. Lord hear us.
2. On this day when Jesus was baptised by John we pray that people everywhere will recognise him as the Lord's anointed. Lord hear us.
3. On this day when Jesus was manifested to his people we pray that the People of God will have the courage to manifest him in our world. Lord hear us.
4. On this day when the Spirit descended on Jesus we pray that the Spirit will descend on all who are in darkness or who are despairing. Lord hear us.
5. On this day when Jesus heard the voice of the Father we pray that all who have died may be called to be beloved sons and daughters. Lord hear us.

President
Father, we have been made your children by adoption in baptism; so as you look upon your beloved Son, look also on us, and grant our needs for we pray to you in Jesus Christ, our Lord. Amen.

Eucharistic Prayer
Preface of the Baptism of the Lord (P7), (*Missal*, p 410).

Invitation to the Our Father
The beloved Son of the Father made us his sisters and brothers, and so we can pray:

Sign of Peace
The Messiah announced the new relationship of peace when he welcomed people to his table. Let us celebrate this new relationship now in the sign of peace.

Invitation to Communion
This is the Beloved of the Father, who now invites us to share his life at his table.

Communion Reflection
The hymn given in the *Breviary*, 'When Jesus comes to be baptized' (vol 1, p 371), for Evening Prayer 1 of this feast is appropriate as a reflection today.

Conclusion
Solemn Blessing 3 for the Beginning of the New Year (*Missal*, p 368) is appropriate as for most people what is most obvious about this time is that is the beginning of the new year – and we should within our Eucharistic assembly formally ask God's blessings on the coming year.

First Reading: Is 55:1-11

This reading from Isaiah can be replaced with that given for
Year A. Is 55:1-11 is the concluding prophecy of Deutero-Isaiah's
book: it began with the cry 'Comfort, comfort my people, says
your God' (Is 40:1); now it ends with this solemn statement that
the Lord is in full control of the destiny of his people. As it is
read within the church it is the announcement that the time of
the Messiah has now begun; that is the reign of the Christ which
begins with the baptism in the Jordan.

Psalm: Is 12:2-6

This text from Isaiah has so many psalm-echoes that one could
easily forget that it is not found within the Psalter. It is a hymn of
thanksgiving that was composed after the time of [First-] Isaiah
and inserted as a finale to chs 2-12. The original meaning of the
phrase 'you [plural] will draw water from the wells of salvation'
is obscure, but has become fixed in the memory of the church as
a prophecy of Christian baptism and it is, presumably, for that
reason it was chosen for use here.

Second Reading: 1 Jn 5:1-9

The use of Year A (Acts 10:34-38) is preferable. The reading from
1 Jn can be seen as adding another early witness to the
Trinitarian theology found in the gospel. Like many sections of
this letter, today's reading is a very well developed piece of catechesis on the identity of Jesus and his mission. The significant
feature is the manner in which the beliefs of the community are
inseparable from its life as the community of the baptised. The
whole passage, with its short phrases and careful use of repeti-
tion, is likely to have been a text that was intended to be committed to memory; and given the references to baptism in the passage it may be that this was part of a baptismal catechesis.

Gospel: Mk 1:7-11

This presentation of the baptism scene is earlier than that in

Matthew, but it is one of those passages in the synoptics where all three have very similar perspectives; hence, look at the notes given for Year A. One point to remember, however, is that here in Mark the baptism scene is the far more stark opening to the whole gospel than in either Matthew or Luke where there are already the manifestations of the identity of Jesus that form part of the infancy narrative. In Mark the baptism scene is far more obviously the answer to the question 'Who is this Jesus whose gospel we are beginning to hear?' He is the one who is uniquely the Son of the Father and the bearer of the Spirit.

HOMILY NOTES

1. Today is a day of celebrating beginnings in the liturgy: the beginning of the preaching and the public ministry of Jesus which is announced with the great cry from heaven of the Father's joy in the work of his beloved Son. Yet Mark expects that as you hear this opening blaze of heavenly light and glory, you know and remember that his story will end in the darkened Friday of the crucifixion. We also are now at a beginning: the beginning of a year. The initial excitement of New Year is over, the champagne has been corked and drunk; so we can now stop and reflect that a new period of our lives in the world is beginning.

2. The public ministry of Jesus today is that which is carried out by you and me, the individuals that go to make up the Body of Christ, the church. Preaching the truth, doing the truth in love, bearing witness to the Father, caring for the poor, being attentive to the Spirit, recognising the presence of God in respecting the environment, seeking justice and peace, offering thanksgiving to the Father in the liturgy – all these are the public works of the Son carried out by his people. Now is the time to take stock and ask are we being attentive to this public ministry with which we are charged.

3. There is no end to the variety of public ministry to which we are called in imitation of Christ, to do the will of the Father, being empowered by the Spirit. However, let us take three examples.

4. Bearing witness to the truth. We live much of our lives being buffeted by propaganda of one sort or another: whether it is formal propaganda intended to create great lies that oppress people, to advertising, to manipulating numbers to prove a point, to putting a spin on a story. There is even the realisation that if you repeat an idea often enough, people will become so familiar with it that they will assume it is some basic fact. Do we simply acquiesce with this, or do we seek to get behind the bald headlines, strap-lines, and tags? Do we confront the part we may be playing in the propagation of falsehoods out of selfishness or the desire for power? Honesty is the obedience that we owe to the structure of the creation, doing the truth is a holy activity because God is the source of all truth. The lie, big or small, is the witness to all that is not of God and has no place in the kingdom; as we see in just three words in the name Jesus gave Satan: 'The Father of Lies' (Jn 8:44).

5. Caring for those who suffer oppression. The oppressed are all those who are in need and cannot escape from that situation by their own exertions: be it illness, or poverty, or ignorance, or as a result of injustice. We believe in a God who forgives and gives us chance after chance, and who challenges us to do to others as we would have them do unto us. To acknowledge the goodness of God to us is to accept that we have an obligation to show that same goodness. This care is not something 'added on' to being a Christian, but what makes us a holy people. God is holy in his action towards us: he loves us in our needs; we act in a holy way in imitation of God when we seek to act with love to those in need. Thus a holy people can pray: forgive us our trespasses as we forgive those who trespass against us.

6. Respecting the creation. Because the environment in which we live is material does not mean that we can look on it with indifference or as something simply to be used and discarded. We believe that the whole of the creation is God's gift and that all that was made was made through the Word: it is 'shot

through' with the character of the Word who in the fullness of time took on our humanity for our salvation. But if the world is God's gift and bears the traces of the Creator within it, then we must respect it and use it with care, conscious that it is here to sustain life not just for us but for all the generations to come. We live in a world where we march through the creation like vandals, but this is incompatible with acknowledging the Father, or calling ourselves disciples of the Son, or claiming that the Spirit enlightens us.

7. In all of these it is often quite acceptable 'to mouth the truth': to talk for example of being less exploitative or less consumerist, but when this starts to become actual in deeds it starts to become painful. It is one thing to say one abhors falsehoods; it is another thing to actually point it out. It is easy to fret over care for the elderly or the poor, another thing to actually visit an elderly relative or give enough money to groups that work with the homeless. Here Christianity confronts us with the reality of the cross. Ours is not a polished philosophy of rhetoric and good intentions: the public witness to the Father's will ended for Jesus in his death, his humble obedience right to the bitter end. It is the willingness to embrace this reality of the pain inherent in doing the good in the midst of a sinful world that sets us apart. It is only in grasping this reality, that the true and the good cost, and building the kingdom makes demands on us, that we become the beloved daughters and sons of the Father.

8. To recall the scene of the baptism of Jesus is to resolve anew to being his public witnesses in the world.

Baptism of the Lord (Year C)

Note

See Year A.

Introduction to the Celebration

Today we celebrate the identity of Jesus our Lord: he whom we follow is the one who is the beloved Son of the Father and the one who is uniquely empowered by the Spirit. This is the great mystery of faith: Jesus is not just some teacher of wisdom or some guide to a happy or holy life, he is the one with whom the Father is well-pleased, and he brings us into the presence of the Father and sends his Spirit among us. We can gather here now for the Eucharist because the Spirit is giving us divine life, Jesus is in our midst, and so we stand and offer our thanks to the Father.

Rite of Penance (or consider Option A: the Asperges)

Lord Jesus, at your baptism John recognised you as the Christ, Lord have mercy.

Lord Jesus, at your baptism heaven opened and the Holy Spirit descended upon you in the shape of a dove, Christ have mercy.

Lord Jesus, at your baptism the Father's voice was heard: 'You are my Son, the Beloved, my favour rests on you', Lord have mercy.

If you do opt for a Rite of Penance, then the third option for the opening prayer is most appropriate.

Headings for Readings

First Reading

The reading for Year A is more accessible for today; but if you use the option for Year C, then:

> The prophet announces that when the Anointed of the Lord

would come among his people a new time of peace would dawn. We believe this new era of peace between God and humankind began with Jesus the beloved Son of the Father.

Second Reading

One can use the option for Year C, but Acts 10:34-38 (the reading for Year A) is to be preferred because it is the only passage in the New Testament outside the gospels that mentions today's feast. Moreover, since this year we are reading Luke's account in the gospel, it is most appropriate to have this reading from Luke also; in effect, we are getting two views of the same aspect of the kerygma.

However, if you use the Year C option:

God's love was shown by sending us Jesus who has freed us from our sins and renewed us with the gift of the Holy Spirit.

Gospel

When we look on Jesus we see the beloved Son of the Father and the one who sends us the Holy Spirit.

Prayer of the Faithful

President

Today we celebrate the mystery of Christ with whom the Father is well pleased and upon whom the Spirit rests, now may the Spirit give voice to our prayers as, gathered in Christ, we make our needs known to the Father.

Reader(s)

1. That the whole church of God may offer praise to the Father. Lord in your mercy, hear our prayer.

2. That this church gathered here may bear witness to the Christ. Lord in your mercy, hear our prayer.

3. That every Christian will be attentive to the promptings of the Spirit. Lord in your mercy, hear our prayer.

4. That we may respect and care for the creation as the gift of the Father. Lord in your mercy, hear our prayer.

5. That we may minister to all who are oppressed, all who are sick, all who are suffering injustice, all who are poor or hungry, following the example of the Christ. Lord in your mercy, hear our prayer.

6. That we may have the courage to profess our faith and to follow the road of discipleship empowered by the Spirit. Lord in your mercy, hear our prayer.

President

Father, you listened to the prayers of your Son our Lord; listen now to these prayers from us his disciples for we make them in the power of the Holy Spirit through that same Christ, our Lord. Amen.

Eucharistic Prayer

Preface of the Baptism of the Lord (P7), (*Missal*, p 410).

Invitation to the Our Father

The Father's voice was heard declaring Jesus his Son, the Beloved; now in the voice of Jesus let us pray to the Father:

Sign of Peace

The work of the Messiah whose beginnings we are recalling was to bring peace and reconciliation on earth. Let us embark on a year of peacemaking.

Invitation to Communion

This is the Son of God, the Beloved of the Father. Happy are we who are called to share his table.

Communion Reflection

The hymn given in the *Breviary*, 'When Jesus comes to be baptized' (vol 1, p 371), for Evening Prayer 1 of this feast is appropriate as a reflection today.

Conclusion
Solemn Blessing 3 for the Beginning of the New Year (*Missal*, p 368) is appropriate as for most people what is most obvious about this time is that is the beginning of the new year – and we should within our Eucharistic assembly formally ask God's blessings on the coming year.

First Reading: Is 40:1-5, 9-11
If you use the Year A readings, see the notes for Year A; if you use the optional reading for Year C, see the notes for the Second Sunday of Advent B.

Second Reading: Tit 2:11-14, 3:4-7
The use of Year A (Acts 10:34-38) is preferable. However, if you do decide to use the optional reading for Year C bear in mind that the two passages that go to make up this reading do not fit well together. Indeed, it is really only the latter passage (3:4-7) that has any connection with today's celebration. It was selected because of its reference to 'the water of rebirth' and the renewal of each Christian by the Spirit, but these relate to the sacrament we receive rather than to the event of the Baptism of Christ (where they would be inappropriate).

Given how unconnected, and unsuitable, both the first and second readings are to the day being celebrated, one suspects that the choice indicates either haste in selection or desperation to find some reading that was even remotely connected with the feast – and in these two readings the connection is truly remote!

Gospel: Lk 3:15-16, 21-22
As edited for today's reading, Luke's account of the Baptism of Jesus is almost identical to that of Mark. Hence while we announce the name of a different gospel writer each year over the three years of the liturgical cycle, we read only one account of this 'event'. The three have been made to fit a single image of the day that we celebrate. This means, in effect, reducing Matthew

and Luke to what is found in Mark: John meets Jesus, announces one greater than him who comes after him, then follows the theophany. For comment on the scene within the kerygma and memory of the first-century church, see the notes given in Year A.

HOMILY NOTES

1. Between today and the end of next November, except for some special days around Easter, we will be reading passages from St Luke's gospel each Sunday at the Eucharist. This year is known in the order of our readings as 'the year of Luke'.

2. We can divide his gospel into three parts: the first deals with the events before and around the birth of Jesus (and we have just read this portion over Christmas; the third part deals with the last week of Jesus's life in Jerusalem, his passion, death, and resurrection (and we will read this at Easter); and in between we have all the preaching and miracles of Jesus during his public ministry which St Luke sets out as taking place as Jesus moves along the road from Nazareth to Jerusalem.

3. This central part of the gospel – the teaching and preaching with recollections of healings and meals – all belong to what we traditionally call the public ministry of Jesus, his adult life, his activity among the people of Israel. It is this central part of the gospel that provides the passages for the ordinary Sundays during the coming year. This central part opens with the great scene of the baptism in the Jordan we have just read when Jesus takes over from John the Baptist. The work of the time of preparation is over; the time of the work of the Christ has begun.

4. Luke places this wondrous scene – the two great prophets meeting, and then the Father's voice being heard and the Spirit appearing in the form of a dove – at the beginning of the public ministry to show us that this is the mysterious in-auguration of the new age of the Christ. He also does it so

that when we hear what follows – Jesus doing this or that, saying this or that, meeting this person and then that person – we will keep in mind the full identity of the One we call 'Lord'.

5. Luke presents us with a highly visual mysterious scene – picture it in your minds – of Jesus and John in the river, crowds of followers around and then from above the heavenly voice and the dove: this is the true identity of Jesus. Jesus is a human being like us, the final prophet, the uniquely beloved Son of God, the one empowered by the Spirit, the revelation of the Father, Emmanuel – God with us, the glory of God made manifest to us.

6. We have to keep this wondrous image of Jesus in the Jordan, the revelation of his true identity, in our minds as we move onwards in our recollection of his words and deeds in the weeks and months ahead.

7. There are now between 345 and 351 shopping days before next Christmas.